AF647104

THE EARLY RULERS OF KHAJURĀHO

Acknowledgment of Plates

Photographs by Sri Amiya Banerji Nos. 1, 2, 3, 4, 5, 6, 7, 8, 11 & 16. *Sri S. Chaudhuri Nos.* 9, 14, 15 & 17. *Sri A. Mitra No.* 10. *Indian Museum, Calcutta, No.* 20. *State Museum, Lucknow. Nos.* 12 & 13.

Frontispiece—1. *Kandarya Mahādeva Temple, Khajurāho*

THE EARLY RULERS OF KHAJURĀHO

Dr. SISIR KUMAR MITRA
M.A., LL.B., D. PHIL., F.A.S.
READER, ANCIENT INDIAN HISTORY & CULTURE DEPARTMEMT,
CALCUTTA UNIVERSITY

Foreword by

Dr. B. C. SEN
M.A., LL.B., P.R.S., PH.D. (LONDON)
PROFESSOR OF INDOLOGY (RETIRED), GOVERNMENT SANSKRIT
COLLEGE, CALCUTTA

MOTILAL BANARSIDASS
Delhi :: Varanasi :: Patna

First Edition : Calcutta, 1958
Second Revised Edition : Delhi, 1977

ISBN 978-81-208-1997-9

© MOTILAL BANARSIDASS
Indological Publishers and Booksellers
Head Office: BUNGALOW ROAD, JAWAHAR NAGAR, DELHI-7
Branches : 1. CHOWK, VARANASI-1 (U.P.)
2. ASHOK RAJPATH, PATNA-4 (BIHAR)

Printed in India
BY SHANTILAL JAIN, AT SHRI JAINENDRA PRESS, A-45, PHASE-I, INDUSTRIAL AREA, NARAINA, NEW DELHI-28 AND PUBLISHED BY SUNDARLAL JAIN, FOR MOTILAL BANARSIDASS, BUNGALOW ROAD, JAWAHAR NAGAR, DELHI-7

To

My Parents

CONTENTS

FOREWORD

Dr. Sisir Kumar Mitra's book, entitled "The Early Rulers of Khajurāho" constitutes a welcome addition to the existing literature on the history of the Candellas of Bundelkhand. The Candellas, as is well known even to the very casual students of Indian history, formed one of the most prominent dynasties that flourished for some centuries preceding the establishment of Islam as an imperial power in this subcontinent. In all probability they started from a humble beginning, but they ultimately succeeded in founding and organizing an independent kingdom, seizing every opportunity to extend its frontiers and spreading their reputation far and wide by daring military expeditions. The sturdy defences of Kālañjar provided them with a comparative security against external enemies. The policy underlying their relations with other powers seems to have been largely based on an appreciation of the strategic implications of the position, held by their territory in the political map of India during their time. The measures, which they took to help a Pratihāra ruler facing an acute crisis, and subsequently to punish another Pratihāra ruler, who had been humiliated by a Muslim invader; to associate themselves with co-operative efforts to protect the freedom of allied kings threatened by violent attacks from outside, and the way in which they rapidly succeeded in restoring their position which had been rudely shaken by the forces of the Kalacuris, testify to political sagacity and discernment of no mean order, a capacity for swift and determined action, and a stubbornness of spirit, which could not be reduced with ease. In an age of strife and turmoil they were able, by providing their own people with a strong and stable government, to prevent the disruption of the prevailing social and economic order in a fairly wide area. They were able, moreover, to maintain their independence much longer than most of the other rulers who quickly surrendered to Muslim aggressions.

Dr. Mitra gives a comprehensive and fascinating account of the varied activities of this distinguished family of rulers, based on a minute and detailed study of the material which he collected with great industry and thoroughness from diverse sources, indigenous and foreign, literary and archaeological. Though most of his data have been compiled from epigraphic sources, he is not over-zealous in his estimate of the importance and reliability of inscriptional material which he examines as critically as any piece of literary evidence that is usually discarded as unhistorical and exaggerated. He has discussed the controversial issues connected with his subject without any bias. Although there may be differences of opinion regarding some of the conclusions he has attempted to draw from his own interpretation of the evidence compiled, unstinted praise is due to him for the reasonableness of his views, precision of expression and sobriety of judgment. His chapters on administrative, social, economic and religious history will be specially useful to those interested in the compilation of epigraphic material bearing on the evolution of ancient Indian culture. I sincerely hope that Dr. Mitra's work will receive wide appreciation as a very valuable and original contribution, and stimulate further research in the field.

University of Calcutta. BENOY CHANDRA SEN.
April 16, 1958

PREFACE TO THE SECOND EDITION

The first edition of the book published in 1958 had long gone out of print. But as it has been included in the list of prescribed books in some of the Universities, Indian and foreign, there has been a sustained demand for it among students and scholars in the field all these years. Hence a fresh edition is considered necessary. Thanks to Sri N. P. Jain of Messrs Motilal Banarsidass of Delhi, for his proposal for a photoprint edition of the book some time last year, which I readily accepted. Because I felt that in the absence of new materials, epigraphic or literary, revision of my findings incorporated in the treatise would become unnecessary. No major work has also been published in the meantime, nor any new theory expounded necessitating change in my opinion.

A few inscriptions relating to the Candellas, edited or re-edited since the publication of my work, have been noticed under Supplement to the List of Inscriptions in Appendix I.

Dr. R.S. Sharma's treatise on Indian Feudalism (300-1200 A.D.) includes references to Candella land grants as indicative of development of feudal traits in Central India. Dr. D. C. Sircar has however ably refuted the arguments of Dr. Sharma in an article entitled 'Indian Landlordism and European Feudalism'. While agreeing with Dr. Sircar about the hollowness of the European analogy, I am constrained to observe that the term 'landlordism' is also not an appropriate expression to describe the peculiar system of land organisation prevalent in the early medieval period of our history. The system had its roots in the past and was evolved by Indian genius. I have however discussed the matter for whatever it is worth in Appendix III of the present edition. In this connection I must frankly admit that I am much indebted to my friend Professor Adhir Chakravarti of West Bengal Senior Education Service, for his discussions with me on this topic, which have been incorporated in my note.

A short note on some of the features of Candella architectural style has also been added as Appendix IV to supplement my observations in Chapter XIV.

My sincere thanks are due to Dr. Ashok K. Bhattacharya, my former pupil and now colleague in the Department of Ancient

Indian History & Culture, Calcutta University, for his assistance in the reproduction of the book. I must also record my thanks to my publishers, Messrs Motilal Banarsidass of Delhi for their cooperation in bringing out the present edition.

Calcutta University
February 2, 1976

S. K. Mitra

PREFACE TO THE FIRST EDITION

This work embodies the results of an intensive study of the history of the Candella dynasty, which I commenced about six years ago. Much work has already been done in the field of the political history of India, but when I undertook my task, the history of the Candellas, like that of some other contemporary dynasties, had not yet been treated on the lines followed in this book, but more or less as a part of the wider history of India as a whole. It was my object to gather in one place all the information that could be compiled from the different sources and study it critically. The application of such a method was expected to result in a larger accumulation of material on the basis of which it might be found necessary to revise some of the current theories. I have tried to collect in one place all the available information relating to my subject, and with its help to reconstruct the history of the Candellas in its different stages and aspects. I am not claiming originality for everything said in this treatise. My indebtedness to all previous writers has been duly acknowledged. I have, however, examined every suggestion or theory pertinent to my subject, and have also endeavoured to offer my own views for what they are worth. I have already tried to indicate my lines of research in a number of papers published in the *Indian Historical Quarterly*, the *Bharatiya Vidya*, Bombay, and the *Proceedings of the Indian History Congresses* (*1951-54*).

This work consists of 14 Chapters and a number of Appendices including one which contains a detailed notice of the inscriptional records relating to the Candella dynasty. In the different chapters I have incorporated the political history of this family in its successive phases as well as accounts of their administrative system, the social, economic and religious conditions in Bundelkhand, and a brief survey of the art and architecture of Khajurāho, with systematic references to the archaeological remains discovered in the regions associated with the memory of the Candellas. In Appendix II I have given a genealogical table of the family with approximate dates

I may be permitted to express my gratitude to Dr. Hem Chandra Ray, M.A., PH.D., D. LITT. (Lond.), Professor & Head of the Department of History, University of Colombo, Ceylon, for having suggested to me the subject of the present work. The work itself was undertaken and completed under the supervision of my revered teacher, Dr. Benoy Chandra Sen, M.A., P.R.S., PH.D. (Lond), Reader in the Department of Ancient Indian History & Culture, Calcutta University, and submitted as a thesis for the D. Phil. (Arts) degree of our University. My indebtedness to Dr. Sen can hardly be expressed in words. While revising my treatise for publication I received valuable information and suggestions from late Dr. N. P. Chakravarti, M.A., PH.D. (Cantab), and Dr. D. C. Sircar, M.A., PH.D., then Epigraphist to the Government of India, regarding unpublished materials bearing on my subject, which with their kind permission I have utilised and incorporated in my work. I am extremely grateful to Dr. Sircar for the kind interest he always took in my researches, and place on record my sincere homage to the memory of late Dr. Chakravarti. I am also grateful to Dr. J. N. Banerjea, M.A., PH.D., Carmichael Professor of Ancient Indian History & Culture, and Prof. S. K. Saraswati, M.A., Reader in the same department, for their valuable help and advice, particularly with regard to the section which deals with art and architecture. In this connection I would also admit that the book would not have been published except for the constant inspiration and encouragement that I received from the venerable Pandit Anantakumar Nyaya-Tarkatirtha and my Principal Dr. Gaurinath Sastri, M.A., P.R.S., D.LITT., of the Sanskrit College. My sincere thanks are also due to my esteemed colleague, Dr. C. C. Dasgupta, M.A., P.R.S., PH.D. (Cal et Cantab), who takes a special interest in my research activities. I shall be failing in my duty if I do not acknowledge my sincere thankfulness to my young pupil, Sri Bratindranath Mukherji, M.A., who arranged for the publication of the book and cheerfully took upon himself the trouble of preparing the index; I am also thankful to two other pupils, Sri Dipak Sen, M.A., and Srimati Rajeswari Natarajan, B.A., and my brother Sri Mihir Mitra for their help at various stages of my work. I would like also to take this opportunity to tender my gratitude to Sri Jagadish Chandra Bhattacharya, B.A., the teacher of my school days, who in the formative period of my life implanted in me a love for the study of our glorious past.

My thanks are also due to Sri R. C. Kar, M.A., Superintendent, Archaeological Section, Indian Museum, Calcutta, and Sri M. M. Nagar, Director, the State Museum, Lucknow, through whose kind help I could procure a few select photographs, and these have been used to illustrate my book with their permission. For other photographs used by me I sincerely thank my friends, Sri Amiya Kumar Banerji, Deputy Secretary, Cottage & small scale Industries Department, Government of West Bengal, Sri Sudhangsu K. Chaudhuri, Sri Devabrata Mukherji, and also my brother, Sri Aroon Mitra of Nagpur. The Map of the Candella territory, attached to this volume, has been kindly prepared by my friend Sri Anil Mukherji. In conclusion I offer my sincere thanks to Sri K. L. Mukhopadhyay, my publisher, and Sri Jibapriya Guha of Sree Saraswaty Press Ltd, for the personal interest they took in the printing and publication of this book.

Sanskrit College,
Calcutta, 14th April, 1958

SISIR KUMAR MITRA

CHAPTER I

THE CANDELLAS, THE EARLY RULERS OF KHAJURĀHO, AND THEIR TERRITORY

The Candellas were the builders of Khajurāho. It was the Candellas, who endowed it with a high political status and gave a distinctive position to this ancient city of temples, for which it enjoys a unique celebrity even today. But they had a humble beginning, which is almost lost in obscurity. Gradually they reached a feudatory status owing allegiance to the Imperial Pratihāras, and, at a critical moment in the latter's history, earned distinction by rendering effective assistance to Kṣitipāladeva[1], humiliated by his powerful antagonists. As the hour of the break-up of the Pratihāras drew nearer, the Candellas went on increasing their strength by enlarging their dominion, especially by the capture of the strategic fortresses of Kālañjar and Gwālior[2], ultimately emerging as an independent power in Central India, obviously actuated by the policy of building up an empire under some of their energetic and ambitious rulers. They ruled for a period of over three centuries, from the 10th to the beginning of the 14th century A.D., when after a protracted resistance they were finally overwhelmed by the invasions of the Turks. Thus the Candellas were among the last defenders of Hindu rule against the onslaught of the Muslims.

The region, in which the Candellas were dominant as can be ascertained from epigraphic records, was known as Jejābhukti[3], Jejābhuktika[4] or Jejākabhukti[5], the ancient name of modern Bundelkhaṇḍ. The name Bundelkhaṇḍ, which became current later, was associated with the Bundelā

[1] *E.I.*, I., p. 122, L. 10.
[2] *ibid.*, p. 129, V. 45.
[3] *ibid.*, p. 221, V. 10.
[4] Ratnapur Stone Inscription of Kalacuri Jājalladeva. *E.I.*, I. p., 35., V. 21.
[5] Madanpur Stone Inscription No. 10, Ll. 2-3; A.S.R., XXI., pp. 173-74.

Rājputs, who appeared as a political power in this region in the 14th century. Evidently this name had no connection with the Candellas. To the Candellas the region was known as Jejābhukti. This name, as they claim in one of their own inscriptions, owed its origin to Prince Jayaśakti of this family, whose name is also given in different forms, like Jejjāka[6], and Jejā[7]. The Mahobā Inscription says, 'as Pṛthu gave his name to Pṛthivī, so Jejā gave his name to Jejābhukti[8]'.

The extent of the Candella kingdom, as mentioned in V. 45 of the Khajurāho Inscription of V.S. 1011[9], was marked by the town of Bhāsvat on the river Mālava (*i.e.*, Bhilsā on the Betwā) on the west, the Jumnā on the north with Gopādri or Gwālior in the north-east. The southern frontier may have been the Kāimur hills on the Narmadā river. This statement of the Khajurāho Inscription (V.S. 1011) regarding the limits of the Candella kingdom is generally supported by the references to the districts or viṣayas owned by them which are to be found in their land-grants and other inscriptions. The area indicated approximately coincides with the modern Bundelkhaṇḍ, comprising in its wider extent all the country to the south of the Jumnā and the Gaṅgā, from the Betwā river on the west to the temple of Vindhyavāsinīdevī (South Mirzāpur) on the east, including the districts of Chanderi, Saugor and Bilhari, near the sources of the Narmadā on the south[10]. The Candella territory, according to Smith, included the districts of Hamirpur, Bāndā, Lalitpur (a subdivision of Jhānsi), with parts of Allahabad and Mirzapur in the United Provinces (Uttar Pradesh), the Saugor and Dāmoh districts in the Central Provinces (Madhya Pradesh), and a large intermediate space, which under British rule was occupied by a number of small native states[11]."

Once the region was known as Jijhoti, Jajhoti, or Jajāhuti.

---

[6] *E.I.*, I., p. 122, L. 6.
[7] *ibid.*, p. 221, V. 10.
[8] *ibid.*,
[9] *ibid.*, p. 129.
[10] *Anc. Geog. of India* (Cunningham), p. 552.
[11] *I.A.*, XXXVII., p. 130.

This name is preserved in the epithet 'Jajhotiya' (Jijhotiya) applied to Brāhmaṇas and Bāniyās resident in the area, and distributed in different parts of Bundelkhaṇḍ. The expression 'Jajhoti' may be equated with the Chinese 'Chih-chi-to[12]' or 'Chi-ki-to' (according to Beal), the names of the country visited by Hiuen Tsang in 641-42 A.D.[13]. According to the pilgrim Chih-chi-to lay "more than 1,000 li to the north-east of Ujjain, and more than 900 li to the south of Maheśvarapura" (Gwālior). The indications given, according to Smith, bring us to the western frontier of Jijhoti on the Betwā river[14]. As regards the capital of the ancient state of Jijhoti, the Chinese pilgrim does not refer to it by name, he only records, "its capital about 15 li in circuit....The king, who was a Brahmin, was a firm believer in Buddhism, and encouraged men of merit and learned scholars of other lands collected here in numbers"[15]. Later records, both indigenous and foreign, refer to Khajurāho as the capital of Jajāhuti[16]. There is no other indication to show that Khajurāho acquired any importance prior to the rise of the Candellas early in the 10th century A.D. V. A. Smith, on the other hand, suggests that Eran (Erakāna) on the Binā river, a tributary of the Betwā, 45 miles west-north-west from Saugor, was the capital of Jijhoti in the 7th century A.D., as it agrees with the distance referred to by Hiuen Tsang[17], which is not impossible.

From the facts stated above it appears most probable that Jijhoti or Chih-chi-to and Jejākabhukti denoted more or less the same area, now known as Bundelkhaṇḍ. The Candella claim as to the origin of the name Jejākabhukti cannot be

---

[12] *Y.C.*, II., p. 251.

[13] Cunningham. *A.S.R.*, XXI., p. 58.
Smith's note., *Y.C.*, II., p. 342.

[14] I.A., XXXVII., p. 131. Chih-chi-to, according to Watters, is modern Chitor (*Y.C.*, II., p. 251), which is also supported by Dr. H. C. Ray (*D.H.N.I.*, II., p. 670).

[15] *Y.C.*, II., p. 251.

[16] Ābu Rihān refers to Kajurāhah as the capital of Jajhoti or Jajhāoti (Reinaud, *Fragment Arabes*, p. 106); Ibn Bātutā (1335 A.D.) calls it Kājurā or Kajarrā (*Ibn Bātutā* by Gibb, pp. 226 & 363); Āl Biruni mentions that the capital of Jejāhuti was Kajurāha (Trans. by Sachau, I., p. 202); Kharjuravāhaka is the Sanskritised version of Khajurāho (*Khajurāho Insc.*, V.S. 1059., E.I., I., p. 147. Ll. 32-33.

[17] I.A. XXXVII., p. 131.

accepted without further investigation. Some are of opinion that 'Jejākabhukti' was shortened into 'Jijhoti' in the same way as 'Tīrabhukti' became modern 'Tirhut'[18]. But it must be noted that Jijhoti was the earlier name, if its equation with the name given by Hiuen Tsang is to be accepted. The Candella records trace the name Jejākabhukti back to the time of Jayaśakti, who was also called Jejjāka and Jejā. He seems to have been the first ruler in the Candella family to have assumed a definite political status, at least that of a feudatory[19]. It is not unlikely that the Candella region was organised into a 'bhukti' and placed under him as a feudatory so that it came to be known after his name, the bhukti of Jejā or Jejāka. The similarity between the different forms of the ancient name of Bundelkhaṇḍ is obviously very striking, viz., Jijhoti, Jajhoti, Jajhāoti, Jajāhuti, Jajāhoti, Jejāhuti, Jejābhukti, Jejākabhukti, Jejābhuktika and the Chinese form, Chih-chi-to or Chi-ki-to. This seems to account for the suggestion that Jijhoti is an abbreviation of Jejākabhukti.

Almost the whole of the eastern part of Central India, known as Bundelkhaṇḍ, is a low-lying tract, marked by the outlying branches of the northern range of the Eastern Vindhyas. These hills are not higher than 2,000 feet[20]. The Pānnā range, which is a branch of the Vindhyas in Bundelkhaṇḍ, extends from south-west to north-east, and plays the dominant role in the geological formation of the region. The other Vindhyan range, known as the Kāimur range, north of the Śon, stands as a boundary between Bundelkhaṇḍ and Bāghelkhaṇḍ. From these hills a number of rivers flow north or north-east towards the Jumnā, of which the most important are the Betwā, the Dhāsan, the Ken and the Tons. Besides, there are a number of minor rivers in the region, viz., the Pahuj, the Jāmni, the Birmā, the Bhagain and the Paisuni.

The rivers and the hill-ranges divide this part of

---

[18] *A.S.R.*, XXI., p. 58; *E.I.*, I., p. 218.

[19] *D.H.N.I.*, II., p. 670. See also my paper on "The status of Early Candella Rulers". *I.H.Q.*, Sept., 1953., pp. 304-09.

[20] *I.G.I.*, IX, p. 68.

Central India into separate zones with differing physical characteristics, as mentioned below :—

(*i*) Between the Sindh (Sindhu) and the Dhāsan (Daśārṇā) lies the first segment of Bundelkhaṇḍ, which includes the valley of the Betwā or the Vetravatī, one of the important rivers of northern India. It rises in Bhopal State and flows in a north-easterly direction to meet the Jumnā near the town of Hamirpur. The Dhāsan itself is one of its tributaries[21]. The Pahuj is also in this area, rising near Datiā and meeting the Sindh a few miles before the latter's confluence with the Jumnā, and the Jāmni is a small tributary of the Betwā, meeting the latter near Orchā. Till recently the two important Bundelā states, Datiā and Orchā, the Rājput state Samthār, and some petty principalities like Dhurwāi, Bijnā, and Jigni and the intervening districts of Jhānsi and Jalaun comprised the area.

(*ii*) The stretch of territory between the Dhāsan and the Ken (Karṇavatī) rivers formerly comprised states of Pānnā, Chārkhāri, Chātārpur and the states of Sarilā, Bānkāpāhāri, Ālipurā, Bijāwār, Gaurihār and Gārrāuli, and the important district of Hamirpur. Immediately after the Ken, rises the Pānnā range, which traverses right across Bundelkhaṇḍ. Below the Ken, near its confluence with the Jumnā, but to the north of the Pānnā range, is located the Bāndā district which should also come in this group. It is watered by the small river named Baghain, which pours itself into the Jumnā.

(*iii*) Between the Pānnā range and the Kāimur there is a low-lying tract, generally sloping towards the Gangetic basin. The eastern portion is watered by the river Tons, rising from the Kāimur hill to the south of Maihār. Further below are the districts of Dāmoh and Saugor of the Central Provinces (Madhya Pradesh) bounded on the south by the hill range known as Bhānrer or Bhāṇḍer. Below the Kāimur is the Śon, which issues from the Amarkaṇṭaka and flows north and turns right only from the base of the Kāimur.

---

[21] *I.G.I.*, VIII., p. 16.

The boundaries of the Candella dominion, of course, varied from time to time. But it always included Mahobā, Kālañjar, Khajurāho and Ajaygaḍh, all of which are situated in the central segment of Bundelkhaṇḍ. Mahobā, now a small country-town in the Hamirpur district, 54 miles to the south of Hamirpur town and 34 miles to the north of Khajurāho, is associated by tradition very closely with the Candella dynasty. The bardic account entitled, the Mahobā Khaṇḍ[22], is the popular legend of Parmāl's war with Pṛthvīrāj Cauhān. Many spots and buildings at and near Mahobā preserve the memory of Candella kings and princes. Some of the kings are remembered for having excavated lakes or built temples, viz., Rāhilya-sāgar and a granite temple on its embankment (named after Rāhila), Kirāt-sāgar and a Śiva temple, the remains of which are found near the dargāh (Kīrtivaraman), Madansāgar and the granite temple, Kākrā Marh (Madanavarman). The remains of the palace of Paramardi (Parmāl), on the top of a slightly fortified hill known as 'the Fort', are still noticeable, though later turned into a mosque[23].

Khajurāho (Khajurāha, Kharjuravāhaka), 27 miles to the east of Chātārpur, with its group of magnificent temples, was according to Smith, the religious city of the Candellas[24]. There are more than thirty temples at Khajurāho and the neighbouring village Jaṭkāri, all testifying to the grandeur of Candella rule and its patronage of art, sculpture and architecture. In the opinion of competent scholars they are some of "the finest groups of Hindu temples in Northern India[25]". It is believed that the splendour of Khajurāho reached its peak in the 10th-11th century A.D. under Candella rule.

Of the eight forts ascribed to the Candellas by tradition, Kālañjar, 90 miles west-south-west of Allahabad, is the most important and believed to have been the military centre of

---

[22] Ed. by Sri S. S. Das under the title, *Parmāl Rāso*. *Pṛthvīrāj Raso* by Cānd Bardāi also describes it in the chapter, 'Mahobā Samaya', pp. 2507-2615.

[23] *I.A.*, XXXVII., p. 134.

[24] *ibid.*, p. 132.

[25] *ibid.*, p. 133.

the kingdom[26]. It has a long antiquity and from the very ancient times the hill had been a favourite resort of Śaiva ascetics. It is included in the list of holy places of Northern India given in the Purāṇas and the Mahābhārata[27]. The Candellas came to occupy it under Yaśovarman early in the 10th century A.D., and the Candella rulers thenceforward were decorated with the title 'Kālañjarādhipati' until the time of the last known ruler of the family, Hammīravarman[28]. It is interesting in this connection to note that all these places (Mahobā, Khajurāho and Kālañjar), which played important parts in the history of the Candellas were located in the central segment of Bundelkhaṇḍ.

Barring Garhā and Maihār, which are near Jabalpur (Madhya Pradesh), other Candella forts are also situated in the central sector, between the Dhāsan and the Ken, as specified in the list of natural sub-divisions of Bundelkhaṇḍ mentioned above (No. ii). Of them the fortress of Ajaygaḍh (Jayadurga) played a no less significant role in the Candella history. Though the main portion of the state of Ajaigarh is in the southern part of Bundelkhaṇḍ the fortress of the name was on the fringe of the Pānnā hills, just below the Ken to the south-east of Mahobā and south-west of Kālañjar. Trailokyavarman, who succeeded Paramardi early in the 13th century A.D., had his headquarters at this fort. A tank in the fort is ascribed to Parmāl (Paramardi), and there are inscriptions of his successors, Trailokavarman, Vīravarman, Bhojavarman and Hammīravarman[29]. Smith believes that after the capture of Kālañjar by Kutubuddin in 1203 A.D., the Candella chiefs resided ordinarily at Ajaygaḍh, which was about 20 miles from Kālañjar[30].

Bārigarh, Maniyāgarh, Marphā and Maudhā are other

[26] *ibid.*, p. 131.

[27] *Matsya Purāṇa* XIII., 32; *Matsya* & *Padma Purāṇas* quoted by Hemādri in his '*Caturvarga-cintāmaṇi*' (Śrāddha Kāṇḍa), p. 30; *Mbh.* (Vana Parva), Bengal Recension, Chap. 85, V. 56-57. It is also mentioned in the *Kāśikā*. IV., 2, 125 "Vṛddhājjana-padāvadheḥ—Kālañjaraḥ—Kālañjarakaḥ".

[28] *E.I.*, XX., p. 135.

[29] *A.S.R.*, XXI., pp. 50-52; *E.I.*, I., pp. 325-38; *E.I.*, XX., p. 134, 135 f.n. 2; *E.I.*, XXVIII., pp. 98-107.

[30] *I.A.*, XXXVII. p. 135.

forts ascribed to the Candellas by tradition. Bārigarh is in Chārkhāri, about 10 miles from Mahobā. Maniyāgarh is a large ruined fort on the left bank of the Ken river on a hill overlooking the town of Rāigarh in the former Chātārpur State[31]. It is believed by some scholars to have been the original seat of the Candella clan. Marphā is in the Bāndā district, 12 miles to the north-east of Kālañjar[32] and Maudhā in the north-eastern corner of the Hamirpur district.

Epigraphic records refer to some of the viṣayas or districts of the Candella dominion. Karigāva viṣaya[33], roundabout modern Kargāwān, 9 miles north-east of Pachār (Jhānsi district), was in the northern sector. The royal encampment at Vilāsapura, from where a number of land-grants were issued, is to be identified with Pachār, which was known by the name Vilāsapura[34] even some 10 or 15 generations ago. Dudāhi viṣaya,[35] the modern place of the same name (Dudhāi), and Vaḍavāri viṣaya[36], modern Berwārā, were both in the Lalitpur sub-division of the same district. Kīrtigiri[37] (Deogaḍh), on the left bank of the Betwā, was also in the Lalitpur sub-division. Vikaura viṣaya,[38] identified with modern Beekore, 4-5 miles south-west of Madanpur, in the northern part of the Saugor district, was to the north of the Dhāsan.

Though located further south in Mālwā, Bhāsvat[39] or Bhaillasvāmin (modern Bhilsā) on the bank of the Betwā near Sānchi, may also be included in this group. Suḍāli viṣaya, mentioned in the Nānyaura Plate 'C' (V.S. 1190)[40],

---

[31] *A.S.R.* XXI., p. 69.
[32] *ibid.*, p. 18.
[33] Pachār Plate (V.S. 1233), *E.I.*, X., pp. 44-49.
[34] Recently found Bhārat Kalā Bhavan Plate of Paramardin (V.S. 1239) was issued from Sallakṣaṇa-Vilāsapura encampment of King Paramardin. According to Dr. D. C. Sircar it may be the same as Vilāsapura mentioned above, only with the addition of "Sallakṣaṇa", the name of the elder brother of Pṛthvīvarman, great-grand father of Paramardin.
[35] Semrā plates (V.S. 1223) E.I., IV., pp. 153-70.
The Bhārat Kalā Bhavan Plate of Paramardin (V.S. 1239) mentions Duḍuhi viṣaya, which is evidently identical with Dudāhi. I am indebted to Dr. D. C. Sircar for this information.
[36] Semra Plates, V.S. 1223.
[37] Deogaḍh Rock Inscription (V.S. 1154) *I.A.*, XVIII., pp. 237-39.
[38] Semrā Plates (V.S. 1223) *E.I.*, IV., pp. 156, 157.
[39] *E.I.* I., pp. 124., 129.
[40] *I.A.*, XVI., pp. 202, 207.

was possibly located near Bhilsā, as the grant was issued while Madanavarman was in residence there.

On the north-western side of Bundelkhaṇḍ we find mention of the town of Padmāvatī[41] (identified with Narwar, also known as Nalapura) on the bank of the Sindh. Beyond the river the Candella territory for sometime extended up to the hill-fortress of Gopādri (Gwālior)[42].

The central sector of Bundelkhaṇḍ, the hub of the Candella dominions, also comprised a number of viṣayas. Beginning from the north-east we find references to (*i*) the Eracha viṣaya[43], modern Erich on the Betwā, 60 miles from Mahobā in the Hamirpur district, (*ii*) the Nandāvana viṣaya[44], which included the village Nandinī or Nandandeo or Nundodeo, some 10 miles south-west of Icchāwār in the Bāndā district, (*iii*) the Navarāṣṭramaṇḍala-viṣaya[45] stated to have been situated on the bank of the Jumnā, either in the Bāndā or in the Allahabad district. All these districts belong to the Candellas, according to their own inscriptions. A land grant was issued by Candella Dhaṅga from Kāśikā (Banaras)[46]. It is also known from the Khajurāho record of V.S. 1059 that Dhaṅga died voluntarily sacrificing his body at the sacred confluence of the Ganges and the Jumnā, Prayāga[47].

The Kirayiḍa viṣaya[48], being identifiable with Kiraḍi, 5 miles from Mahobā, may have been situated near the capital of the Candella territory. In the south-western portion of the central segment may be located the Pāniulī viṣaya[49] (the former state of Pānnā) and the Dahī viṣaya[50] (the former Bijāwār state). The Gārrā plates of V.S. 1261[51] refer to a village, Lohasihani (identified with modern Lohani in Bijāwār) as included in the viṣaya of Vikrauni. Vikrauni

---

41 *E.I.*, I., pp. 148-49, 151, L. 6.
42 *ibid.*, p. 129, V. 45.
43 Mahobā Plates of Paramardideva (V.S. 1230) *E.I.*, XVI., pp. 9-15.
44 Icchāwār Plates (V.S. 1228) *I.A.* XXV., pp. 205-08.
45 Chārkhāri Plate (V.S. 1108), *E.I.* XX., pp. 125-28.
46 Nānyaura Plate 'A' (V.S. 1055) *I.A.*, XVI., p. 203., L. 7.
47 *E.I.* I., pp. 139, 146. V. 55.
48 Chārkhāri Plate (V.S. 1236) *E.I.*, XX., pp. 128-31.
49 Gārrā Plates (V.S. 1261) *E.I.* XVI., pp. 272-77.
50 Chārkhāri Plate (V.S. 1311) *E.I.*, XX., pp. 132-34.
51 *E. I.*, XVI., pp. 272-77.

of this record and Vikaura of the Semrā Plates are taken to be identical[52].

There is a reference to a viṣaya, named Vedesaitha,[53] in the Chārkhāri Plate, which, however, is not identifiable. But this record was issued from Vilāsapura, believed to be identical with the modern village of Pachār, as has already been mentioned. If this identification is accepted it will appear that the Vedesaitha viṣaya was also somewhere in the central sector of Bundelkhaṇḍ. The Bhārat Kalā Bhavan Plate of Madanavarman (V.S. 1192)[54] mentions the name of Mahisineha Viṣaya (and Pattalā), which has not yet been identified. But from its association with places such as, Eraccha, Nandāvena, &c., it may be suggested that like the latter the Mahisineha viṣaya also was situated in the central part.

In the south-eastern part of Bundelkhaṇḍ, on the borders of Bāghelkhaṇḍ, between the Pānnā range and the Kāimur range, was the feudatory state of Kakareḍikā, modern Kakreri, on the table-land at the head of the principal pass, the Mamani Ghat, leading to the west towards Bāndā, Kālañjar and Mahobā. A series of copper plates of the Mahārāṇakas of Kakareḍikā reveals that they owed allegiance to the Cedis[55], but later became feudatories of the Candellas, when Trailokyavarman wrested control of the region from the Cedis sometime before 1239 A.D.[56]

The geological formation of southern Bundelkhaṇḍ, marked by the branching ranges of the Vindhyas, already referred to, has greatly influenced the character of the plain country lying between the hills and the Jumnā, which is alluvial due to the course of the rivers, rising from the different parts of the Vindhyan ranges, which run across the north-eastern and western parts of Bundelkhaṇḍ. It is estimated that about 8,000 sq. miles, to the west of the Pānnā

---

52 *E.I.*, XVI., pp. 274-.
53 *E.I.* XX., pp. 134-36.
54 Edited by Dr. D.C. Sircar in *E.I.*, XXXI.
55 *I.A.*, XVII., p. 224.
56 *ibid.*, pp. 230-36.

range, is level country, and the remainder falls in the rugged tract formed by that branch of the Vindhyas.[57]

Compared to Mālwā or the western part of Central India, the soil of Bundelkhaṇḍ is poor, being sandy and often strewn with boulders. Even comparatively fertile portions of the land require artificial irrigation. In spite of this physical handicap the people of the country were predominantly agricultural, and their prosperity depended on favourable agricultural conditions.[58] Epigraphic records show that the people of Bundelkhaṇḍ were anxious to raise the fertility of the soil by excavating tanks, wells and canals, and by constructing embankments.[59]

Varieties of soil that are still found in the different parts of Bundelkhaṇḍ, are locally known as "the Mār, the Kābar and the Rākar'. The Mār type of soil is of black or dark colour and is specially suitable for growing wheat, cotton, &c. The Kābar soil is a variety of lighter black colour with differing qualities. The Mār and the Kābar are found in most of the Bundelkhaṇḍ districts, specially in the plains. But from Jhānsi to Lalitpur the prevailing colour of the soil is largely red or yellow[60]. This is locally known as 'rākar' or 'rānkar'. A red or yellow loam, called 'Parwā', resembling the ordinary loam soil of the Doab, occurs in many parts of the Bāndā districts.[61]

In this connection it may be interesting to note that the Ajaygaḍh inscription of the time of Bhojavarman mentions 'Pītaśaila-viṣayesu-adhipatinām'[62] (Lords of the Yellow-mountain districts), as an epithet of the Candella rulers, which has not so far been properly explained, as the viṣaya of that name could not be identified. The term, as it appears to me, was used in a figurative sense to indicate the 'rākar'-soil districts of Bundelkhaṇḍ, which constituted the centre of the Candella kingdom.

---

[57] *I.G.I.,* IX., p. 75; *C.R.,* XX. Pt. I, p. 28.
[58] *C.R.,* XX., Pt. I., p. 24.
[59] Māu Stone Insc., *E.I.,* I., pp. 195-207., Ajaygaḍh Stone Insc. (V.S. 1227) *A.S.R.,* XXI., pp. 49-50; Ajaygaḍh Rock Insc. (V.S. 1317) *E.I.* I., pp. 325-30.
[60] *I.G.I.,* IX., p. 68.
[61] *ibid.,* VI., p. 351.
[62] *E.I.,* I., pp. 333, 336, V. 9. For S. L. Katare's suggestion vide *E. I.,* XXX, p. 89.

CHAPTER II

LEGENDS ABOUT THE ORIGIN OF THE CANDELLAS

The origin of most of the Rājput dynasties of Northern India is somewhat obscure and uncertain. Traditional theories with regard to most of them are generally associated with some legends contained either in laudatory verses or in bardic ballads or even in unwritten folk-tales or songs. The dynasties like the Cāhamānas, the Pratihāras, the Caulukyas and the Paramāras are regarded as the four fire-born races (agnikula). Their founders are said to have sprung from the fire-altar of the sage Vaśiṣṭha on the Mount Abu[1]. The Kalacuris claim to have descended from Yayāti, the Kachwāhas from Kuśa, the son of Rāma, and the Guhilots directly from Rāma.

The Candellas, in the same way, trace their descent from the Moon, in which respect the inscriptions of the dynasty as well as current traditions are almost unanimous. 'Candrātreya' has been adopted as the clan-name of the family in their epigraphic records, after the name of the sage Candrātreya, who has been claimed to be the progenitor of the family ('Candrātreya-muner mahīyasi kule'[2], 'Candrātreya narendrānām vaṁśa')[3]. The Khajurāho Inscription of V.S. 1011 is the earliest available record to refer to this mythical origin of the family. It states that the renowned sages of pure character, viz., Marīci, Atri and others, arose from the Primordial Being, the Maker of the Universe (Viśvasṛk Purāṇapuruṣa). Of them Atri begat Candrātreya, a sage, who acquired great power by ceaseless

---

[1] *Annals and Antiquities of Rajasthan* by J. Tod (Ed. by Wm. Crooke) Vol. I. pp. 112-13.

[2] *Nānyaura Plate* 'A' *I. A.* XVI., p. 201, Ll. 1-2.

[3] I.A., XVI, p. 208; *ibid.* XXV., p. 206; *E. I.* IV., p. 157; *ibid.* XVI., p. 12; *ibid.* XX., pp. 129, 133, 135.

austerities[4]. Thereafter the record merely states that 'in the family of the sage Candrātreya was born Nannuka', the first king of the dynasty. The Khajurāho Inscription of V.S. 1059[5] and the Baṭeśvar Stone Inscription of V.S. 1252[6] also trace the origin of the family from the eponymous sage Atri, from whose eye sprang the Moon, from whom was born the sage Candrātreya. Kielhorn suggests that the form 'Candrātreya' may have been the Sanskritised form of the term, 'Candrella' (Candra and suffix-'illa', meaning 'descended from Candra'), found in the Dudāhi Stone Inscription of Devalabdhi[7]. The colloquial terms, 'Candela' and 'Candella' used in folk literature are also noticed in some of the inscriptions, viz., the Deogaḍh Rock Inscription mentions 'Caṁdella'[8], the Benares Grant of Lakṣmī-Karṇa, 'Candella'[9], the Madanpur Stone Inscription of Cāhamāna Pṛthvīrājadeva III[10] and the Chārkhāri Plate of V.S. 1108, 'Candela'[11]. Obviously all these terms indicate the association of the Moon with the origin of the family. A direct descent from the Moon is also described in the Mahobā Inscription[12] and the Ajaygaḍh Rock Inscription of V.S. 1317[13]. Thus mythical details about the lunar origin such as are generally found in the records of other ruling families, viz., the Kalacuris[14] and the Yādavas of East Bengal,[15] are not furnished in the Candella inscriptions.

The local traditions have preserved curious stories explaining the place of the Moon-God in regard to the origin of the family. The material, which is derived from these sources, is hardly of much historical value, but even in these absurd stories some points are found which may have some

---

[4] *E. I.* I., p. 125.
[5] *E. I.* I., p. 140.
[6] *E. I.* I., p. 208-09.
[7] *I. A.* XVIII., pp. 236-37.
[8] *ibid.* pp. 237-39., L. 1.
[9] *E. I.* II., p. 306., V. 8.
[10] *A. S. R.* XXI., p. 174, No. 10., Ll. 2-3.
[11] *E. I.* XX., p. 127., L. 9.
[12] "Tasmād-ajani rajanī-vallabhād viśva-kāntaḥ" *E. I.* I. P. 217.
[13] *E. I.* I., p. 325
[14] *Jabalpur Plate of Yaśaḥkarṇa E. I.* II., pp. 1-7; *Goharwā Grant ibid.* XI., pp. 139-46; *The Kāhlā Grant* (V.S. 1135) *E. I.* VII., pp. 85-93.; *The Kāsiā Stone Inscription ibid.* XVIII. pp. 121-37.
[15] *Belāva Grant of Bhojavarman I. B.* (III) pp. 14-24.

significance. The whole tradition as to the origin of the Candellas, as embodied in the Mahobā Khaṇḍ, should be placed before scholars, so that they may be helped to form a proper estimate about the character of the legendary material available. The work has only been cursorily mentioned by other writers. It is given here in detail from the original text.

The Mahobā Khaṇḍ is generally taken to be a part of the Pṛthvīrāj Rāso of the well known Central Indian bard, Cānd Bardāi. The question of the authorship of the Mahobā Khaṇḍ is a matter of controversy. Sri Shyamasundar Das, who edited the text under the caption, Parmāl Rāso, holds that it can never be a part of the Pṛthvīrāj Rāso, and that its authorship cannot be ascribed to Cānd Bardāi. He suggests that it would not be unnatural for a Bundelkhaṇḍi poet to compose the Rāso (Mahobā Khaṇḍ) on the lines of either Cānd Bardāi's story, or Jāgnik Rāi's Ālhā Rāso, or similar other works and incorporate in it the materials derived from traditions. According to Sri Das, the extant Mahobā Khaṇḍ could not have been composed earlier than the 17th or 18th century of the Vikram Era, *i.e.*, much later in point of time than the Pṛthvīrāj Rāso of Cānd Bardāi, who was a friend and contemporary of Pṛthvīrāj Cauhān[16].

The first chapter of the Mahobā Khaṇḍ relates the story of the birth of Candravarman (Candra Brahma (Varman) Utpatti Khaṇḍa), who is described as the first ruler of the Candella lineage. While describing the birth of the first prince of the Candella clan, the author introduces the story of Hemavatī, the daughter of Hemrāj, a priest of the Gahirawārs, and her union with the Moon-God. Reference to this story has been already made by Cunningham[17] and Dr. H. C. Ray[18].

The story has been rejected as a 'silly legend' by V. A. Smith[19]. But a critical examination of the leg end may

[16] *P. R.* Introduction p. 2.
[17] *A. S. R.* II., pp. 445-6.
[18] *D. H. N. I.* II., p. 665.
[19] *I. A.* XXXVII., pp. 136-7.

reveal, in spite of its apparent absurdities, a substratum of fact. I have carefully examined the manuscript of the Mahobā Khaṇḍ in the Library of the Asiatic Society of Bengal. It is, however, entered in the catalogue of the Library of the Society under the title, "Pṛthvīrāj Rāso by Cānd Bardāi". The only printed edition of the work has been published from the Kāśī Nāgri Pracāriṇī Sabhā under the title, 'Parmāl Rāso' (now out of print).

The story opens in the Puranic style in the august presence of Anaṅgapāla, the Tomara king. The poet introduces the story thus, "Listen now to the three dynasties, their early history is being narrated."[20]

The three dynasties referred to by the poet are mentioned in the following order:

First the Goḍas, then the Gahirawārs, and after them the Candels, born of the daughter of Hemrāj, the family-priest of the Gahirawārs[21].

The main purpose of the poet is to give the history of the Candellas, who came to power by supplanting the Gahirawārs. As to the Goḍas, who are mentioned as having ruled prior to the Gahirawārs, nothing definite can be said. In another place of the text there is a reference to the Gauḍas associated with Māhiṣmatī[22].

It appears that the Gauḍas have been referred to as Goḍas in the above verse. In fact the Asiatic Society Manuscript gives the reading 'Gauḍa' for Goḍa. It may be suggested that the word Goḍa or Gauḍa may have been applied to the indigenous tribes inhabiting Mahobā and its neighbourhood (Bundelkhaṇḍ), who later came to be known as the Gonds. J.C. Nesfield points out on the basis of the Census Report of 1882 that the aboriginal Gond of the Central

---

[20] सुनहु श्रवन त्रय वंस अव, पूरव कथा सुनाइ ।। ७६ ।

[21] प्रथम गोड़ ककाशी नृपति गहिरवार फिर होइ ।।
ता नृपके प्रोहित भयौ हेमराज कहि सोइ ।। ७७
ता दुजवर की कन्यका प्रगटे वंस चंदेल ।
M. K. (Ms.) has a variant reading—प्रथममेव पुन गोड़ नृप . . . .

[22] लई जीति माहिष्मती गौड़ भाजा (८६) ।

India should not be confused with the Gonds of the Gangetic valley, and the name of the former should properly be spelt as 'Gaud'[23].

The reference to the Gahirawārs, following the Goḍas but preceding the Candellas, is curious, though it is to be found in all the versions of local traditions. A number of antiquated embankments, dry beds of lakes and tanks are ascribed to the Gahirāwar rulers by local people. V. Smith recognised their antiquity and placed them in the pre-Candel period[24]. If the Gahirawārs are to be regarded as identical with the Gaharwārs (Gāhaḍavālas), it is difficult to find a place for them prior to the rise of the Candellas. The official records of the Gāhaḍavālas mention their first ruler, Yaśovigraha, as appearing after the end of the families of the Sun and the Moon[25], i.e., the Gurjara-Pratihāras and the Kalacuris respectively. Thus the Gāhaḍavālas came to power not earlier than the first quarter of the 11th century A.D. In these records there is no information about the Gāhaḍavālas ruling in Mahobā or anywhere else earlier than the 9th century A.D., when the rise of the Candellas took place.

Smith in this connection refers to a Gorakhpur tradition, mentioned in Martin's Eastern India II (quoted in Beames' Elliot I, p. 124) that the Gaharwārs are descendants of the famous Rājā Nala, and they came to Kāśī from Nalapura (mod. Narwar, near Gwālior)[26]. He surmises that while migrating southwards during the period of political instability following the decline of the empire of Harṣavardhana, some of them branched off from the main stream to settle at Mahobā. While Yaśovigraha, who seems to have been a commoner[27], bringing distinction to his family, founded the well-known Gāhaḍavāla dynasty of Benares and Kanauj, these Gahirawārs (Gāhaḍavālas), who are supposed to have

---

[23] A brief view of the caste system of N. W. Provinces and Oudh together with an examination of the names and figures as shown in the Census Report of 1882. p. 6.

[24] *J. A. S. B.* (1881). L., Pt. I., p. 1.

[25] *I. A.* XXIII., p. 11.

Āsīd-asitadyuti-vaṁśa-jāta kṣmāpālamālāsu divaṁ gatāsu/Sākṣād-Vivaśvān-iva bhuridhāmnā Yaśovigraha ityudāraḥ//

[26] *J. A. S. B.* (1881)., p. 3.

[27] *I. A.* XVIII., p. 11.

settled at Mahobā, may have owned a principality there and ruled before the rise of the Candels of the Mahobā Khaṇḍ.

There are a few verses regarding the Gahirawār dynasty in the Mahobā Khaṇḍ, which give us a genealogical account of the Gahirawārs, described as connected with Kaśī. Karamcānd, the first ruler of the line, was a very upright administrator, under whom every subject was happy and contented. His son, Ranasiṁha, was as beautiful as Cupid; and his son Naranāth, was a valiant soldier. He was succeeded by his son, Jayasiṁha, and after him came Jagannātha Rāya, who conquered the fort of Ratnadurga. His son was Narasiṁha, who seized Māhiṣmatī and defeated the Gauḍas. Next came his son, Indrajit, to whom the goddess Vindhyadevī appeared in person. (P. R., Book. I., V. 84-87).

The dynastic history, as described above, can hardly be regarded as authentic. None of the names occurring in the list of Gahirawār kings is to be found in the records of the Gāhaḍavālas. Then, again, the description of the Gahirawārs as belonging to Benares[28], can hardly be accepted. For the Gāhaḍavālas of Benares can by no means be carried back to a period earlier than the 11th century A.D., on the basis of the historical materials at our disposal. But if the Gorakhpur tradition, mentioned earlier, has any value, it may, as already suggested, indicate an earlier settlement of the Gahirawārs at Mahobā. That the Gahirawārs mentioned by the author, were, in his opinion, the same as the Gāhaḍavālas, is apparent from the reference to the Kāśī region. The connection with the Gāhaḍavālas is not directly shown in the verses quoted above, but most probably the author means the Gāhaḍavālas when he refers to Kāśī in the manner he has done so in the verse. The memory of the Gāhaḍavālas, it appears, had not entirely faded away from the minds of the people for whom the Mahobā Khaṇḍ was meant. It is not unlikely that while referring to the Gahirawārs, who were known only from ballads and songs current in Mahobā, the poet, struck by the similarity of the two names—Gahirawārs and Gaharwārs

28 "गहिरवार काशिय भयव" ।

(Gāhaḍavālas), introduced a link between the two by connecting the former with Kāśī, and thus raised the status of the Gahirawārs, the local rulers of Mahobā, in the estimation of the people.

Now the poet takes up the third dynasty, the Candels, stated to have been given birth to by Hemavatī, the daughter of the priest of the Gahirawār rulers.

The story, about the origin of the Candella dynasty, as preserved in the Mahobā Khaṇḍ[29], finds little corroboration from the epigraphic records of the time of the Candella rule. The only point of agreement between these traditions and the inscriptional documents is the theory of the descent from the Moon-God. But the inscriptions trace the lineage in the conventional way, as has already been mentioned, either directly from the Moon, or from Atri, the progenitor of the lunar race of Kṣatriyas. This evidence from their own records, coupled with the inclusion of the Candellas in the list of 36 Rājput families of noble rank by Cānd Bardāi[30], have led C.V. Vaidya to regard the Candellas as of high birth and of Aryan origin[31].

But Smith and a few other scholars reject the theory attributing a high pedigree to the Candellas. According to them the attempt of the Candellas to trace their ancestry from Candra is only for the purpose of hiding the real origin, which was probably from such aboriginal tribes as the Bhars and the Gonds[32].

In analysing the story of the Mahobā Khaṇḍ, however, it appears, that although the origin of the family is connected with the Moon-God, the irregular nature of the association did constantly trouble the poet as well as his listeners. This is evident from the details given in the story as well as the enquiry made by the Tomara king, before whom the story was narrated. The King asks, "How is it that a Kṣatriya caste was

---

[29] See Appendix. 'A'.

[30] वरणे वंस छतीस, Pr. R. (Cānd). *Pahila Samaya* p. 54.

[31] *History of Mediaeval India.* Vol. II., pp. 130-33.

[32] *I. A.* XXXVII., p. 137; *E. H. I.*, p. 379.

born of a Brāhman[33] ? A direct answer to this question is evaded by the poet, who only gives the story by way of an explanation. The story, as narrated, reveals the following irregularities regarding the origin of Candravarman and his dynasty :

(*i*) The origin of a Kṣatriya dynasty from a Brahmin woman,

(*ii*) Her widowhood, when the intercourse takes place, which is prohibited in the Śāstras, and,

(*iii*) The character of the union requiring Candravarman to be treated as of impure birth.

We may next analyse the incredible features included in the story.

(*i*) Apart from the connection with the Moon-God, other divine or semi-divine personalities are associated with Candravarman in different periods of his career, viz., (*a*) Bṛhaspati writing his horoscope, (*b*) Celestial women performing auspicious rites at the time of his birth, marriage, consecration, etc., (*c*) Bṛhaspati, Kubera and Candra teaching him polity.

(*ii*) The exhibition of a rather unusual feat of strength and courage in killing a tiger and a lion merely with stones and missiles. Reference may in this connection be made to similar incidents in the lives of Sher Shāh[34] and Bābar.

(*iii*) The gift of a touchstone by the Moon-God and procurement of immeasurable wealth, thereby making it possible for Candravaraman to organise a strong four-fold army and occupy Kāliñjar and other adjacent tracts by defeating their rulers[35].

(*iv*) Building temples and constructing lakes and gardens by the divine architect, Viśvakarman, at Khajurāho in course of only four hours.

Instances of Brahmins becoming Kṣatriyas (i.e., Brahma-

---

[33] व्रह्मनतें छतियनकी कैसे उतपति होति ?

[34] *C. H. I.* IV., Chap. III., p. 46.

[35] The military exploits ascribed to this prince hardly agree with the facts known from authentic sourcc. According to Khajurāho Inscription of V. S. 1011 Yaśovarman occupied Kālañjar. *E. I.* I., pp. 127-28., V. 31.

Kṣatriyas)[36] on assumption of royal power were not unknown. The case of the Candellas was evidently not similar to them. Otherwise the poet would not have experienced so much difficulty in giving a direct answer to the question of the Tomara king.

Where the origin of a dynasty is not pure from the orthodox point of view, but still has to be glorified, stories are manufactured in which some irregular features can be detected from which alone in the absence of any other internal evidence, an impure origin can be inferred. For example, Naraka, the progenitor of the earliest of the Kāmarupa kings, is stated to have been born of the Earth Goddess as a result of an intercourse with Viṣṇu in His Boar incarnation. But it was an irregular intercourse as the Earth Goddess was 'unclean' at the time[37].

On the whole, the Mahobā Khaṇḍ, though unacceptable, gives an idea as how legends were connected and mythical elements introduced to explain the origin and early history of a ruling dynasty, when real facts about it have already been forgotten. It cannot be treated as totally useless in so far as it agrees with the materials found from inscriptions and other sources, showing the continuity of a tradition that was not completely lost, even after some centuries.

The Candellas became a considerable power and made useful contribution to the greatness of Mahobā. The existence of songs and ballads about them which the author of the Mahobā Khaṇḍ must have utilised show that they were remembered for many centuries. Even in their own time the Candellas had been given a lunar origin. The aryanisation of an indigenous tribe must have been completed when they began to rule.

---

[36] *Deopārā Praśasti*, L. 5. I. B. (III) p. 46; *Mādhāinagar Grant*, L. 36 I. B. (III) p. 111.

[37] *Kālikā Purāna* Ed. by Pañcānan Tarkaratna. Chap. XXXVI, 8.

APPENDIX A

The Story of Candravarman in the Mahobā Khanḍ.
चन्द्रब्रह्म उत्पत्ति खंड (Book I)

Hemrāj, a man of amiable disposition, was a priest to King Indrajīt Gahirawār, as तिन राजाके evidently refers to the last named king of the Gahirawār family. The priest was blessed with the birth of a daughter, whom he named Hemavatī. She was not only as beautiful as a picture but her manners also were charming.

तिनराजाके विप्र हुव हेमराज[1] सुखदाय ।
ताके एक सुता भई मनहु सुक सो श्राय ।। ८८
कासी कल भय कन्यका हेमवती[2] धरि नांव ।
श्रति सुन्दर तनु चित्रनी सोभत सील सुभाव ।। ८९

But unfortunately when she was only sixteen years old, she became a widow by the curse of Lord Indra (षोड़सवर्ष सुता भई । इन्द्र श्रापते विधवा भई ।......१०१)

Then we are introduced to the queer anecdote of the union of the Moon-God and the beautiful woman, Hemavatī (हेमवती वर सुन्दर नारिय ।). It was a sultry summer night. Hemavati felt very uneasy and went out to have a bath. (सुक्रमास गरमी तनश्राइय । निसि श्रस्नान करत सुखदाइय ।) While she was taking her bath, the Moon-God, the friend of Kumuda flowers, appeared on the sky. (ग्रीष्म रितु श्रस्नान जु किन्निव कुमुदवन्धु तव दरसन दिन्निव । ९०) Seeing this exquisitely beautiful lady in that position, the Moon-God felt exceedingly delighted. He came down on the earth near her and embraced her passionately. (दिक्खि कलानिधि काम सताइव । उतरि तासु कंह कंट लगाइव ।।.....१०२)[3] The incident is described in further details in verses 91-94. The God sported with Hemavatī for the whole night, but the latter was not aware of his identity. (चारिजाम जामिनि रितु मानिय । देव तेज त्रिय कछुव न जानिय ।)

[1] Variant in M. K. (Ms.) हंसराज
[2] Variant in M. K. (Ms.) हेमावती
[3] *P. R.*, pp. 9-10.

Now when he was preparing to return to the skies, his own region, Hemavatī ran after him and caught hold of him by his hands. Further she threatened to curse him for having spoilt her life.

उदधिनन्द रितु दै चलिव धरिव धाइ तिय हथ्थ ।
मोहि कलंकित करि चलिव लै सराप समरथ्थ ।। १०३

At this the Moon-God turned round and said,—'You need not curse me, rather be happy to note that your son will be a King. He will be a vigorous ruler enjoying the whole world, and from him will spring a thousand branches'[4]. Now, of course, she had to compose herself and in consideration of the assurance given by the Moon-God, she gave up the idea of cursing him. (विचारि नारि नित्तय सराप मुंचि चित्तय) But what tormented her most was the fear of social degradation that would result from this union, as she was a widow. So she prayed to the Moon-God,—'How shall my dishonour be effaced ? (म्हा कलंक को मिट्टइय उड़पति कहहु विचारि) I am a poor widow without a lord or husband though I may possess a youthful body'.

'Fear not' replied Candramā, 'your son will be born on the bank of the Karṇavatī river (modern, the Ken), and he will be a valiant hero. (शुभ कर्णवती के तीर तुव पुत्र होय सुवीर) Then go to Khajjurapura (modern Khajurāho or Khajrāho), offer gifts and perform sacrifices. (षज्जुरपुर फिरि जाय दिय दाय जज्ञ कराय). He will reign in Mahobā with extensive possessions acquired by defeating other monarchs through the efforts of his four-fold army. He will possess a philosopher's stone, which will turn iron into gold. He will build numerous temples and excavate lakes and tanks. He will also build a fortress at the holy Kālinjar.'

But all these promises of glory waiting for the son could not remove Hemavatī's apprehensions of social stigma in this world and future sufferings in the next. So in utter agony she cried out, 'You would make my son a king no doubt, but I shall be made to suffer in Hell'. (भुव पुत्र करि है राजु म्हा कहतु नर्क समाजु ।। ११३)

---

[4] *P. R.* p. 10.

Then the Moon-God prescribed some expiatory rites for her. 'When your son will be of sixteen years of age, he will perform a Bhāṇḍya Yajña, whereby your sin will be washed away'.

> षोड़स वर्ष कुमार तव होइ भुर वल दाय ।
> भांडय्र जज्ञ करि भुमितल पातक पुंज वहाय ।। ११७

'So, Hemavatī, you now realise that you have nothing absolutely to be afraid of; your son will be a Kṣatriya of a high order (हेमवती तुव पुत्र वड़ छोनी छत्रिय होई)'. With these words the Moon-God disappeared from the scene.

Then comes the section describing how the prophecy came true.

> काशिय तजि कालिंजर ग्राइय । चारमास तिय तँह विलमाइय ।।
> करि तीरथ ग्रस्नान सुदाये । पुत्र काज सव देव मनाये ।।
> छड़ि कालिंजर सुंदरिय गइय धाम इक सोय ।।
> रहिय ग्रामपतिके सदन मेंह भयौ पुत्र इक जोय ।। १२४

After leaving Kāśī Hemavatī came to Kāliñjar and passed four months there taking purificatory baths and offering sacrifices for the birth of a son. From Kālinjar she went to a village and stayed there at the house of the village headman, where she gave birth to a son. The new-born child, Candravarman by name, was like another moon (विंधुविय होय). He was born at dawn on Monday, the 11th day of the waxing moon in the month of Mādhava (Vaiśākh), when joyous notes were sounded and auspicious ceremonies were performed by the women of the celestial abode.

> पाहर निशा रहि प्रातकी सोमवार गन सोय ।।
> माधव सुदि एकादशी चंद्रव्रह्म नृप होय ।।
> ग्रन्तरिक्ख ग्रानन्द वजि सुरतिय मंगल जोय ।। १२६

The Moon-God appeared again and repeated his prophecy but warned her that the dynasty founded by her son would continue to rule only as long as its rulers retained the surname 'Varman'. Bṛhaspati, the preceptor of the gods, came and wrote the horoscope of the child (जनमपत्र सुरगुरु लिखित) and the Moon-God held a festival (mahotsava) there in the presence of a large gathering.

The next incident refers to the time when Candravarman

was sixteen years old. He was so powerful and courageous that he killed a tiger with a piece of stone only, and a lion, twelve cubits long, by means of a missile of the type of a short staff.

भयौ कुँवर षोड़स वरस गये केदार सम्हार ।
लरिव ग्रानि इक वाघवर लयौ उपल इक मार ।।१३६
द्वादस हथ्थ मयंदवर भिंडपाल लिय मारि ।

At the news of this achievement of her son, Hemavatī felt exceedingly glad and she recited a hymn to the Moon-God, and forthwith he appeared.

हेमवती मिलि सुवन कँह उर ग्रानन्द वढ़ाइ ।
पठन करयो ता मंत्रको निशिकर पहुचे ग्राइ ।।१३६

The Moon-God kissed his son and called him a ruler among men (नरवाहन). He brought with him a touchstone, which he now places at the disposal of Candravarman.

चुंमि वदन विधुपुत्र कर नरवाहन वुलवाय ।
पारस मनि स्यो ल्याइय । चन्द्रव्रह्म थपि जाय ।।१४०

Almost all the prominent gods made their appearance at Khajurāho to bless Candravarman on the occasion of his consecration. The God of Wealth came with all his forces (सव सेना सह धनपति ग्रायव) and presented them to Candravarman. He was also taught polity by the three gods, viz., Kubera the Dhanapati, Bṛhaspati, the preceptor of gods, and the Moon-God himself. (राजनीति सिख दै सवै धनपति गुरु निशानाथ).

The next verse relates to the marriage of Candravarman when we find the Moon-God once again warning him that the surname 'varman' should never be given up (व्रह्म शब्द नहि जाय).

Next, there is a description of the achievements of King Candravarman rendered possible mainly by his acquisition of wealth through the touchstone, presented to him by the Moon-God. The occupation of Kāliñjar was his first achievement.

चन्द्रव्रह्म ग्रायस सिला पारस लाइय छुवाइ ।
करिय हेम सत कोटि लिय कालिंजर कँह जाइ ।।१५६

After taking Kāliñjar he took bath and worshipped the God Nīlakaṇṭha and thereafter on an auspicious day offered gifts worth a hundred crore of gold coins to Brahmins and ascetics. Then he devoted himself to the task of extending his possessions.

तीस सहस सादिय सुरखि करि धावा नृपराय ।
पंच प्रहर भीतर लिये जनपद जुगल छिड़ाइ ।।१६१

He set out on an expedition accompanied by no less than thirty thousand soldiers, and in course of only five 'praharas' he occupied two 'janapadas'. The achievement of the Candel king frightened the Gahirawārs, who fled away leaving their own dominion of Kāśī, which also came under the occupation of Candravarman.

गहिरवार भय मानि भगि काशी तजि अकुलाइ ।
चन्द्रब्रह्म अवतार सब जनपद लये छिड़ाइ ।।१६३

Candravarman is also stated to have built a fort at Kāliñjar (गिरिदुर्ग वनाय). The sanctity of Kāliñjar as a holy place is stressed in the following verse:

कहो महातम विप्रवर कालिंजर अव कौन ।
जँहा होत अस्नानके करत देवपुर गौन ।।१६४

A bath at Kāliñjar will earn more religious merit than a visit to the heavenly region.

चन्द्रवंश वर्णन खंड (Book II)

From Kāliñjar the king accompanied by his queen came to Khajurāho and sat at the feet of his mother, Hemavatī. (परिव भूप वनिता सहित हेमवती के पाय). The mother described to the son the agony that she had to endure when most uncharitable references were made to her past life by all sorts of people. (कान मंडि कामिन कहतु मम सु वैन ढहराय).

So she earnestly requested her son to perform the Bhāṇḍya Yajña as prescribed by the Moon-God and thus relieve her of this mental torture.

भांडग्र जज्ञ तुम किज्जियौ भांडय चित्र लिखवाय ।. . . २८
मोहि उधारो भुमितल भांडय जज्ञ वनवाय ।।३२

She further directed him to construct 85 temples with a lake and a garden attached to each and to give sufficient gifts and offerings to brahmins.

पञ्चासी मढ देवजुत तव तुव पातक जाय ।२८
निकट निकट सरसी रचौ निकट निकट पर वाग ।।

Candravarman carried out the directions of his mother and performed the sacrifice with all the attendant rites and ceremonies. For the construction work, however, he invoked the aid of the Divine Builder. Viśvakarman, who built 85 temples in course of only four hours.

पञ्चासी मढ देवसव वाहन जुत त्रिपुरारि।
विसु कर्म्मा कौ रचतही लगीं न घटिका चारि ।।५४

At the conclusion of the ceremony all sins of Hemavatī were washed away ((धन्य धन्य दुज देवन रट्टे हेमवती के पातिक कट्टे), and free from all blemishes, she went directly to Heaven.

हेमवती तन छुट्टियव वैढिव देव विमान ।
मृत्यलोक निर्म्मल भई जानी सकल जहान ।।६२

After having faithfully performed the sacrifice, Candravarman set himself to the task of building up his new capital at Mahobā.

करिव जज्ञ खज्जुरपुर वहु धन दीन लुटाय।
रानिय चन्द्रावती सहित वस्यो महोवे अाय ।।६४
रच्च्यो सहर जोजन जुगल षट् जोजन विस्तार।
रैयत अतिराजी वसे घर घर मंगलचार ।।६५

CHAPTER III

BEGININGS OF CANDELLA HISTORY : FROM NANNUKA TO HARṢA

The earliest prince of the Candella dynasty, according to the evidence of the Khajurāho Inscriptions, is Nannuka. In the Khajurāho Inscriptions nos. 2 and 4 he has been mentioned as 'nṛpa'[1] and 'mahīpati'[2] respectively. The records however do not furnish any definite data about him or the circumstances leading to the foundation of the Candella State. Nannuka has been extolled in vague and conventional phrases, which describe him as 'a touchstone to test the worth of the gold of the regal order', (Kṣatra-suvarṇṇa-sāra-nikaṣagrāvā) and 'one who playfully decorated the faces of the women of the quarters with the sandal of his fame' (yaśaścandana-krīḍālankṛta dik-purandhri-vadanaḥ)[3]. He is said to have forced even the enemy princes to bow down their heads before him, and made them carry his commands on their heads like diadems. Another verse (no. 11)[4] describes him as a conqueror of many hosts of enemies (bahuvairivargajayinaḥ). Verse 15 of the Khajurāho Inscription no. 4[5] refers to him as one 'whose skill in the use of bows and arrows reminded people of the great Epic hero, Arjuna'.

He was succeeded by his son, Vākpati, who has been mentioned as the lord of the country ('kṣitipa'), the most favourite of his subjects (janānanda-sundaraḥ śrīmān)[6]. He must have achieved this popularity by granting them freedom

[1] *E. I.* I., p. 125, V. 10.
[2] *ibid.*, p. 141, V. 11.
[3] *ibid.*, pp. 125, 131.
[4] *ibid.*
[5] *E. I.* I., p. 141 :
Tena vikramadhanena dhanvinā krāmatā yudhi vadhāya vidviṣām/ Dhunvatā dhanuradhijyaṁ Arjunaṁ smāritā divi vimāna-gāminaḥ//
[6] *ibid.*, V. 16.

from fear by the display of his valour (prajānām-ātaṅka-śankum-akalaṅkita-vikramena)[7]. Besides his military abilities in defeating enemies in battle (parājitāreḥ), he possessed wisdom and power of speech like his namesake, 'Vākpati' (Bṛhaspati, the preceptor of the Gods). ('Srī Vākpatir-Vākpati-tulya-vācaḥ[8]'; 'Vākpatiriva Vākpatiḥ kṣitipaḥ')[9]. In combining in himself wisdom and valour Vākpati is said to have excelled the mythical kings, Pṛthu and Kakutstha[10].

The traditional accounts, preserved in the folk-ballads and stories, do not make any mention of Nannuka. They unanimously refer to one Candravarman as the founder of the Candella dynasty. The Mahobā Khaṇḍ or the Parmāl Rāso, current in the Bundelkhaṇḍ region, gives a fanciful story about the birth of Candravarman[11]. The military exploits ascribed to the prince in these bardic legends hardly agree, as I have shown, with the facts known from authentic sources. The legendary account has, therefore, generally been rejected by scholars.

In one of the MSS. of the Mahobā Khaṇḍ, however, Cunningham noticed Saṁ 225, mentioned as the date of the consecration of Candravarman[12]. Presuming it to be dated in the Harṣa Era, Cunningham concluded that the founder of the Candella State began to rule from c. 831 A.D. The date of the Khajurāho Inscription of Yaśovarman, 6th in descent from Nannuka, the founder of the family, is V.S. 1011 (A.D. 954). Calculating on the basis of an average of 20 to 25 years per reign, Cunningham placed the founder in the beginning of the 9th Cent. A.D. This, he pointed out, supported his theory that the date in the Mahobā Khaṇḍ should be assigned to the Harṣa Era.

V. Smith[13] and H.C. Ray[14] accept the view of Cunningham as regards the date of the founder of the Candella dynasty.

[7] *ibid.*, V. 17.
[8] *ibid.*, p. 125., V. 12.
[9] *ibid.*, p. 141., V. 16.
[10] *ibid.*, V. 17.
[11] *P. R.*, Chap. I.; A. S. R. II., pp. 445-46.
[12] *ibid.*
[13] *J. A. S. B.* (1881), L., p. 5.
[14] *D. H. N. I.*, II., p. 667, f. n. 4.

Smith suggests further on the basis of the traditional accounts, preserved in the Qānungo families of Mahobā, that Nannuka might have been the leader who wrested Mahobā from the Pratihāras.

With regard to the status of Nannuka and his successor, Vākpati, Smith holds that they are not referred to simply as ancestors, but that they must have enjoyed some sort of sovereign power, as indicated by the use of such epithets as 'nṛpa' and 'mahīpati' in the Khajurāho inscriptions.

H. C. Ray controverting this assumption of Smith, holds that it was rather unlikely for the early Candellas to establish a sovereign state ousting the Parihārs (Pratihāras), while the latter were at the height of their power. Though suggesting that the name Candravarman might have been the 'biruda' of Nannuka, Dr. Ray thinks that Nannuka was at best a feudatory to the Imperial Gurjara-Pratihāras, probably to Nāgabhaṭa II (815-833 A.D.)[15]. But why should it be presumed that from the very beginning the Candellas were feudatories to the Gurjara-Pratiharās ?

A survey of the political condition of Northern India during the beginning of the 9th cent. A.D. reveals the utter instability that was prevaling in the region due to the continued struggle for supremacy between the three contemporary powers,—the Gurjara-Pratihāras, the Rāṣṭrakūṭas and the Pālas of Bengal[16]. During these troublesome days it might have been possible for a local tribal leader in the Bundelkhaṇḍ region to establish an independent chiefship, not necessarily owing allegiance to any suzerain power. It need not be supposed that the Candellas during this period wrested Mahobā region from the Parihārs, as suggested by Smith. In fact, there is no positive evidence of any direct conflict between early Candellas and the Gurjara-Pratihāras. It may be assumed that Nannuka, the leader of a local tribe, found a suitable opportunity in the prevailing circumstances to organise it on a military basis, and that it

---

[15] *D. H. N.* I., II., pp. 667-68.

[16] *J. D. L.*, X., pp. 42-43; *D. H. N. I.*, I., pp. 567-68; *History of Kanauj*, Tripathi, pp. 230-32.

was under his leadership that the nucleus of the Candella State was founded in the region, which later came to be known as Jejābhukti or Jejākabhukti[17]. As the Pratihāras were preoccupied with deadly struggles against their powerful enemies, it may have been possible for the Candellas to lay the foundation of their chiefship.

But the picture of the Pratihāra power, as drawn by Dr. Ray, seems to be, I am afraid, a little exaggerated. The Gurjara-Pratihāra power did not rise to its height even by the end of Nāgabhaṭa II's reign. Dr. R. C. Majumdar thinks that the evidence of the Jain text Prabhāvaka Carita, connecting Kanauj with Nāgabhaṭa II, is not reliable[18]. Thus Kanauj may not have formed a part of the Gurjara-Pratihāra dominion even during Nāgabhaṭa II's time, i.e., 833 A.D. He was followed by Rāmabhadra (833-36 A.D.) on the Pratihāra throne, who again was a weak ruler. Down to about the middle of the 9th century A.D. the Pālas were still a considerable power in Northern India. If all these circumstances are taken into account it does not become necessary to presume that the Candellas could not have existed except as a feudatory to the Pratihāras.

In V. 13 of the Khajurāho Inscription of V.S. 1011, however, it is stated that the Vindhyas became the pleasure-mount (Krīḍā-giri) of Vākpati, where he was entertained by the Kirāta women[19]. Dr. H.C. Ray concludes from it that 'Vākpati succeeded in extending to some degree the limits of his small ancestral principality'.[20] He has not however specified the extent of this increased power. As mentioned in the Introduction[21] there were hills connected with the Vindhyas in the territory which later came to be known as Jejākabhukti. It is quite probable that some of these ranges may have been meant, and comprised in the territory originally held by the Candellas. The passage need not

[17] *Mahobā Inscription, E. I.* I., p. 221; *Madanpur Inscription of V. S.* 1239. *A. S. R.*, XXI., pp. 173-74; *Ratnapur Stone Inscription of Cedi Sam* 866., *E. I.*, I. p. 35, spells it as "Jejābhuktika".

[18] *H. B.* I., p. 12, f. n. 3.

[19] *E. I.*, I., p. 125., V. 13.

[20] *D. H. N. I.*, II., p. 669.

[21] Vide ante

necessarily be taken as indicating any definite advance of territorial power without concrete details.

Vākpati had two sons, Jayaśakti and Vijayaśakti, both of whom appear to have been closely associated in the task of consolidating their political status. In connection with Vijayaśakti, it may be observed that he is described as having carried on expeditions to the far south to help the cause of an ally.

Suhṛd-upakṛti-dakṣo dakṣiṇāśāṁ jigīṣuḥ
punaradhita payodher-bandha vaidhūyamaryaḥ/v. 20[22].

If Jayaśakti and Vijayaśakti were feudatories to the Pratihāras, then to whom should this epithet 'suhṛd' be applied? It would not be an appropriate epithet for a Gurjara-Pratihāra king, if he was their overlord. Further, nothing is known about any expedition of the Pratihāras to the extreme south of India, in which they may have been helped by the Candellas. R. C. Majumdar[23] thinks that the Candella Chief, Vijayaśakti might have helped Devapāla in the latter's southern expedition[24], and earlier, Vākpati might have similarly been associated with Devāpala in his exploits in the Vindhya region[25]. If this view is accepted it will appear that the Candellas were free to help other powers, such as the Pālas, who were the bitter enemies of the Pratihāras. If the Candellas were really feudatories to the Gurjara Pratihāras, as supposed by some scholars, it would have been unusual for them to do so. Thus it appears that the feudatory status of the Candellas in relation to the Gurjara-Pratihāras during the early stages of their history, is not clearly established.

Dr. Majumdar suggests that the 'Candellas had helped Devapāla in his fight against Bhoja (Pratihāra) and were rewarded, after the latter's defeat, with the sovereignty of the territory near Khajurāho, perhaps under the suzerainty of Devapāla'. In the absence of positive evidence, I am afraid, it is difficult to accept the view that the early Candella rulers were feudatories of the Pālas of Bengal.

[22] *E. I.*, I., pp. 141-42.
[23] *H. B.*, I., p. 119, f. n. 4.
[24] "Āsetoḥ prathita daśāsya-ketu-kīrteḥ" *E. I.*, XVIII, p. 304. *G. L. M.*, p. 38.
[25] "Ā-Revājanakān-mataṅgaja...." V. 5, I. A., IV., p. 366; *G. L. M.* p. 72.

The Candella ruler, Yaśovarman, however, was a feudatory of the Pratihāras.[26] Before him Harṣa had helped the Gurjara-Pratihāras, possibly in a domestic strife.[27] There is no definite indication of his status in relation to the Gurjara-Pratihāras. When, then, did the Candellas first accept the position of a feudatory to the Pratihāras ?

From about the middle of the 9th century A.D., there was a progressive weakening of the Pāla power[28] and a temporary cessation of the Rāṣtrakuta attacks. The Candellas in all probability, may have accepted the suzerainty of the Pratihāras during this time, as no other power was stronger than the Pratihāras in Northern India then. By doing so they gained for themselves a recognised political status, though it was that of a feudatory. Jayaśakti's importance in the family is indicated in the statement found in its records that Jejā gave his name to Jejābhukti as Pṛthu did to Pṛthivī.

Jejākhyayātha nṛpatiḥ sa babhūva Jejābhuktiḥ
Pṛthoriva yataḥ Pṛthivīyam-āsīt[29]

Further it may also be observed that the later Candella rulers generally invoke Jayaśakti and his brother, Vijayaśakti as the early ancestors of the family in the opening verse of their records.

Jayatyāhlādayan-viśvam Viśveśvara-śiroddhṛtaḥ
Candrātreya narendrānāṁ vaṁśaścandra iv-ojjalaḥ
Tatra pravarddhamāne virodhi vijaya bhrājiṣṇu
Jayaśakti-Vijayaśaktyādi-vīrāvirbhāva bhāsvare.[30]

The importance appears to have been due to the fact that he (Jayaśakti), by submitting to the overlordship of the Pratihāras, the greatest power in Northern India in his time, was able to win a recognised status for his family. But this must have happened sometime after Vijayaśakti's expedition

---

[26]This is evident from the reference to Vināyakapāla as ruling over the earth in the Khajurāho Inscription of V. S. 1011., L. 29. "Sri Vināyakapāladeve pālayati vasudhāṁ" *E. I.*, I., p. 129.

[27]*E. I.* I., p. 122, L. 10.

[28]*H. B.*, I., p. 129 : D. H. N. I., I., p. 305; H. I. B., Sen, p. 360.

[29]*Mahobā Inscription*. E. *I.*, I., p. 221, V. 10.

[30]*I. A.*, XVI., p. 208; *ibid.* XXV., p. 206; *E. I.*, IV., p. 157; *ibid.* XVI., p. 12; *ibid.* XX., pp. 129, 133, 135.

to the south, when he might have been assisting the Pālas as suggested by Dr. Majumdar.

Nannuka founded the nucleus of the Candella dominion, but he was a tribal chief only. For about fifty years the Candellas profited by the political disturbances in which other powers were seriously involved. Afterwards when the superiority of the Pratihāras was firmly established they submitted to their overlordship, as there was no other alternative.

Rāhila, the son of Vijayaśakti, is mentioned in two of the Khajurāho Records. He is, however, only vaguely eulogised as a great warrior,—'never tired at the sacrifice of battle'[31] and 'thinking of whom the enemies enjoy little sleep at night' (nidrā daridratāṁ yānti yaṁ vicintya niśi dvisaṁ).[32]

Rāhila undertook works of public interest, viz., excavation of tanks and lakes and construction of temples, remnants of which are still visible at Ajaygaḍh and Mahobā. At Ajaygaḍh a temple bears some stones inscribed with his name,[33] and an old lake with a fine cruciform granite temple on its bank, near Mahobā, is still called 'Rāhilya Sāgar' after his name.[34] The traditional account of the Parmāl Rāso, ascribes to him the construction of the township of 'Rasau',[35] which is now identifiable with a village of the same name in the Parganā Badausā, 20 miles north-east of Kālañjar, where A. Cadell noticed some old fortifications and a temple of the usual Candella type.[36]

It was during the time of Harṣa, who succeeded Rāhila, that the Candellas appear to have made a steady progress towards the attainment of a significant status in the political history of Northern India. Their position seems to have been greatly strengthened by matrimonial alliances with other contemporary powers. Khajurāho Records eloquently refer to

[31] *E. I.*, I., p. 131, V. 17.
[32] *ibid.* V. 16.
[33] *A. S. R.*, VII., p. 41.
[34] *J. A. S. B.* (1881), p. 8.
[35] *P. R.*, p. 27. V. 88.
[36] *J. A. S. B.* (1881), p. 8.

the marriage between Harṣa and Kañchukā of the Cāhamāna dynasty (Cāhamāna kulodbhavāṁ).[37] The Benares Grant of Lakṣmī-Karṇa (Kalacuri) alludes to the marriage of the Kalacuri king Kokkalla I with Naṭṭa or Naṭṭākhyadevī, a princess of the Candella lineage.[38] As Harṣa, mentioned in the same record, is identical with Candella Harṣa, Naṭṭa was possibly related to him. The Kalacuris appreciate this marriage as an ideal one like the celestial unions of Śacī with Indra, Kamalā with Upendra, and Umā with Candramaulī.

An additional indication of friendly relations between the Kalacuris and the Candellas during this time is furnished by the same record, which states that Harṣa, along with three other rulers including Bhoja II of the Pratihāra dynasty and Vallabharāja (i.e. Rāṣṭrakūṭa Kṛṣṇa II) had been granted freedom from fear by the Kalacuri king Kokkalla (c. 875-925 A.D.).[39] It seems that Kokkalla assured Harṣa of his intention not to injure the interest of the Candellas, and at the same time to secure indirectly protection for them by allying himself both with the Gurjara Pratihāras and the Rāṣṭrakūṭas, who had been bitterly opposed to each other for a long period.

It is, however, well-known that the hostilities between the Pratihāras and the Rāṣṭrakūṭas took a serious turn after 915 A.D., when Indra III sacked even the Imperial city of Mahodaya (Kanauj).[40] But the Gurjara Pratihāras were able to recover substantial portion of their dominions after the death of Indra III. Kṣitipāla (Mahīpāla) in his attempt to rebuild the Pratihāra power, was aided by some of his feudatories including the Candellas. The Chātsu Stone Inscription[41] refers to an expedition of conquest led by the

---

[37]Sonurūpaṁ surūpāṅgah Kanchukākhyām-akuṇṭhadhīh savarṇṇāṁ-vidhinovāha Cāhamāna-kulodbhavāṁ//V. 21., *E. I.* I., p. 126.

[38]Sacīmivendrah Kamalāmūpendro Nagendra-kanyām-iva Candramaulīh/
Candella-vasa (vaṁśa) prabhavā susilā (suśīlā) Naṭṭākhyadevī sa tu parjjanaiṣit//8. *E. I.*, II., p. 306., C. I. I., IV p. 242.

[39]Bhoje Vallabharāje Srī-Harṣe Citrkūṭa-bhūpāle Saṁkaragaṇe ca rājani yasyāsīd-abhayadaḥ pāṇiḥ/7. *ibid.* Mm. Mirashi identifies Harṣarāja (Guhila) of the Chātsu inscription with Srī Harṣa of the Bilhari record. (C. I. I., IV., p. lxxv.)

[40]*E. I.*, VII., p. 38.

[41]E. I., XII., pp. 12, 16., V. 26.

Guhilot prince, Bhaṭṭa, against the kings of the south, evidently the Rāṣṭrakūṭas, at the behest of his overlord, generally identified with the Pratihāra ruler, Mahīpāla. The Khajurāho Inscription similarly claims for Candella Harṣa the unique distinction of restoring Kṣitipāladeva on the throne.[42] It is therefore quite reasonable to believe that the Candella king Harṣa by his successful intervention in the affairs of the suzerain power enhanced his status in contemporary politics, which, as pointed out by Dr. H. C. Ray, 'in the end proved fatal to it'[43] (the Imperial Pratihāras). An almost similar situation developed in the history of Bengal in the latter half of the 11th century A.D., when Rāmapāla secured the help and cooperation of his 'Sāmanta-cakra' (feudatory powers) to recover 'Varendrī' (North Bengal) from the clutches of his enemy.[44]

The allusion to this important political incident in the Khajurāho Record is a clear indication of the growing power of the Candellas. It provides the missing link to the circumstances that led to the rise of the Candellas as an independent power free from political subservience to the Pratihāras. Henceforth the Candellas retain only a nominal show of allegiance to their overlord, which continued till the days of Yaśovarman.

[42] "Punar-yena Sri Kṣitipāladeva-nṛpatiḥ siṁhāsane sthā-(pitah)." E. I., I., p. 122, L. 10.

[43] D. H. N. I., I., p. 582. Hoernle believes that Yaśovarman is the King indicated therein and not Harṣa (J. R. A. S., 1904, p. 665., f. n. 1.)

[44] *H. I. B.*, Sen., pp. 432-35; H. B., I., pp. 156-58.

CHAPTER IV

THE RISE OF THE CANDELLAS : YAŚOVARMAN

Yaśovarman was practically the first independent ruler of the Candella dynasty, who may be regarded to have laid the foundations of the greatness of the family. The Candellas, as has already been shown, became feudatories of the Gurjara-Pratihāras. But the imperial power had to fight the Rāṣṭrakūṭas of the Deccan repeatedly. This must have heavily told on their resources, compelling them to seek the aid of their feudatories, the Guhilots and the Candellas. The feudatories felt that their help was of paramount importance in maintaining the Pratihāra overlordship and would naturally seek the earliest opportunity to shake off their allegiance.

The Candellas, by their successful interference in the affairs of Kanauj,[1] had earned for themselves a distinction in North-Indian politics and carried themselves one step forward. Such was the position of the Candellas when Yaśovarman came to the throne, succeeding his father, Harṣa. The Rāṣṭrakūṭas had in the meantime been enfeebled by disruptive dynastic quarrels which made it difficult for them to play a decisive role in Northern India. The dismemberment of two great Imperial dynasties of India almost simultaneously in the middle of the 10th century A.D., offers a golden opportunity to subsidiary powers to take the best advantage of the resulting situation.

Yaśovarman, the Candella ruler, did not miss this chance of increasing his family's power and prestige; he began to engage himself in military operations with a view to extending

[1]*E. I.*, I., p. 122., L. 10.

his territorial possessions, while not refusing formal allegiance to the Pratihāras.

Early life.—Information regarding his early life is however scanty. One inscription says that his mother, Kañchukā of the Cāhamāna family, having given birth to a beautiful and robust child, became an object of pride for the family. As she has been raised to the status of Devakī, the mother of Lord Kṛṣṇa, the conqueror of the demon Madhu[2], it may be imagined that even in his early days he achieved certain exploits, though not specified, which were remarkable for his age. As to the date of Yaśovarman's accession to the Candella throne no precise information is available. The Khajurāho Stone Inscription of V.S. 1011 (953-54 A.D.) records the erection of a temple of Viṣṇu under the name of Vaikuṇṭha(nātha) by Yaśovarman. But the inscription appears to have been engraved after the death of Yaśovarman, when the throne was occupied by his son and successor, Dhaṅga, who is introduced in V. 44 of the record.[3] All that can be safely inferred is that Yaśovarman ruled prior to the date of the record, i.e. 953-54 A.D.

Occupation of Kālañjar.—The occupation of Kālañjar hill (Kālañjārādri) was a significant achievement for Yaśovarman, which enhanced the prestige of the family, and the Candellas came to be recognised as a political power. V. 31 of the inscription tells us that Yaśovarman conquered Kālañjar with ease. (Jagrāha krīḍayā......Kālañjarādriṁ).[4] This conquest must have happened sometime before 953-54 A.D. But from whom did Yaśovarman conquer the Kālañjar hill ? The records of the Pratihāras reveal that Kālañjara-maṇḍala was under their possession in 836 A.D.[5] It is however well known that soon after 915 A.D. the Rāṣṭrakūṭa onslaught on Northern India developed into serious proportions, and 'the city of Mahodaya, which is greatly renowned among men by the name Kuśasthala' had been completely

[2] *E. I.*, I., p. 128., V. 34.
[3] *ibid.*, p. 129.
[4] *E. I.* I., pp. 128, 133.
[5] *E. I.*, XIX., p. 18., L. 6.

uprooted by Indra III.[6] But after the death of Indra III the Gurjara-Pratihāras recovered much of their dominions with the help of their feudatories including the Candellas. As Asiatic Society's Plate, dated 931 A.D.[7], which records a grant of land included in the Vārānasī viṣaya and other territories, testify to the continuing greatness of the family, it is generally presumed that the dominions of the Pratihāras during this time included Kālañjara-maṇḍala. Consequently it has been suggested that this territory must have been conquered from the Pratihāras.[7a]

With the revival of Rāṣṭrakūṭa attacks, as recorded in the Deoli and Karhād Plates the recovery of Pratihāra power was checked, and it hastened the dismemberment of the empire. V. 30 of the Karhād Plates of Kṛṣṇa III says that, —'on hearing of the conquest of all the strongholds in the southern region simply by means of his angry glance the hope about Kālañjara and Citrakūṭa vanished from the heart of the Gurjara'.[8] Kṛṣṇa III must have attacked the Gurjara dominions from the south-west and the south-east (before the middle of the 10th century A.D.), and succeeded in capturing the famous forts of Citrakūṭa (Chitor), and Kālañjara from the Gurjara Pratihāras. The Jurā Inscription[9] of the same king also shows that his claim to have captured Kālañjara may not be baseless. Most of the victories of Kṛṣṇa III had been achieved during the lifetime of his father, i.e. sometime before 940 A.D. Dr. Ray thinks that, 'it is not unlikely that Yaśovarman may have captured the famous hill-fort not from the Gurjara Pratihāras, as was so

---

[6] *Cambay Plates*, V. 19; *ibid.* VII, p. 38.

[7] *I. A.*, XV., pp. 138-41; *J. B. R. A. S.*, XXI., pp. 405 ff.

[7a] The Bhārat Kalā Bhavan, Banaras, possesses an inscription dated V. S. 1040 issued by King Harirāja, son of Nīlakaṇṭha of the Pratihāra family, which has been edited by Dr. D. C. Sircar. He identifies this family with the one whose fragmentary record was found at Chanderi. (Bhandarakar's list No. 1207). He further suggests that this Pratihāra family was defeated by Candella Yaśovarman who is described as "Saṁjvaro Gurjjarānām" in the Khajurāho inscription. His suggestion is based upon the assumption that these Pratihāras were a branch of the Imperial Pratihāras of Kanauj to whom they originally owed allegiance, acting as their viceroys of the Kālañjara region. (E. I., XXXI).

[8] *E. I.*, IV., pp. 284, 289.

[9] *J. B. O. R. S.*, Dec. 1928., p. 476 ff.

long believed, but from the Rāṣṭrakūṭas'.[10] As Yaśovarman is thus supposed to have conquered Kālañjara from the Rāṣṭrakūṭas, and not from the Gurjara Pratihāras, it will explain why even after this conquest he continued to regard the Pratihāra ruler as his overlord. It must be noted, however, that there is no positive evidence showing that the Candellas conquered Kālañjara from the Rāṣṭrakūṭas.

The inscriptions of the Kalacuris and the Candellas throw light on their mutual relations at different stages of their history. In the Khajurāho inscription of Candella Yaśovarman dated V.S. 1011 mention is made of a severe defeat inflicted by him on the Kalacuris. Verse 28[11] of the inscription says that the Cedi king, whose forces were countless, was conquered by Yaśovarman (saṁkhye-saṁkhya-balaṁ vyajeṣtha gatabhiryas-Cedirājaṁ haṭhāt). In another place of the same inscription also (verse 23),[12] where other expeditions of Yaśovarman are mentioned, there is an allusion to his victory over the Cedis. No doubt the same episode has thus been referred to in these different parts of the record. It is in verse 23 that we come across the phrase 'sīdat sāvadya Cediḥ' in connection with the Candella expedition against the Cedis. The intrinsic significance of the term '*sāvadya*', which means 'one liable to condemnation', as applied to the Cedi king, has not been explained in the inscription itself. But with the help of other contemporary inscriptions, which refer to the history of the Kalacuris, an attempt may be made to explain why this epithet has been used in a record of the victorious Candella ruler, Yaśovarman against the defeated Cedi king.

The attitude of the Candellas towards the Kalacuris in the time of Yaśovarman, as shown by the use of this expression, was strikingly different from what it had been in the earlier period. It may be remembered that Yaśovarman's father, Harṣa had been granted freedom from fear by the

---

[10] *D. H. N. I.*, II., p. 674. Dr. Altekar and Dr. Tripathi also hold the same view. (*Rāṣṭrakūṭas & their times*, P. 113., *History of Kanauj* p. 271).

[11] *E. I.*, I., pp. 127, 132.

[12] *E. I.*, I., pp. 126, 132.

Kalacuri king Kokkalla (c. 875-925 A.D.) as recorded in the Benares Grant of Karṇa.[13]

It implies that the two powers were in a sort of friendly political alliance, which had most probably been cemented by the marriage of Kokkalla with a Candella princess, Naṭṭa or Naṭṭākhyadevī. The Kalacuris equated this union with the divine couples of Śacī and Indra, Kamalā and Upendra, and Umā and Candramaulī.[14] Although there is no reference to the early relations of the Candellas with the Kalacuris in the records of the former prior to the time of Yaśovarman, it seems highly probable in view of the evidence of Kalacuri epigraphy, that such relations were not unfriendly. But when in a record of Yaśovarman's reign the Kalacuris are spoken of with evident contempt, as in the inscription already referred to, it definitely means that not only the Candellas were now hostile to the latter, but that there were some special reasons for their being provoked against the Kalacuris.

The Candellas were no doubt emboldened to proceed against the Kalacuris during the time of Yaśovarman, relying on their increased power due to the effective part they played in securing the throne for Kṣitipāla,[15] to their matrimonial alliance with the Cāhamānas[16], and to some conquests which must have already been achieved by the Candellas as the Khajurāho inscription mentions.

The aggressive policy in this new situation can be well understood. But the question is : why did they use the term '*sāvadya*' while mentioning their enemy, the Kalacuris ?

The policy of friendship pursued by the Kalacuris, as shown in a verse of the Benares Grant, already alluded to, and in another verse in the Bilhari inscription,[17] was subsequently changed. They became more and more definitely attached to the Rāṣṭrakūtas, thus allying themselves with a power which had aggressive intentions in the north.

---

[13] *ibid.*, II., p. 306.; V. 7.; The identification of Harṣa the 'lord of Citrakūṭa' with Candella Harṣa is not accepted in *I. H. Q.*, XIII., pp. 482 ff.
[14] *E. I.*, II., p. 306, V. 8.
[15] *ibid.*, I., p. 122, L. 10.
[16] *ibid.*, p. 126, V. 21.
[17] *E. I.*, I., p. 256., V. 17.

There was a series of political marriages between the Rāṣṭrakūṭas and the Kalacuris:

(*i*) Kṛṣṇa II married the younger sister of Saṅkuka (Saṅkaragaṇa), a daughter of Kokkalla I.[18]

(*ii*) Jagattuṅgadeva, son of Kṛṣṇa II, married Lakṣmī[19] and Govindāmbā,[20] both daughters of Saṅkaragaṇa, son of Kokkalla.

(*iii*) Indra III married Vijāmbā, grand-daughter of Arjuna, another son of Kokkalla.[21]

It will appear from the above that in every case the bride came from the Kalacuri family. This may suggest admission of an inferior status by the Kalacuris in their relations with the Rāṣṭrakūṭas.[22] This policy of courting favour of the Rāṣṭrakūṭas could not have been liked by the North Indian powers. It was definitely against their interests, as strategically the Kalacuri dominion might be used as a spring-board of Rāṣṭrakūṭa attacks against them. They also lowered themselves in the estimation of those powers whose interests were linked up with the political fortunes of Northern India, particularly the Candellas.

The Rāṣṭrakūṭa invasions of the early 10th century A.D. dealt a servere blow to the Gurjara Pratihāra power. In some of their campaigns the Rāṣṭrakūṭas seem to have received actual help from the Kalacuris, who are mentioned in the Amodā Plate,[23] as having carried on plunderous raids on a number of territories including that of the Gurjaras.

The Candellas themselves could not but regard their attachment to the Rāṣṭrakūṭas as hostile to their own interest. The establishment of Rāṣṭrakūṭa authority in Kālañjara, however temporary it might be, was possibly facilitated by this alliance. The subsequent occupation of Kālañjara by

---

[18] *I. A.*, XII., p. 265. An almost identical reference to Kṛṣṇa's marriage to a girl of the Cāhamāna dynasty. *ibid.*, XII., p. 250.

[19] I. A., XII., p. 265; also in P. 250.

[20] *ibid.*, p. 265.

[21] *ibid.*, Ll. 21-22.

[22] Ref. 'kanyopāyanadāna', ('present of daughters' to the suzerain ruler by vassal kings. *C. I. I.*, III., p. 8.

[23] *E. I.*, XIX., pp. 75, 78.

Yaśovarman marked the turning point of the fortunes of the family. If Kālañjara was conquered from the Rāṣṭrakūṭas the Candellas must have regarded them as their enemy. Association with their enemy on the part of the Kalacuris caused irritation to the Candellas particularly, because the Kalacuris, compared with the Rāṣṭrakūṭas, were a weaker power, and as such might have appeared as depending on the patronage of the Rāṣṭrakūṭas.[24] In the circumstances it was quite natural for the Candellas to have described the Kalacuris as '*sāvadya*'.

It is necessary to consider the question of the identification of the Cedi ruler, so impetuously defeated by Yaśovarman. The history of the Kalacuri dynasty shows that after Mugdhatuṅga, son of Kokkalla I, three rulers occupied the Cedi throne in quick succession (viz. Bāla-Harṣa, Yuvarāja and Lakṣmaṇarāja), and all of them appear to have been contemporaries of Yaśovarman. It is, therefore, difficult to say who among these three was defeated at Yaśovarman's hand. As Bāla-Harṣa, the eldest son of Mugdhatuṅga had a very short reign, and is not prominently mentioned, it was most probably this ruler, whose career was cut short by Yaśovarman.[25] This may also explain the omission of his name from some of the records of his successors. The identification of the Cedi king defeated by Yaśovarman with either Lakṣmaṇarāja or his predecessor, Yuvarāja I,[26] is less probable, as on the evidence of the Bilhari Record, definite improvement in the position of the Cedi dynasty may have taken place during their reigns.[27]

Eulogies about Yaśovarman's exploits.—With regard to the achievements of Yaśovarman, we notice that the Candella records, like the Khajurāho Inscriptions of V.S. 1011,[28] and of V. S. 1059,[29] and the Nānyaura Plate 'A' of Dhaṅga-

[24]A similar attitude was expressed by Nāgabhaṭa II against Cakrāyudha for his 'lowly demeanour' in acting as a protege of the Pāla king, Dharmapāla. E. I., XVIII, p. 99.

[25]*D. H. N. I.*, II., pp. 759-60.

[26]E. I., II., p. 301., Mm. Mirashi suggests that the Cedirāja Yuvarāja was defeated by Candella Yaśovarman. (*C. I. I.*, IV., P. lxxxiii)

[27]*ibid.*, I., p. 265., Vv. 24, 28.

[28]*ibid.*, pp. 123-35.

[29]*ibid.*, pp. 137-47.

deva of V.S. 1055,[30] are all eloquent about them. Thus V. 26 of the Khajurāho Inscription of V.S. 1011 in a conventional manner reads,—"When dust rose on the expeditions of his forces the river of Heaven had its current diverted midway by the embankments formed in it; the sun, having its lustre covered, was pleasant like a mirror; seeing the sky covered with clouds the elephants of the Lord of the gods became delighted and the swans eagerly looked upwards, and a thousand eyes of averted enemies became closed".[31] As the praśasti does not give any specific details there is no historical value in it. In another verse Yaśovarman is stated to have surpassed Pārtha (i.e., Arjuna) in military prowess (sa śūraḥ Pārthopi prathitamahimānaḥ).[32] It is also said that "in battle the impetuous massive arms of that ocean of regal splendour (kṣatra tejomburāśeh) engaged in conquering the earth. did not cease to itch even though the enemies had clearly disappeared nobody knew whither".[33] Amongst this mass of exaggerated statements we come to find a somewhat practical suggestion in verse 23 which reads thus—

Gauḍa-krīḍālatāsis-tulita-Khaṣabalaḥ kośalaḥ Kośalānāṁ
Naśyat-Kaśmīravīraḥ śithilita-Mithilaḥ kālavan-Mālavānāṁ
Sīdat-sāvadya Cediḥ Kurutarusumaruṭ-saṁjvaro Gurjjarāṇāṁ
Tasmāt-tasyām sa yajñe nṛpakulatilakaḥ Śrī Yaśovarmarājaḥ[34]

(Trans.)—"Who was a sword to (cut down) the Gauḍas, as if they were mere pleasure-creepers; equalled the forces of the Khaṣas (treated the Khaṣas with contempt, according to R. C. Majumdar),[35] and carried off the treasures of the Kośalas; before whom perished the Kāshmīri warriors; who weakened the Mithilas, and as it were a God of Death to the

[30] *I. A.*, XVI., pp. 201-04.
[31] *E. I.*, I., pp. 127, 132.
[32] *ibid.*, pp. 126, 132., V. 24.
[33] *ibid.*, pp. 128, 133., V. 36.
[34] *ibid.*, pp. 126, 132.
[35] *I. H. Q.*, XXV., p. 213.

Mālavas; who brought distress to the shameful Cedis; who was to the Kurus what a storm is to the trees, and a scorching fire to the Gurjjaras".

This verse claims that Yaśovarman undertook a number of campaigns over a vast area in Northern India, from the Himālayas to Mālava and from Kāśmīr to Bengal.[36] There must be an element of exaggeration in this account, but the consensus of opinion among scholars is that Yaśovarman must be credited with military successes in some regions, at least Bihar and Bengal.

Yaśovarman's Expedition to Bengal.—It is to be particularly noted that the military power of the Gauḍas in the opinion of the praśastikāra was so insignificant that it could be subdued as easily as a pleasure-creeper is cut down with the help of a sword. If this statement is to be believed, the military weakness of the Gauḍa rulers must have been one of the main factors responsible for their defeat. The decline of the Pāla power at this stage (prior to 953-54 A.D.)[37] is a well-known fact and is borne out by independent data.

The Khajurāho Inscription, by referring to the Gauḍas, undoubtedly meant the Pālas. The Candella invasion took place before 954 A.D. This was the time when Rājyapāla (c. 908-40 A.D.) and after him Gopāla II (c. 940-60 A.D.) occupied the Pāla throne.[38] They were admittedly weak rulers and were unable to retrieve the lost furtunes of their family, whose decline started shortly after Devapāla's reign.

As the history of the Pālas show, there were different successful attempts made by these rulers to recover their lost power in the 10th and 11th centuries. The recuperative power of the Pālas could not be overlooked by the Candellas, who regarded them as their potential enemy. This explains the reason why Yaśovarman led his expedition against Gauḍa. In fact, he was only following a line of action which is demanded by the recognition of a danger inherent in a political situation which had menacing potentialities. The

---

[36] *D. H. N. I.*, II., p. 675; *H. B.*, I., P. 132.
[37] *D. H. N. I.*, I., pp. 303-04; *H. B.*, I., pp. 125-30; *H. I. B.*, Sen, pp. 360-61.
[38] *H. B.*, I., Chap. VI., App. II. (*The chronology of the Pāla kings*), pp. 176-77.

Pālas were the '*prakṛtyamitra*' of the Candellas in terms of the Arthaśāstra of Kauṭilya.[39]

The reference in the Khajurāho inscription to Yaśovarman's attack on Gauḍa does not imply that any attempt was made by him to incorporate the dominion of the defeated Gauḍa king in his realm. But it may be assumed that his expedition made the Pāla power still weaker and less able to resist any attack. The confusion which the Gauḍa invasion created gave an opportunity to the Kāmbojas to capture north and western Bengal and to found a separate kingdom.[40]

The Dinājpur Rāj Palace Pillar Inscription[41] refers to a Gauḍa king of Kāmboja lineage (Kāmbojānvayaja-Gauḍapati), and the Irdā Copper Plate Grant[42] mentions a line of Kāmboja rulers (Kāmbojavaṁśatilakaḥ) dominating considerable portions of West Bengal. The scholars are generally of the opinion that the Kāmboja rule began from about the middle of the 10th century A.D. The establishment of the Kāmboja power seems to have been preceded by the invasion of Gauḍa by Yaśovarman. Thus it appears that although the Candellas did not occupy Gauḍa, their invasion created a situation in which it was possible for another family to occupy the territory.

The Bāngaḍ Grant of Mahīpāla,[43] who re-occupied Gauḍa, says that those under whose possession this territory had remained had no real title to it, and were merely usurpers. The expression '*vilupta*' used in this connection clearly shows the complete loss of power of the Pālas in this area. There is no indication in this passage to show that this loss was the culmination of any serious fight put up by the Pālas against their enemy. The enemies' victory seems to have been simply a case of usurpation (anadhikṛta viluptaṁ). The Pālas with their army greatly impaired (as shown by the Khajurāho Record of V. S. 1011), had been so much

[39] *K. A.* (Shamasastry) *Book* VI., 260, p. 290.

[40] There is a sharp difference of opinion among scholars regarding the origin and identity of the Kāmboja rulers. *H. B.*, I., pp. 190-91.

[41] *J. A. S. B.* (N. S.), II., p. 619.

[42] *E. I.*, XXII., pp. 150-59; *ibid.*, XXIV., p. 43.

[43] *ibid.*, XIV., p. 324; *G. L. M.*, p. 91.

weakened by the Candellas, that they had no means of efficiently resisting this usurpation.

Invasion of Mithilā.—The other state of the same region mentioned in the Khajurāho record is Mithilā, which received a shake-up at the hands of Candella Yaśovarman. Mithilā or North Bihar, therefore, seems to have been outside the political jurisdiction of the Pālas at the time of Yaśovarman's invasion. It may be remembered that Mahendrapāla of the Gurjara-Pratihāra family succeeded in establishing his control over Bihar and North Bengal during the reign of the Pālā ruler Nārāyaṇapāla.[44] Even it is suggested by some scholars that the Cȃndras of East Bengal, who trace their origin from Rohitagiri (identifiable with Rohtasgarh[45]), were original residents of North Bihar, but most probably they migrated eastwards due to the pressure of the army of Mahendrapāla.[46] Thus it appears that Mithilā was the seat of a tributary ruler, or, in any case, it enjoyed some amount of autonomy or separate political entity.

The Uddaṇḍapur Image Inscription of the 54th year of Nārāyaṇapāla testifies to the restoration of authority in portions of East Bihar,[47] which has led scholars like Dr. Ray to presume that Mithilā also was then restored to the Pālās,[48] and as such, separate mention of Mithilā in the Khajurāho record was of no historical value. But it may be pointed out that no direct reference to the region north of the Ganges is found in any of the Pāla records so far. It is only during the reign period of Mahīpāla I that we come to find some evidence regarding the recovery of North Bihar by him (Imādpur Image Inscriptions of the 48th year of Mahīpāla).[49] It may not therefore be impossible that Mithilā was an autonomous political unit, the *de jure* authority of which might have rested either with the Pratihāras or with the

---

[44]*H. B.*, I. p. 129; *D. H. N. I.*, I., pp. 302-03; *ibid.*, II., p. 676, f. n. 1.

[45]*I. B.*, III., p. 3. There is a controversy about the correct reading of the term as well as its location. Bhattasali identifies it with modern Lālmāi hills near Comilla.

[46]*H. I. B.*, Sen, p. 372.

[47]*I. A.*, XLVII., p. 110.

[48]*D. H. N. I.*, II., p. 676.

[49]*I. A.*, XIV., p. 165, f. n. 17; *J. A. S. B.* (3rd series), VII, p. 218.

Pālas. If that is accepted, then, of course, it may be suggested that Candella king, Yaśovarman might have fought this small power, practically at the entrance of the Pāla dominion. But in the absence of more definite data we cannot be sure on the point.

Relation with the Mālavas.—In the south-western region, the Khajurāho record refers to the Mālava country. It is claimed in the verse that Yaśovarman was like the Lord of Death to the Mālavas (kālavan Mālavānām). The claim is, however, rejected on the ground of Mālwā being still under the Gurjara rulers of Kanauj.[50] It is well known however that the Rāṣṭrakūṭa hold over Mālwā continued till about the first quarter of the 10th century A.D., when taking advantage of some dynastic struggles among the successors of Indra III, the Pratihāras asserted their supremacy and established their control over this region once again. The Paramāras, who were practically agents of the Rāṣṭrakūṭas in running the administration of Mālwā were now driven out to Gujarat. The Paramāra king, who met this tragic fate has been identified with Vairisiṁha II (c. 918-46 A.D.), and it is believed that this incident came about towards the latter part of his reign. But Dr. D. C. Ganguly while admitting Vairisiṁha II's exile in Lāṭamaṇḍala, observes on the evidence of the Udaipur Praśasti that before his death Vairisiṁha II re-established the Paramāra hold in Mālwā, presumably with the help of the Rāṣṭrakūṭas.[52] He was succeeded by his son, Siyaka II, alias Harṣa, who, it is generally held, was a contemporary of Candella Yaśovarman. Siyaka II, who came to the throne after 949 A.D., claims to have defeated the Hūṇa chief to the north-west of Mālwā[53] and probably had plans of further expansion of his territories. But his progress must have been retarded by Candella Yaśovarman. As there is no direct reference to any open conflict between the two in the records of either dynasty,

---

[50] *D. H. N. I.*, II., p. 676.
[51] *D. H. N. I.*, II., p. 847.
[52] *H. P.*, Ganguly, p. 36.
[53] *ibid.*, pp. 39-40.

we can possibly take the expression used in the Khajurāho record, 'kālavan Mālavānām' to denote only the menacing potentiality of the Candellas poised against the Mālavas, i.e. the Paramāras. The real significance of it was that both the former feudatories of the Imperial Pratihāras now gathered sufficient strength in the absence of the suzerain power to provide a check to each other against further consolidation.

Invasion of Kośala.—The record also refers to the Kośala country, whose treasures were carried away by the Candella king (kośalaḥ Kośalānām). Scholars have taken this to be an expression of poet's skill in the use of figurative language only,[54] because, it is held that the Kośala country was within the limits of the Pratihāra empire. Evidently Uttara-Kośala, modern Oudh, was meant. But, in fact, during this period the state of Kośala naturally indicated the region of the upper Mahānadī valley, which was known as Dakṣiṇa Kośala, Mahā Kośala or Kośala. The epigraphic records of this region reveal that a line of rulers claiming to belong to Pāṇḍuvaṁśa ruled there. They used the title, 'Kośalādhipati' (lord of Kośala). Palaeographically their records are assigned to about the 6th and 7th centuries A.D.[55] As most of their inscriptions were issued from Śrīpura (modern Sirpur, Rāipur Dist.), they are commonly designated as Śrīpura line of kings. They are believed to be connected with the 'Kośalendra-Somavaṁśi' kings of Sambalpur (Orissa),[56] whose records are placed between the 10th and 12th centuries A.D. on palaeographic considerations.

The Bilhari inscription of the Cedi rulers eulogised Mugdhatuṅga, son of Kalacuri Kokkalla as having 'conquered the lines of country by the shore of the eastern sea, and wrested Pāli from the Lord of Kośala'.[57] 'Pāli' has been located by scholars at the village of the same name (12 miles to the north-east of Ratnapur in the Bilaspur Dist.),

---

[54] *D. H. N. I.*, II., p. 675.
[55] *I. H. Q.*, XX., p. 80.
[56] *E. I.*, XI., p. 186.
[57] *ibid.*, I., pp. 256, 265.

and Śivagupta of the Orissan branch, has been identified as the 'Kośalendra' of the Bilhari record, defeated by the Cedi king. Śivagupta is generally placed round about 950 A.D. The Kalacuris gradually ousted the Somavaṁśi rulers from their possessions in Chatisgarḥ and restricted their power in western Orissa.[58]

Therefore it is not unlikely that in spite of highsounding titles and designations that the Somavaṁśi rulers might have been using in their own records, they were most probably under the influence of the Cedi rulers, if not their feudatories. The idea is further strengthened by the adoption of the *Gajalakṣmī* symbol by the Somavaṁśis of Orissa on their seals and inscriptions, a feature particularly associated with the Kalacuris.

A Kalacuri record (Ratnapur Stone inscription of Jājalladeva)[59] shows that of the 18 sons of Kokkalla, the eldest one succeeded to the throne while others became 'maṇḍalādhipatis' or feudatory chiefs, including one Kaliṅgarāja, the founder of the Tummana branch. Similar family ties between the Kośalendras and the Kalacuris may not be unlikely. But there is no direct evidence to pursue the point further.

Remembering the Cedi-Candella hostilities, already referred to, it may not be impossible that the political ties between the Somavaṁśis and the Kalacuris were responsible for the irritation of the Candella ruler, Yaśovarman, who might have raided the kingdom of the Kośalas of the south during the reign of Śivagupta (c. 950 A.D.). The expression, 'kośalaḥ Kośalānām' is also indicative of a snap raid than any pitched battle or a long-drawn war.

The verse (V. 23) in the Khajurāho record (V.S. 1011) also refers to the northern regions of the country. With regard to the claim of Yaśovarman to have vanquished the forces of Kāshmīr (naśyat Kaśmīravīrah), it may at once seem absurd and nothing but poetic exaggeration. From the

[58] *D. H. N. I.*, I., p. 396; *I. H. Q.*, XX., p. 80; *A.I.K.*, p. 145.
[59] *E. I.*, I., pp. 34, 37, V. 5.

practical point of view, as also from the standpoint of sound politics, taking out of an expedition to such a far off region by a rising power, however virile, is well nigh impossible. The history of Kāshmīr during this period, i.e. the middle of 10th century A.D., however, reveals a sorry state of affairs. Dynastic conflicts and palace intrigues vitiated the political atmosphere of Kāshmīr since the death of Yaśaskara of the Utpala dynasty in 948 A.D., in the midst of which the child king Saṁgrāmadeva was murdered by one of the ministers, named Parvagupta, who seated himself on the throne in 949 A.D.[60] Such a time is undoubtedly highly suitable for an enterprising neighbour, who may, in the words of Kauṭilya, be a 'vijīgiṣu rājā', to deal an effective blow and cripple it for some time at least. But the situation of the Candella territory and the political condition in northern India during the period can hardly make us believe in the claim put forward in the Khajurāho Record. Rather it is clear from Kalhaṇa's Rājataraṅginī that all its strength and weakness were due to internal factors with no extraneous elements having any hand in it.

In the same way we may examine the claim of Yaśovarman having reduced the Khaṣa forces to a position of contempt (tulita Khaṣabalaḥ). The term '*tulita*' was interpreted by Kielhorn as 'equalled',[61] but Dr. Majumdar has shown that the term has also uses in Sanskrit texts to denote 'treated with contempt',[62] which is more appropriate in the context of the complete statement here. The Khaṣas, it may be mentioned, were the masters of the Lohara country on the borders of the Kāshmīr state. It seems that the composer of the record had a fair knowledge of the geography of the country, and in establishing the claims of his patron he utilised it wisely.

Invasion of the Kuru country: Clash with the Pratihāras

Another state which finds mention in the record is that of Kuru, which suffered the storm of the Candella invasion

[60] *D. H. N. I.*, I., pp. 128-30; *A. I. K.*, p. 119.
[61] *E. I.*, I., p. 132.
[62] *I. H. Q.*, XXV., p. 213.

(Kuru-tarusu marut). The Kuru country was in the Delhi region, and as such, it was definitely included in the Pratihāra dominion. So this claim of Yaśovarman is highly doubtful, particularly in view of the fact that he used an expression of allegiance to the Imperial power at the end of the Khajurāho record of V.S. 1011.[63] But at the same time it cannot be denied that simply by the occupation of the fortress of Kālañjar Yaśovarman earned a unique status for his family, and that together with some military expeditions in spheres originally held by the Pratihāras, the Candellas have already grown to be a serious menace to the Imperial power. The show of allegiance in official documents was nothing but a mere formality. On the other hand verse 23 clearly stated that Yaśovarman became 'saṁjvaro Gurjarānām'. This was the expression of the real feeling between the effete Imperial power and an almost liberated feudatory ruler. In the very next generation, when Dhaṅga, the son of Yaśovarman, was on the Candella throne, he claims to have defeated a Kanauj prince (nikhila nṛpam yaḥ Kānyakubja-narendraṁ samara bhuvi vijityaḥ—Māu Stone Inscription of Madanavarman)[64]. Therefore it may be quite likely that since the occupation of Kālañjar occasional clashes of interest between the Pratihāras and the Candellas were not uncommon, and such an incident might have come about in the Kuru country, which has been alluded to in the vague expression, 'Kurutarusu-marut'.

It is, however, quite clear that Yaśovarman was a successful military leader who did not fail to take the best advantage of the decay of the Imperial power in North India and truly laid the foundation of the Candella state which wielded a strong influence in Indian politics from the middle of the 10th century A.D.

Extent of the kingdom.—The Khajurāho Record of V.S. 1011, it has already been shown, endows Yaśovarman with an unchallenged authority over the whole of Northern India from Kāshmīr to Bengal, and from the Kuru country

[63]"Sri Vināyakapāladeve pālayati vasudhāṁ" *E. I.*, I., p. 129, L. 29.
[64]*E. I.*, I., pp. 197, 203, V. 3.

to Dakṣiṇa Kośala. But from the analysis of the account, as has been attempted in the previous pages, it appears that barring the exaggerated portions of the statement, Yaśovarman may be credited to have gained some successes against the Cedis to the south-west of his dominion, and against Bengal and Bihar to the east. But it is quite clear that none of these areas were incorporated into his dominion, nor even any attempt was made to establish authority over the regions concerned.

The only positive evidence that is available from the Khajurāho Inscription is the reference to Yaśovarman's conquest of the Kālañjar fort,[65] and naturally occupation of the adjoining area. The findspot of the inscription and its evidence of the erection of the temple dedicated to Vaikuṇṭha(nātha) at Khajurāho undoubtedly indicate inclusion of the area within the ambit of his direct administration. That is to say, Yaśovarman was the ruler of Bundelkhaṇḍ proper.

Verse 39 of the Khajurāho Inscription[66] further describes how Yaśovarman, alias Lakṣavarman, in course of his expeditions turned the Yamunā and the Gaṅgā into his pleasure-lakes (keli-sarasi) and their waters became muddy by the bathing of his furious mighty elephants (majjanmatta karīndra paṅkila-jalām Śrī Lakṣavarmābhidhaścakre Śakrasamaḥ Kalindatanayāṁ Jaḥnohsutām ca kramāt). This verse indicates that Yaśovarman was able to establish his authority over the Ganges-Jumna valley, i.e. the area roundabout Allahabad. In consideration of the proximity of the area to the Candella territory, and in view of the possibility of clashes with the Imperial Pratihāra power, who must have been holding the region till at least 931 A.D. (the date of the Asiatic Society's Plate, donating lands in the Vārāṇasī viṣaya),[67] the occupation of this area by Yaśovarman does not seem impossible. Rather the reference

---

[65] "Jagrāha krīḍayā.....Kālañjarādriṁ" *E. I.*, I., pp. 127-28, V. 31.
[66] *ibid.*, pp. 128, 134.
[67] *I. A.*, XV., pp. 138-41; *J. B. R. A. S.*, XXI., pp. 405 ff.

to his son Dhaṅga's voluntary death at the confluence of the Ganges and the Jumna, near Allahabad, as recorded in the Khajurāho inscription of V.S. 1059,[68] makes it all the more probable.

The Dudāhi Inscription,[69] found in a village in the southern portion of the Lalitpur district, records the existence of a prince named Devalabdhi, claiming to be a grandson of Yaśovarman through Kṛṣṇapa and Āsarvā (Mahārājādhirāja Śri Yaśovarmā-naptṛ Śri Kṛṣṇapasuta mātri Śrī Āsarvā-udarodbhava Candellānvaya Śrī Devalabdhiyaṁ). Evidently this Kṛṣṇapa was another son of Yaśovarman who did not succeed to the throne. Dr. N. P. Chakravarti identifies him with Nṛpa Kaṇhapa of the Jhansi fragmentary inscription.[70] From the findspot of the inscriptions it appears that Kṛṣṇapa (Kaṇhapa) must have been placed by Yaśovarman on the Mālava-Candella frontier, like the Warden of the Marches. Thus it becomes clear that to the south-west the Candella territory touched the borders of the Mālavadeśa, or the kingdom of the Mālava people, to whom the Candellas were like the "Lord of Death" (kālavan Mālavānām).

His family.—The Khajurāho Inscription no. 4 of V.S. 1059 introduces us to the queen of Yaśovarman, named Puppā[71].

It is stated in the verse that Puppādevi hailed from a reputed family (the name of the family is however not mentioned therein) and that she was as pious as the holy Narmadā. In the following verse (V. 41) she has been equalled to Śacī, the wife of Indra, the lord of the gods (sā devī naradevād devādhipateh Śacīva saccaritām), and it may be presumed that their domestic life was quite happy and peaceful. Puppādevi was the mother of the renowned son Dhaṅgadeva, who succeeded Yaśovarman on the Candella throne. Kṛṣṇapa was most probably another son of Yaśovarman,

[68] *E. I.*, I., p. 146, V. 55.
[69] *A. S. I.*, X., p. 90; *I. A.*, XVIII., pp. 236-37.
[70] *A. S. R.*, 1936-37, pp. 94-95.
[71] *E. I.*, *I.*, p. 144., V. 40.

as mentioned in the Dudāhi inscriptions. But nothing else is known about him. The Maser Stone Inscription records that Narasiṁha of the Śulki family defeated and killed a Kalacuri King at the command of Kṛṣṇarāja,[72] who has been identified by some scholars with Kṛṣṇapa of the Dudāhi Inscriptions.[73] The proposed identification is not inherently improbable but it must be noted that the two names are not fully identical, and that the subservience of the Śulkis to the Candellas is not indicated by any independent evidence.

Estimate.—The career of Candella Yaśovarman, it will thus appear, was marked with significant political developments. From the position of a petty subordinate ruler of Central India under the Pratihāras, Yaśovarman not only liberated himself and laid the foundations of the independent Candella kingdom, but by his forceful and vigorous military measures, he made his influence acutely felt by the Imperial power as well as other contemporary powers of the north and central India in the second quarter of the 10th century A.D. Naturally with the weakening of the Pratihāras, the Candellas under Yaśovarman came to play more and more important roles in the politics of North India. This by itself is no mean achievement for any sovereign.

Yaśovarman was not only a military genius, as is proved by this successes in the political field, but he must have also taken adequate measures for the well-governance of his realm, without which he could hardly have found it possible to undertake these military expeditions. Materials are however scanty for a detailed study of the measures adopted by him, but from whatever material that is available for his reign it may not be wrong to believe that he introduced in his own kingdom the system of administrative bureaucracy that was current generally in North India during this period.

His records do not mention the name of any of his ministers, but we find reference to one of the important functionaries of the state, viz., the writer of legal documents (karaṇika)

---

[72]Annual Report of the Arch., Deptt. of Gwalior State, (1930-31) p. 10.
[73]C. I. I., IV., p. lxxxvii.

Jaddha the Gauḍa, who was well versed in Sanskrit language.[74] The name of the court-poet, who composed the lengthy Khajurāho Record, is Poet Mādhava, son of Dedda the grammarian.[75]

As for other public works undertaken by Yaśovarman the Khajurāho Inscription no. 4 refers to the construction of a big tank (taḍāgārṇavaṁ).[76] Another inscription (no. 2) from the same place records the erection of a magnificent temple dedicated to Viṣṇu. 'The golden pinnacles of the temple illuminated the sky and became, it is said, the object of attraction for even the inhabitants of the heaven.[77] This temple has been identified by Cunningham with the Vaiṣṇava temple at Khajurāho, also known as the Caturbhuja temple. The image that was installed in the temple was also a very valuable one. It was, as stated in the record, 'obtained by the Lord of Bhoṭanātha (Tibet) from Kailāśa, and from him, Sāhi, the king of the Kīras (near Kāshmir) received it as a token of friendship, and from him afterwards Herambapāla obtained it for a force of elephants and horses, and Yaśovarman himself recieved it from Hayapati Devapāla, the son of Herambapāla'.[78] The text of the inscription however reveals that king Yaśovarman was above petty jealousies of sectarian worshippers and even while founding a temple for Viṣṇu showed respects to Śiva and his consort as well as to Sāvitṛ, the Sun God.[79]

---

[74]*E. I.*, I., p. 129, V. 48.
[75]*ibid.*, V. 47.
[76]*ibid.*, p. 144, V. 38.
[77]*E. I.*, I., pp. 129, 134, V. 42.
[78]*ibid.*, V. 43. For Pt. G. S. Ojha's views, see *E. I.*, xiv. p. 180.
[79]*ibid.*, pp. 124-25, 129, Vv. 1-4 and the opening expression "Om Namo Bhagavate Vāsudevāya" as well as the last sentence "Namo Bhagavate Vāsudevāya// Namo Savitre//"

CHAPTER V

THE GROWTH OF THE CANDELLA POWER : DHANGA

Yaśovarman was succeeded on the Candella throne by his son, Dhaṅga, sometime before V.S. 1011 (953-54 A.D.), as is evident from the fact that the Khajurāho Inscription no. 2, which had been composed during the lifetime of Yaśovarman was set up after his death, when Dhaṅga was on the throne.[1] Presumably Dhaṅga had an undisputed succession. Dudāhi Inscriptions, as it has already been mentioned before, refer to another son of Yaśovarman, named Kṛṣṇapa, whose son, Devalabdhi,[2] was most probably guarding the Mālava frontier during Dhaṅga's time. It may not be unreasonable to presume that this important function was most probably entrusted in the first instance to Kṛṣṇapa, the father of Devalabdhi by Yaśovarman, who it may be remembered, claimed to be as fierce as the 'Lord of death to the Mālavas'.[3] Evidently Kṛṣṇapa does not appear to have contested the claim of his brother, Dhaṅga to the throne.

Yaśovarman, we have seen, laid the foundations of the greatness of the family, and Dhaṅga, it must be admitted, ably and steadfastly followed the footsteps of his father, and by his own achievements established the claim of the Candellas to be ranked among the leading contemporary powers of Northern India.

It was during the reign of Dhaṅga that we meet with for the first time a definite demarcation of the limits of the

---

[1]*E. I.*, I., p. 129, V. 44.

A curious suggestion has been made that "Vināyakapāladeva" in L. 29 of the Khajurāho Inscription was none other than Dhaṅga, 'Dhaṅga being the nickname or a popular name of the King.' (H. C., p. 42). This is a pure assumption for which no evidence is available.

[2]*A. S. I.*, X., p. 90; I. A., XVIII., pp. 236-37.

F. I., I., pp. 126, 132, V. 23.

Candella kingdoṁ, as indicated in the Khajurāho inscription of V.S. 1011, V. 45 of which reads as follows:

Ā-Kālañjaraṁ ā-ca Mālavanadī-tīrasthite Bhāsvataḥ
Kālindī-saritas-taṭādita itopyā Cedideśāvadheḥ/
Ā-tasmādapi viṣmayaika-nilayād-Gopābhidhānagireryaḥ
śāsti kṣitimāyatorjjita-bhuja-vyāpāra līlārjitāṁ/.[4]

(Trans.).—He playfully acquired by the action of his long and strong arms, as far as Kālañjara, and as far as Bhāsvat situated on the banks of the river of Mālava, from here also to the bank of the river Kālindī, and from here also to the frontiers of the Cedi country, and even as far as that mountain called, Gopa.

Thus it appears from the verse that the Candella kingdom during the reign of Dhaṅga included two strategic fortresses of Northern India, viz., Kālañjara and Gwālior. The territory thus brought under the control of Dhaṅga took the shape of almost a triangle with Gwālior fort forming the vertical point and an irregular line drawn from Bhāsvat, identified with Bhaillasvāmin (modern Bhilsā) on the Betwā river or Mālavanadī, to the confluence of the Ganges and the Jumna (Kālindī), forming the base of the triangle. This, when compared to the area held directly by Yaśovarman, reveals the achievements of Dhaṅga.

Conquest of Gwālior: *Relation with the Kacchapaghātas*—

Just as the occupation of Kālañjar fort by Yaśovarman earned for the Candellas a distinctive status among the contemporary powers, so the conquest of Gwālior fort (28° N. Lat. and 78°E. Long.) situated on the principal route to reach the Central Indian valley, in the reign of Dhaṅga, was his principal achievement. This, in fact, enabled Dhaṅga to declare himself as an independent ruler, as in none of the subsequent records do we find any indication of acknowledgment of Pratihāra overlordship by the Candella rulers.

The Sās Bahu Temple Inscription of Mahīpāladeva of V. S. 1150[5] reveals the existence of a Kacchapaghāta family

[4] *E. I.*, I., pp. 129, 134.
[5] *I. A.*, XV., pp. 33-46.

in possession of the Gwālior fort and its environs in the 10th and 11th centuries A. D. Vajradāman, the second in descent from the founder of the family, has been credited with the capture and occupation of the 'Gopādridurga' from the 'Gadhīnagarādhīśa',[6] who has generally been identified with a ruler of the Imperial Gurjara-Pratihāra dynasty of Kanauj. The record, however, does not mention the name of the Gurjara Pratihāra ruler, who is thus claimed to have been defeated. The evidence of a Jain fragmentary image inscription at Suhanīyā, dated Samvat 1034 (977 A. D.)[7] mentions 'Śrī Vajradāma' who has been identified with Vajradāman of the Sās Bahu record. Thus the conquest of Gwālior must have been accomplished earlier than 977 A. D. The question naturally arises, who was the 'Gadhīnagarādhīśa', referred to in the inscription ?

The records of the Gurjara Pratihāras would undoubtedly show that the Gwālior region including the strategic fort was in the possession of the Imperial rulers till at least 942-43 A. D., as evidenced by the Rākhetra Stone Inscription of Vināyakapāla, dated V. S. 999-1000.[8] In the circumstances it may be held that the Gurjara Pratihāras must have lost the fort of Gwālior to the Kacchapaghātas sometime between 944 and 977 A. D. Contemporary history shows that great confusion prevailed amongst the Gurjara Pratihāras due to internal dissensions and fresh Rāṣṭrakūṭa attacks.[9] It was during this period of turmoil that the fortress of Gwālior slipped out of their hands.

But, as indicated in verse 45 of the Khajurāho Inscription of V.S. 1011, the conquest of the Gwālior fort by Dhaṅga cannot also be doubted. Moreover Dhaṅga claims to have inflicted a crushing defeat on a Kanauj prince.[10] It is not impossible that this defeat of the Gurjara Pratihāra Chief

---

[6] *ibid.*, pp. 36, 41, V. 6.
[7] *J. A. S. B.*, XXXI., p. 411.
[8] *A. S. I.* (1924-25)., p. 168.
[9] *D. H. N. I.*, I., P. 588.
[10] *E. I.*, I., pp. 197, 203., V. 3.
'Nikhilanṛpaṁ yaḥ Kānyakubjaṁ narendraṁ samara bhuvi vijitya prāpa sāmrājyamuccaiḥ/'

resulted in the further expansion of the Candella territory including the Gopādridurga. Like the Sās Bahu Record, the Māu Inscription also does not furnish the name of the 'Kānyakubja-narendra', who was defeated by Dhaṅga.

We have thus the evidence of the conquest of Gwālior by the Kacchapaghāta Vajradāman, and again by the Candella Dhaṅga. This has given rise to a complicated issue. Dr. H. C. Ray suggests[11] that the Kacchapaghātas were at first feudatories to the Imperial Gurjara Pratihāras till they gained mastery of the Gwālior Fort by defeating the ruler of Kanauj, whom he identifies with Vijayapāla (960 A. D.)[12]. The sovereignty that they thus acquired, according to the same scholar, was short-lived, as they had very soon to yield to the rising power of the Candellas and acknowledge their hegemony.

But, as we have already shown, 'the mountain called Gopagiri' came to be included within the Candella State as early as 954 A. D. If the Candellas conquered it before 954 A. D., how could Vajradāman conquer it from the Pratihāras ? There is no evidence to show that the Candellas lost the Gwālior Fort to the Gurjara-Pratihāras between 954 and 977 A. D., so that it might have been possible for Vajradāman to conquer it again from the latter. Hence it must be concluded that the Candella episode and the Kacchapaghāta episode connected with the conquest of Gopādri are not separate stories, but that they refer to a single event in which the Candellas and the Kacchapaghātas were closely associated together. In short, the Fort was occupied by Vajradāman for the Candellas.

The Sās Bahu Temple Inscription is dated in V. S. 1150 (A. D. 1093) during the time of Mahīpāla, eighth in descent from Lakṣmaṇa, the founder of the family. Counting backwards for six generations, from Mahīpāla to Vajradāman, taking 25 years as an average, we arrive at 940 A.D. for Vajradāman. One of the members, Padmapāla, is mentioned

[11] *D. H. N. I.*, II., pp. 822-23.
[12] *Rajor Stone Insc. of V. S.* 1016. *E. I.*, III., pp. 263-67.
[13] *I. A.*, XV., pp. 37, 43., V. 30.
'yuvaiva daiva pratikūlabhāvāt Saṇkrandan-ānk-āsana-bhāg babhūva'.

to have died young[13]. In view of the possible uncertain element in this calculation, we may hold that Vajradāman's career began in about 950 A.D., and ended in about 980 A.D.[14].

Now with regard to the theory that the Kacchapaghātas were feudatories to the Gurjara Pratihāras, it may be observed that there is no history of any contact between the Gurjara Pratihāras and the Kacchapaghātas earlier than the incident resulting in the loss of Gopādri. Hence it will not be safe to conclude that they were originally feudatories to the Gurjara Pratihāras. In fact, there is nothing on record to show that they ruled over any territory before their conquest of Gwālior.

Regarding the position and status of the Kacchapaghātas subsequent to their occupation of the Gwālior Fort, it is generally assumed that they were under the Candella hegemony[15]. The occupation of the Fort, which was achieved for the Candellas, must have laid the foundation of their vassalage.

Extent of the kingdom.—In describing the boundaries of the kingdom under Dhaṅga, we find it to have extended upto the Cedi country (Cedideśāvadheḥ) on one side, and Bhaillasvāmin or Bhilsā on the other, beyond which was the Mālavadeśa. Therefore in that region Dhaṅga could hardly improve upon the achievements of his father, Yaśovarman. But there can be no doubt about the fact that he maintained a firm grip over the prevailing political situation of the time. Further the bitterness of feeling of the Candellas against the Mālavas as well as the Cedis due to the subservience of both the latter powers to the Rāṣṭrakūṭas, had by this time been reversed[16]. This must have resulted in the abatement of tension between them to some extent.

To the east, Dhaṅga retained his hold on the Ganges-Jumna doab, upto the confluence of the two rivers, where he

[14] Dr. H. C. Ray assigns to Vajradāman a reign-period of 20 years from c. 975-995 A. D. (*D. H. N. I.*, II., p. 835), and Dr. D. C. Ganguly from c. 977-999 A. D. (*H. P.*, p. 106., f. n. 1.). But as has already been shown on the evidence of V. 45 of the Khajurāho Insc. of V. S. 1011, the Fort was under the Candellas during this period.

[15] *T. A.*, I., p. 14.

[16] *D. H. N. I.*, II., pp. 761, 850-52; *H. P.*, Ganguly, P. 43.

ended his life voluntarily by forsaking his mortal coil at the sacred waters of the 'Saṅgam'. That Benares was included in Dhaṅga's dominions is indicated by the Nānyaura Plate of V. S. 1055 (A. D. 998) which was issued by Pb. M. P. Kālañjarādhipati Dhaṅgadeva from Kāśikā, recording the grant of a village to an immigrant Brāhmaṇa Bhaṭṭa Yaśodhara, on the auspicious occasion of a lunar eclipse[17].

Dhaṅga, like his father, undertook expeditions over an wide range in different parts of India beyond the limits of the territory actually held by the Candellas. His achievements in this respect are mentioned in verses 45 and 46 of the Khajurāho Inscription of V. S. 1059[18].

These verses refer to Dhaṅga's possible invasions on some portions of the Peninsular India, beyond the Vindhyas, as well as on some of the states of Eastern India, viz., Kośala, Kratha, Kuntala, Siṁhala, Andhra, Aṅga and Rāḍha. In this case too, like that of his predecessor in verse 23 of the Khajurāho inscription of V. S. 1011, there are some obvious exaggerations. But, in spite of that it is generally admitted that Dhaṅga's military potentiality helped him to rise to an important position in the history of Northern India.

Dhaṅga's Invasion of Bengal.—We have already referred to Yaśovarman's successful military operations in Bengal towards the middle of the 10th century A. D., resulting in the crippling of the Pāla power and the abrupt rise of the Kāmbojas in North Bengal. Some scholars think that they were the Kāmboja-Pālas, and not Kāmbojas, and that there was a division of the Pāla dominion.

The attention of the Candellas towards Bengal affairs was however, not withdrawn after that incident. When the Kāmboja-Pālas consolidated their position and began to assume Imperial titles like "Parameśvara, Paramabhaṭṭāraka and Māhārājādhirāja"[19], the Candellas most probably thought it necessary to be alert, so that the new power may not grow up to be a source of danger to them in future.

---

[17] *I. A.*, XVI., p. 201-04.
[18] *E. I.*, I., p. 145., Vv. 45-46.
[19] *Irdā Copper Plate* E. I., XXII., pp. 150-59., Ll. 18-20.

This policy is presumed to have culminated in Dhaṅga leading an expedition against West Bengal (Rāḍha) as implied in V. 46 of the Khajurāho Inscription of V. S. 1059, corresponding to 1002 A. D.

The expedition indicated in the verse against Rāḍha took place before 1000 A. D., i. e., sometime between 954 and 1002 A. D. The Kāmbojas were ruling in West Bengal (Varddhamānabhukti, Daṇḍabhukti maṇḍala—Irdā Grant)[20] during this time. Hence if the Candellas actually invaded Rāḍha under Dhaṅga, they must have come into contact with the Kāmbojas. It is noteworthy however that this inscription does not refer to Gauḍa. The Kāmbojas, on the other hand, actually ruled in Gauḍa, as the Dinājpur Inscription[21] read with the Bāngaḍ Grant of Mahīpāla I[22], would definitely show. But the Candellas might have contented themselves merely with an invasion on Rāḍha, which must have been an important centre of their power.

Dhaṅga, like his predecessor Yaśovarman, did not take any step to annex Rāḍha to his dominion. The object of such invasions seems to have been merely to weaken the ruling power, so that no attempt could be made by it to extend itself beyond certain limits. With the weakening of the Kāmbojas as a result of Dhaṅga's invasion, the Pālas found an opportunity to reassert themselves and re-conquer their lost territory, as indicated in the Bāngaḍ Inscription. When Rājendra Cola's army invaded Bengal in about 1023 A.D., Uttara-Rāḍha appears to have been included under Mahīpāla's dominion. It is quite likely that this part of West Bengal came into the possession of Mahīpāla after the Candella raid on West Bengal by Dhaṅga. Another part of West Bengal, Dakṣiṇa-Rāḍha (South-western part of Bengal, between the Ajay and Dāmodar rivers), according to the Tirumalai Inscription[23], was at this time under the rule of a Śūra king, Raṇaśūra, and Daṇḍabhukti (*Taṇḍabutti* of

[20] *ibid.*, Ll. 20-21.
[21] *J. A. S. B.* (N. S.), II., p. 619.
[22] *E. I.*, XIV., p. 324; *G. L. M.*, p. 91.
[23] *E. I.*, IX., p. 229.

the Tirumalai Record)—modern Dānton in Midnapur District, was held by one Dharmapāla. Some scholars think that he belonged to the Kāmboja-Pāla lineage of the Irdā Grant.

The reference to Dhaṅga's imprisoning of the wife of the King of Aṅga, as distinguished from the King of Rāḍha, is also not without significance. As the inscriptions of the Pāla rulers since the days of Nārāyaṇapāla to Mahīpāla I, have continuously been found in South Bihar[24], it may be regarded to have been in the continuous possession of the Pālas, particularly since the recovery of the region from the hands of Mahendrapāla of the Pratihāra dynasty. Evidently the Pāla king was meant by the term 'Aṅgendra', if, of course, it did not allude to a feudatory of them. As such the Pāla dominion also was not free from Dhaṅga's raids. But it could not undermine the recuperative power of the Pālas which soon became manifest in Mahīpāla's achievements.

Southern Expedition.—It is hardly possible to believe that Dhaṅga became so powerful as to make his weight felt on the whole of the peninsular India, and even beyond, on the island-state of Ceylon (Siṁhala), as is claimed in the Khajurāho Record. Undoubtedly it is a poetic exaggeration. Dhaṅga might have, however, raided some of the territories in the Deccan, just to the south of the Vindhyas, viz., Kratha and Kośala.

We have already seen that Yaśovarman claims to have carried off the treasures of the Kośalas (Kośalaḥ Kośalānāṁ). There might have been a recurrence of a similar expedition by Dhaṅga on Dakṣiṇa Kośala, when its ruler was compelled to accept the suzerainty of the Candella ruler. Śivagupta (c. 950 A. D.) was succeeded by his son, Mahābhavagupta Janamejaya. The charters issued by Mahābhavagupta[25] contain very little information about the political incidents of the reign of Mahābhavagupta, but it becomes quite evident that he was the ruler of Orissa proper only, though

[24] *H. B.*, I., App. I., pp. 173-74 (List of Pāla Inscriptions).
[25] *E. I.*, III., pp. 341-51; *ibid.*, VIII., pp. 141-43; *ibid.*, XI., pp. 94-95; *ibid.*, XXIII., pp. 250 ff, *J. A. S. B.*, (N. S.,)., I., pp. 12-13.

high-sounding paramount titles might have been used in his records[26]. Dhaṅga's possible invasion of Kośala and the latter's submission to the Candellas, however temporary, may have brought them into conflict with the Cedis, who under Lakṣmaṇarāja, son of Yuvarāja I, claims to have inflicted a severe defeat on the Lord of Kośala (Kośalanātha)[27], who may be identified either with Mahābhavagupta, as suggested by Dr. Ray[28], or with some of his successors.

Kratha is generally located in the Yeotmal district in North Berar, and according to tradition, Kratha is the name of an indigenous tribe inhabiting the particular region of Berar (Vidarbha). The Kāhlā Grant of Kalacuri Soḍhadeva dated V. S. 1134 (1077 A. D.)[29] seems to suggest that the Krathas were in possession of Kālañjara prior to its occupation by the elder brother of Kalacuri Lakṣmaṇarāja. This incident must have happened long before the Pratihāra occupation of the Kālañjara-maṇḍala in the 9th century A.D., of which we have epigraphic evidence.[30] The Krathas, on being ousted from Kālañjara might have settled in Berar, and Dhaṅga on his way to Kośala must have come upon them, whereupon they had to accept his suzerainty, which has been alluded to in the Khajurāho Record of V. S. 1059 (V. 45).

But Dhaṅga's claim to have imprisoned the wives of the kings of Kāñci and Andhra (V. 45), and to have compelled the ruler of Kuntala to obey his commands like a disciple (V. 46), as mentioned in the same record, can only be taken as mere praśasti. Towards the end of the 10th cent. A. D., the Rāṣṭrakūṭa power was fast declining, which relieved the North India rulers immensely from their constant apprehension of invasions from the South. But the revival of the Western Cālukyas under Tailapa II Āhavamalla (973-96

[26] "Parama-bhaṭṭāraka Mahārājādhirāja Parameśvara Soma-kulatilaka Trikaliṅgādhipati Śrī Mahābhavagupta-rāja-devaḥ".

[27] *E. I.*, I., pp. 260, 268., V. 62.

[28] *D. H. N. I.*, II., p. 401.

[29] *E. I.*, VII., p. 89., V. 5.

[30] *ibid.*, XIX., pp. 15-19.

A. D.), who dealt the final blow to the last king of the Rāṣṭrakūṭa lineage[31], and that of the Colas under Parantaka (907-53 A. D.) and Rājarāja the Great (985-1016 A. D.), and the rise of the Eastern Cālukyas of Veṅgi preclude all possibilities of the Candella ruler having undertaken successful invasions on their territories, far less to speak of Siṁhala (Ceylon).

So these references in the Candella records were in all probability incorporated by the court poet, who, it must be admitted, was quite conversant with the political condition of the time, viz., the eclipse of the Rāṣṭrakūṭas, the traditional enemy of the Northern powers, and the rest was mainly a fanciful expression of his pious wish.

Invasion of the Turks: The Role of Dhaṅga—A fragmentary inscription discovered at Mahobā throw an interesting light on the achievements of Dhaṅga. Verse 17 of the record reads as follows:—

> "Nirmmitavairibhaṅgaḥ Śrī Dhaṅgaḥ ityavani-maṅgalamāvirāsīt/
> Sāreṇa yaḥ svabhujayor- *bhuvanātibhāraṁ Hamvīram-apyatibalaṁ tulayaṁ cakāra//*".

"There appeared a blessing for the earth called, Dhaṅga, who caused destruction of his enemies, and who, by the strength of his arms *equalled even the powerful Hamvīra,* who had proved a heavy burden for the earth" [32].

The term 'Haṁvīra' is generally taken by scholars to be derived from the Arabic word, 'Āmir', meaning 'Commander'. Later it came to acquire the use as a title for a Muhammadan prince. The word Haṁvīra has variants like Hammira, and Hamira. But the stray reference in the abovementioned Mahobā record does not enable us to identify accurately the particular Muslim prince mentioned therein. It is, however, generally held that as the Yāmini Sultāns themselves used the honorific 'Āmir', Haṁvīra must refer either to Sabuktigin or his illustrious son, Māhmud of Ghaznā. Hultzsch identifies Haṁvīra of the Mahobā Record

[31] *A. I. K.*, pp. 15-16.
[32] *E. I.*, I., p. 221.

with Sabuktigin[33]. Māhmud, it is well known, played the most significant role in almost all the major expeditions of the Yāminis on Indian territories. Even during the lifetime of Sabuktigin, Māhmud was associated with his father in the latter's invasion on India. It is recorded in the Tabakāt i Ākbari[34] that Āmir Muhammad, the son of Āmir Nāsiruddin showed much courage and great heroism in the battle against Jayapāla, and it was practically Māhmud's strategy that compelled Jayapāla to sue for peace on payment of some 50 elephants and much treasure. Then again, on ascending the throne of Ghaznā in A. D. 999, Mahmud took a vow of taking out a 'holy' expedition to India every year[35], and this vow was not an empty boast. His inconoclastic zeal became almost a nightmare to the Indian princes, which has been very aptly expressed in the Mahobā record by the term 'bhuvanātibhāram',—his weight appeared 'unbearable' to the Mother Earth. So, to equate Dhaṅga with Haṁvīra (Māhmud) in prowess and military achievements must have appeared to the praśastikāra as deserving of the highest reward.

But the question arises, why should the praśastikāra be so modest as merely to equate his hero (*tulayaṃ cakāra*) with another and not to claim to have surpassed him ? √tul has the use of expressing 'treating with contempt', as has already been shown, in a verse of the Khajurāho Record of V. S. 1011[36].

But the circumstances do not permit us to draw that meaning here. The available sources do not indicate that there was any direct fight between the Candella ruler and Sultān Māhmud. That Dhaṅga was not defeated nor his kingdom invaded by Māhmud might have been construed by a later court-poet in taking pride that the predecessor of his master was an equal to the Sultān.

A study of the political condition of the time (towards the

[33]*ibid.*, pp., 218-19.
[34]*T. A.*, p. 3.
[35]Dr. Nazim disagrees with this interpretation. *S. M. G.*, p. 86, f. n. 3.
[36]*I. H. Q.*, XXV., p. 213.

end of the 10th cent. A. D.) reveals that Jayapāla, the Sāhi ruler of the Punjab, anticipating the magnitude of the impact of the impending Turki invasion under Sabuktigin, organised a very strong army. The Muslim sources are almost unanimous about the fact that Jayapāla put into the field no less than 1,00,000 cavalry, many elephants and an innumerable host of foot. Utbi records that the Hindu army appeared like the boundless ocean, and in numbers like the ants and locusts of the wilderness[37]. Dr. Nazim rather inappropriately refers to the formation of 'a league of the Hindu Rājās[38]', of which we have no direct evidence. It cannot be denied however that Jayapāla made a supreme effort to protect his kingdom, but it is highly doubtful as to whether it was possible for him to arouse a feeling of national danger among the North Indian rulers and galvanise them into a confederacy.

Nizāmuddin[39] and Firishtā[40] make only a veiled reference to the assistance in the shape of men and money received by the Sāhi ruler from the different Indian states, a list of whom, viz., Delhi, Ājmer, Kāliñjar and Kanauj, has been furnished by Firishtā only. The latter source, being a much later work, is always susceptible to minor inaccuracies here and there. But there is no doubt about the fact that the 'Rājā of Kāliñjar', referred to herein, was Dhaṅga of the Candella dynasty, who along with the ruler of Kanauj of the Pratihāra family, might have sent some contingents of army only in response to the call of Jayapāla. The defeat of the army of Jayapāla in 977 A.D., as a result of which the territory to the west of the Indus including Lamghān and Peshāwār passed over to the Sultān, had no repercussion on other North Indian States.

Then again in 1006-07 A.D., when Sultān Māhmud in course of his invasion of Multān tried to pass through the territories of Ānandapāla, the successor of Jayapāla, the

[37] *T. F.*, I., pp. 18;19; *T. A.*, pp. 3-4; *K. Y.*, pp. 40-42.
[38] *S. M. G.*, p. 30.
[39] *T. A.*, p. 3.
[40] *T. F.*, I., p. 18.

latter, apprehending a crisis for the whole of India, appealed to the neighbouring Rājās for help. The Rājās of Ujjain, Gwālior, Kāliñjar, Kanauj, Delhi and Ājmer, according to Firishtā[41], readily responded to the appeal and despatched their contingents to swell the Sāhī army. Evidently there is some amount of exaggeration in the statement, but that there was an organised movement is also understood from the account of Utbi. Victory again lay with the Yāmini Sultān, who pursued the fugitives upto the fort of Nagarkot in 1009 A.D., but as on previous occasion, it did not matter very much with those allies of Ānandapāla, including the Candellas just then, as they did not participate directly in the battle and their main source of power remained intact.

Māhmud too did not belittle the potentialities of these rulers, and he took out almost annual expeditions to India and dealt with the states separately[42], thereby consolidating his Indian Empire. The Candellas, it must be admitted, had not to face the Turki onslaught till 1019 A. D., when Vidyādhara, a grandson of Dhaṅga was on the Candella throne. This justifies the claim of the praśastikāra in comparing Dhaṅga with Haṁvīra as an equal in the Mahobā Record, whose reign was not marred by defeat at the hands of the Sultān.

Dhaṅga thus stands out in the contemporary political set-up of Northern India as an important figure, who not only consolidated his own kingdom but also exercised an abiding influence on other neighbouring powers. It may not be an exaggeration to say that Dhaṅga by his military exploits usurped much of the glory of the Imperial Pratihāras, who were then a decadent power. In internal administration it may be noticed that Dhaṅga continued the same organisation as prevailing in time of his father, Yaśovarman. It appears from the study of the Nānyaura Plate 'A'[43], which refers to a gift of a village to an immigrant Brahmin named Bhaṭṭa Yaśodhara, who is generally identified with Yaśodhara

---

[41] *T. F.*, I., p. 46.
[42] *S. M. G.*, App., pp. 232-34.
[43] *I. A.*, XVI., pp. 201-04.

of the Khajurāho Record of V.S. 1059, that Dhaṅga tried to induce learned brahmins to settle within the Candella state by granting revenue-free lands to them and utilise their services in dealing out even-handed justice to his subjects. The Khajurāho Record, alluded to, states that the Purohita of Dhaṅga, Śrīmad Yaśodhara acted as the Dharmmādhikāra or the Chief Magistrate, who followed the principles of law enunciated in the legal texts of ancient India[44].

The Māu Stone Inscription of Madanavarman gives us the name of the Chief Minister of Dhaṅga. He was a brahmin named Prabhāsa of the lineage of Āṅgirasa and Gautama Akṣapāda. He is described as an experienced administator as well as a skillful diplomat[45]. He was appointed after he had been tested on the lines indicated in the Arthaśāstra of Kauṭilya[46] (sarvvopadhā-śuddhi). Besides we get references to two other classes of officials viz., Karaṇika and Kāyastha, the writer of legal documents and the official scribe. All these go to show that there was a perfect bureaucratic machinery functioning in the Candella state which enabled Dhaṅga to focus all his energy and resources in military pursuits.

As for the personal religion of Dhaṅga it may be noted that he was a devout worshipper of Śiva, as it is mentioned in the Khajurāho Inscription, that he had forsaken his life at the sacred confluence of the Gaṅgā and the Yamunā at Prayāga, while concentrating on Rudra. He had a very long life of over one hundred years, as recorded therein, and voluntarily retired from the world[47]. Such cases of voluntary termination of life are, of course, not rare in Indian history. Besides it is also observed that he installed a precious idol of Śivaliṅga, made of emerald (Marakateśvara)[48], and his inscriptions generally begin and end with adoration to Śiva. Still he had no parochialism in him. He was imbued with the

[44] *E. I.*, I., p. 146, V. 56.
[45] *ibid.*, p. 199, Vv. 18-22.
[46] *K. A.* Shamsastry, p. 17.
[47] Jīvitvā śaradām śatam samadhikaṁ Śrī Dhanga-pṛthvīpatih / Rudram-mudrita locanaḥ sa hṛdaye dhyāyañ-japañ Jāhnavī-Kālindyoḥ salile kalevara parityāgād-agānnirvṛtiṁ//" V. 55. *E. I.*, I., p. 146.
[48] *ibia.*, Vv. 48, 63., pp. 145-147.

same spirit of toleration to other religious sects as his father, Yaśovarman. It is interesting to note that it was he who completed the construction of the temple of Vaikuṇṭha-(nātha) begun by his father[49]. The liberal outlook of Dhaṅga is noticeable in bolder relief when we study an unofficial document of the time relating to the gift of some gardens in favour of a temple of Jinanātha by Pahilla, who, it is claimed, was held in high esteem by Dhaṅga[50].

Throughout his career, glimpses of which are available in the Candella records, we find that Dhaṅga was a man of charitable disposition and he made several gifts and endowments for the maintenance of temples as well as brāhmaṇa families. He is credited with having performed the Tulāpuruṣa gift[51], one of the most luxurious of ceremonies. The Nānyaura Plate records that he used to make gifts also on occasions like the Solar eclipse &c., with the belief that it would be meritorious for himself as well as for his departed parents (vṛddhaye puṇyayaśasor-mmātāpitorathātmanaḥ)[52].

The records do not furnish us with the name of his queen or any other matter concerning his family life. But in both the Māu and Mahobā inscriptions we find the name of his son, Gaṇḍadeva[53], who succeeded him on the throne.

---

[49] *E. I.*, I., pp. 122-35.
[50] *ibid.*, pp. 135-36.
[51] *ibid.*, p. 146, V. 52.
[52] *I. A.*, XVI., p. 203, L. 11.
[53] *E. I.*, I., p. 197, V. 4; p. 221, V. 17.

CHAPTER VI

STRUGGLES WITH THE MUSLIMS: GAṆḌA AND VIDYĀDHARA

Gaṇḍa—Dhaṅga, as has already been mentioned, had a very long life extending to more than a hundred years, and evidently he had a long reign, from about 950 A.D. to at least 1002-03 A.D., of which we have epigraphic evidence. But some scholars are of opinion that it is not unlikely for Dhaṅga to have lived upto 1008 A.D., which saw the downfall of the Hindu Sāhī dynasty[1]. If it is admitted then Dhaṅga must have been the ruler of Kālañjar, who is stated to have co-operated with Ānandapāla against the Turuṣka Su'tān. But scholars are not unanimous on the matter, and according to V. Smith, the Kāliñjar prince, referred to in the Muslim records, was Gaṇḍa, the son and successor of Dhaṅga[2]. Though the possibility of Dhaṅga continuing on the Candella throne upto 1008 A.D., cannot be ruled out, still in the absence of positive evidence it is indeed difficult to be definite on the point.

Dhaṅga was succeeded by Gaṇḍa. For the latter's reign we have no epigraphic record or any other contemporary account. He has only been mentioned in rather vague conventional phrases in some late records, issued not less than one hundred years after his demise. Those records are—(*i*) A fragmentary inscription from Mahobā[3] composed after the reign of Kīrtivarman (c. 1098 A.D.), grandson of Gaṇḍa (*ii*) Māu stone inscription of Madanavarman[4], grandson of Kīrtivarman and, (*iii*) A rock inscription of the time of Bhojavarman[5]. These too do not provide us with any informa-

[1] *D. H. N. I.*, II., p. 683.
[2] *I. A.* XXXVII., p. 142.
[3] *E. I.*, I., p. 217-22.
[4] *ibid.*, pp. 195-207.
[5] *ibid.*, pp. 330-38.

tion of historical importance. He has been described as an unrivalled hero (ekavīrah),[6] 'and an expert in annihilating enemies whose massive arms were terrible through the itching of pride (Darpa-kaṇḍugra-dorddaṇḍadviśat-khaṇḍana paṇḍitah)[7]. But there is no mention of any specific occasion when Gaṇḍadeva might have shown his military skill, so eloquently described by the praśastikāra. An examination of the extent of the kingdom and the position of the Candella ruler during the time of his successor, Vidyādhara, reveals that it did not suffer any diminution at the hands of Gaṇḍadeva. Evidently Gaṇḍa was able to preserve his territory without being too much aggressive like his father and grandfather.

The black cloud of the Gaznavid invasions looming large on the north-western horizon of India since the days of Dhaṅga, gradually assumed greater and more menacing proportions. The victory of Sultān Māhmud against the Sāhī ruler in 1008 A.D., opened up the road to India beyond the Sutlej to the Turki depredations, which from now on were almost regularly carried out year after year till they appeared in Kanauj in 409 A.H., i.e., 1018 A.D.[8] It was probably Rājyapāla who was ruling in Kanauj at the time. According to the evidence of Utbi, Rājyapāla was almost deserted by his allies, and finding the situation deteriorating almost beyond his control, he retreated from the field of battle leaving the city and its fortifications to be captured by the Sultān in a single day[9]. Encouraged by repeated successes, Māhmud visited again next year in 410 A.H. (1019 A.D.), but according to Firishtā, Nizāmuddin and others, Māhmud now came on the plea of punishing 'Nandā' of Khajurāho, who had killed the Pratihāra Rājyapāla for his surrender to Māhmud during the latter's invasion in the previous year (409 A.H.). Cunningham took 'Nandā' as a misreading for

---

[6] *ibid.*, p. 219., V. 19.
[7] *ibid.*, p. 197., V. 4.
[8] *T. A.*, pp. 12-13.
[9] *T. Y.* (Elliott., II), pp. 41-46.

Gaṇḍa, which was accepted by Hultzsch, Smith and others[10]. This would take the length of the reign of Gaṇḍa beyond 1018-19 A.D.

But the Dubkuṇḍ Inscription of the Kacchapaghāta Vikramasiṁha dated V.S. 1145 (1188 A.D.) tells us that his great-grandfather, Arjuna, an ally or feudatory to Vidyādharadeva, killed Rājyapala in battle[11]. This complicates the issue. V. Smith explains the discrepancy by supposing that Arjuna joined in a confederacy with Vidyādhara, who was then a crown-prince only[12]. This theory does not hold good after the discovery of the Mahobā inscription, in which the credit for victory over the 'Kānyakubjanarendra' was given to Vidyādhara[13]. Ibu-ul-Āthir in his Āl-Tārikh ul Kāmil also recorded that after Māhmud's return to Ghaznā, "Bidā, the accursed, who was the greatest of the rulers of India in territory and had the largest army, and whose territory was named Kajurāhā, sent messengers to the Rāy of Kanauj, who was named, 'Rājaypāl', rebuking him for his flight and for the surrender of his territories to the Mussalmans. A long quarrel ensued between them, which resulted in hostilities; and as each of them prepared to fight the other, they marched out and met and fought, and Rājaypāl was killed[14]", 'Bidā' of Ibn ul Āthir is undoubtedly a corruption for Vidyādhara, and 'Nandā' of Utbi, Nizāmuddin and Firishtā was nothing but a misreading for 'Bidā' (Vidyādhara), and not for 'Gaṇḍa', as has been shown by Dr. Ray.[15] Therefore Gaṇḍa must have ceased to rule before 1018 A.D.

As for the internal condition of the state during the reign-period of Gaṇḍa, we come to know that Prabhāsa, the Chief Minister (Mantrimukhya) of Dhaṅga continued to be at the helm of affairs.[16] His son, Śivanāga, it appears served Vidyā-

---

[10] *A. S. R.*, II., p. 452; *E. I.*, I., p. 219; *J. A. S. B.* (1881), p 11 *I. A.*, XXXVII., p. 128.
[11] *E. I.*, II., p. 237, L. 12.
[12] *I. A.*, XXXVII., p. 128.
[13] *E. I.*, I., pp. 197, 203., V. 3.
[14] *T. K. A.*, IX., pp. 115-16.
[15] *D. H. N. I.*, I., p. 606.
[16] *E. I.*, I., p. 199., V. 21.

dhara, the successor of Gaṇḍa, as minister. This again supports the contention that Gaṇḍa did not enjoy a long reign.

It has already been noticed that the Candella rulers encouraged learned brahmins to settle within their territory so that their services may be utilised in the administration of the kingdom. But in the bureaucratic administrative set-up the function of the Karaṇikas and the Kāyasthas can hardly be overstated. In recognition of this fact most probably Gaṇḍa granted a village, Dugauḍa by name, to Thakkura Jājuka of the Vāstavya race of the Kāyasthas, who held a position of trust under him[17].

Vidyādhara

Gaṇḍa's successor on the Candella throne was Vidyādhara, one of the greatest rulers of the Candella family. His claim to greatness did not rest on conquests or invasions, but on the gallant part he played in the defence of the country against the Ghaznavid marauders, which could not but be recognised even by the Muslim historians[1].

It has already been seen that Gaṇḍa, during his short tenure, could not play an aggressive role in the face of steadily deteriorating political condition of Northern India due to the repeated incursions of the Turks, which culminated in the flight and surrender of the effete Imperial ruler, Rājyapāla of Kanauj in 1018 A.D. The city of 'Mahodayaśrīh' was laid open to plunder and desecration. But its significance however was much greater. It broke the morale of the Indian rulers, as, in spite of all weaknesses, the halo of imperial status still surrounded the head of the Pratihāra ruler. So the fall of the Pratihāras was considered to be symbolic of the final collapse of Indian resistance. One after another, chiefs of fortresses and rulers of smaller states to the north of the Chambal surrendered to Sultān Māhmud almost without any opposition. This had brought about a situation surcharged with

[17]*ibid.*, Pp. 333, 336, Vv. 5-7.
[1]*T.A.*, P. 12; *T.K.A.*, IX., Pp. 115-16; *K. Z.A.*, P. 76.

grave consequences. The realisation of it must have prompted Vidyādhara, on whom now devolved the responsibility of resisting foreign inroads, to take drastic steps, as recorded by Ibn ul Āthir[2].

Defeat and death of Rājyapāla

We are told in the Kāmil that Bidā, equivalent for Vidyā in the Arabic phonetics,[3] after a long quarrel, had fought and killed Rājaypāl, the ruler of Kanauj for his flight and surrender of his territories to the Mussalmans.[4] This finds eloquent corroboration in the Dubkuṇḍ Inscription, in which Arjuna of the Kacchapaghāta family, a devoted ally of Vidyādhara, is mentioned to have killed Rājyapāla in a great battle[5]. Evidently Arjuna was in close alliance with Vidyādharadeva and probably he was only carrying out the directions of the Candella ruler, who now assumed leadership in the North Indian politics.

This bold and courageous stand of Vidyādhara further enhanced his prestige in the estimation of other rulers of Central India. It was most probably at his instance that Trilocanapāla, referred to in the Jhusi Grant,[6] was installed on the Pratihāra throne after Rājyapāla's assassination. Thus, it may be claimed, Vidyādharadeva gave full effect to the policy of Yaśovarman and Dhaṅga, and justified the assumption of Imperial titles like, Parmeśvara Paramabhaṭṭāraka Mahārājādhirāja &c., (Nānyaura Plate 'B' of Devavarman V.S. 1107)[7]. A fragmentary Mahobā Inscription in this connection describes that 'Bhojadeva together with Kalacuri-candra (the moon of the Kalacuris), worshipped full of fear like a pupil, the master of warfare, who had caused destruction of the King of Kānyakubja'[8]. Bhojadeva of this

---

[2] *T.K.A.*, IX., Pp. 115-16.
[3] *D.H.N.I.*, II., P. 688.
[4] *T.K.A.*, IX., Pp. 115-16.
[5] *E.I.*, II., P. 237., L. 10. "Śrī Vidyādharadeva-kāryaniratah Śrī Rājyapālaṁ haṭhāt kaṇṭhāsthi-cchidaneka vāṇa-nivahair-hatvā mahatyāhave."
[6] *I.A.*, XVIII., Pp. 33-35.
[7] *ibid.*, XVI., P. 205., L. 1.
[8] *E.I.*, I., Pp. 219, 222., V. 22. "Vihita Kānyakubja-bhūpāla bhaṅgaṁ-Samara gurum-upāsta prauḍhabhiṣtalpabhājaṁ saha-Kalacuricandraḥ śiṣyavad Bhojadevaḥ."

record has generally been identified with Bhoja of the Paramāra dynasty and Kalacuri-candra with Kokkalla II[8a]. It cannot be denied that both the Paramāras and the Kalacuris were so long hostile to the Candellas, as all of them were contesting for the supremacy in North India. But circumstances took such a turn that for the time being they had to accept the superiority of the Candella ruler, Vidyādhara. So rightly has it been claimed in a Candella record that king Vidyādhara gathered the flowers of the fame of his enemies. (v. 21). The Māu Stone inscription of Madanavarman also equalled Vidyādhara to Indra, the lord of Gods (Vāsava), whose lotus feet took rest on diadems of all kings without exception[9]. This also agrees with the account of him as recorded by the Muslim chroniclers. Ibu ul Āthir describes Vidyādhara as the most powerful Indian prince of the time, possessing an army of 56,000 cavalry, 1,84,000 infantry and 746 elephants[10] [Nizāmuddin—36,000 cavalry, 1,45,000 infantry & 390 elephants[11]; Firishtā—45,000 infantry[12] (evidently a mistake for 1,45,000)[13]; Kitāb-Zainul Ākhbar—640 elephants[14].] In spite of possible inaccuracies in matters of detail, it is to be admitted that Vidyādhara created for him an unique position in the political set-up of North India, which made Sultān Māhmud of Ghazni no less concerned.

Vidyādhara did not rest content with inflicting punishment on the Pratihāra ruler for his faults of omission and commission. He fully realised that matters would not stop there, and that further clashes with the Turuṣkas were inevitable. So he formed, what may be called an alliance of the rulers of India ready to meet fresh onslaughts from the

---

[8a]Mm. Mirashi believes that the '*Kalacuri-candra* referred to as a pupil' is probably Gāṅgeya. The latter, he points out, appears to have held a subordinate position in the beginning of his career on the evidence of the Makundapur S.I., *C.I.I.*, IV. P. lxxxix and P. 234-35.

[9]*E.I.*, I., Pp. 197, 203., V. 5. "(Tasmād-aśeṣa narapati-mauliṣu viśrānta kāntapadakamalaḥ Śrī Vidyādharadevaḥ)".

[10]*T.K.A.*, P. 216.

[11]*T.A.*, P. 12.

[12]*T.F.*, I., P. 64.

[13]*D.H.N.I.*, II., P. 690., f.n. 2.

[14]*K. Z. A.*, P. 76.

Ghaznavids. Even, according to Ibn ul Āthir[15] and Kitāb Zainul Ākhbār[16], Paru Jaypāl or Taru Jaypāl (equivalent to Trilocanapāla of the Sāhī dynasty) sought the protection of Bidā, who promised to restore to him his country, and to protect him[17].

Renewed invasion of Māhmud.

In the words of the author of the Kāmil, "when the news reached Yāminuddaulāh, he was disturbed and prepared for fight". Thus it becomes evident that the cause of Māhmud's taking out another expedition to India in A.H. 410 (1019 A.D.), was not merely ambition and love of plunder, but necessitated by the fact that the Candella prince had been reorganising the scattered energies of the Indian chiefs with an object to recover the lost territories.

So Māhmud turned again towards 'Hind' with his bold warriors in 410 A.H., and according to Nizāmuddin[18], when he reached the river Jun (Yamunā), Naro Jaipāl, who had several times fled before his armies, encamped in front of it now, in order to help and assist Nandā (i.e., Bidā). The mention of the Jun is rather confusing, as the Yamunā could by no means become the battle ground between Māhmud and Naro Jaipāl, identified with Trilocanapāla of the Sāhī dynasty. Utbi however more accurately records the name of the river as the Rāhib or the Rām-Gaṅgā[19]. Dr. Nazim inferred from the evidence of Fārukhi that the Sultān crossed the river Ganges somewhere near Hardwār and pursued Trilocanapāla upto the bank of the river Rāhut or Rām-Gaṅgā, where a crushing defeat was inflicted upon him.[20] But according to Utbi and Ibu ul Āthir, Trilocanapāla determinedly resisted the passage of the Sultān across the river. A detachment of Māhmud's followers somehow or other crossed the river and effected a landing on the other

[15] *T.K.A.*, P. 216.
[16] *K.Z.A.*, P. 76.
[17] *D.H.N.I.*, I., P. 605.
[18] T.A., p. 12
[19] *I.G.I.*, XXI., P. 175.
[20] *S.M.G.*, P. 94, f.n. 7.

side in the teeth of bitter opposition. Then the Sultān himself with the remainder of his army also crossed over, whereupon a fierce battle was fought between them, resulting in serious losses to Trilocanapāla's army. The latter now sought for peace, which however was turned down by Māhmud. Thus frustrated, Sāhī Trilocanapāla tried to make good his escape with an idea of joining his ally, Bidā. But unfortunately, he was surprised and killed on the way by some unknown Hindus[21]. The identity of these Hindus, who slew Trilocanapāla, cannot be established, for, nowhere have they been mentioned by name nor could any other information be gathered.

After this incident Sultān Māhmud proceeded towards Bāri[22], the new seat of the Pratihāra kingdom under Trilocanapāla[23], possibly a nominee of Candella Vidyādhara. Trilocanapāla, according to the author of Kitāb Zainul Ākhbār, hearing the news of the approach of the Ghaznavid hordes, fled from his kingdom, leaving it to be ravaged by the Turuṣkas.

Then Māhmud prepared himself for the final battle and started in pursuit of Bidā. Bidā was met commanding an immense army on the banks of a river, which filled the heart of the Turuṣka chief with nervousness. The Tabakāt i Ākbari records that, 'when the Sultān, encamped in front of Nandā's army, he first sent an envoy to him and invited him to submit and to accept Islām. Nandā refused to place his neck under the yoke of subjection. After that the Sultān went to an elevated spot, so that he might look at and make an estimate of the strength of Nandā's army. Then, when he saw what a vast host it was, he repented for his coming; and placing the forehead in supplication on the ground prayed for victory and conquest from the Giver of all mercies[24]'. Other sources also agree with Nizāmuddin about the military power of the Candella ruler. The Tabakāt goes on to say that 'in the night

[21] *T.K.A.*, Pp. 116ff.
[22] *ibid; K.Z.A.*, P. 26.
[23] *I.A.*, XVIII., Pp. 33-35.
[24] *T.A.*, P. 12; *K.Z.A.*, P. 76.

a great fear fell on the heart of Nandā, and he fled with a few special companions leaving the army and all munitions of war behind'. That is to say, there was no fight between the two armies, but due to the sudden withdrawal of the Candella chief under cover of night, the Sultān gained, what may be called, an easy victory. The chroniclers are not however unanimous on the point. According to Ibn ul Āthir, before effecting a direct clash the men of the Sultān diverted the course of the river. Only then was it possible for 'Yāminuddaulāh to send a party of his infantry to fight him (Bidā), and the latter also sent out against him a similar number, and both the armies continued reinforcing their soldiers till the two opposing forces increased in numbers, and battle became vehement. At last the night overtook them and parted them[25].' As suggested by Dr. Ray, on account of the diversion of the stream, the strategic importance of the field chosen by Vidyādhara to resist Māhmud must have considerably diminished[26], and Vidyādhara evaded an unnecessary show-down by staging a planned retreat without giving the Sultān an opportunity to force a decision. The amount of frustration of the Sultān at this highly strategic move of the Candella king is evident from the account of Gardizi in Zainul Ākhbār. It is stated therein that the following morning Sultān Māhmud despatched his ambassador to Gaṇḍa (i.e., Bidā), but he returned to report that the enemy's camp was deserted. Gaṇḍa (Bidā) unaccountably stricken with panic had fled from the field under cover of night. The Sultān thanked God for this unexpected good luck, and making sure that no ambush has been laid, he gave orders for the plundering of the camp of the enemy.

As regards the booty obtained by the Sultān in this raid, the Muslim chroniclers generally give an exaggerated report. The Tabakāt-i-Ākbari states that the army of Islām procured immense quantities of booty, including 580 elephants.[27] A similar account is also found in the Kāmil. This shows that

[25] *T.K.A.*, P. 216.
[26] *D.H.N.I.*, II., P. 691., f.n. 2.
[27] *T.A.*, P. 13.

the Candella ruler had surrendered completely to the Sultān. This is hardly consistent with the power and prestige of Candella Vidyādhara even after the defeat at the hands of the Sultān, and it may be noted in this connection that realising this Māhmud had to launch an all-out offensive in about 3 years' time. The nett result therefore might have been that by the tactical move of Bidā the Sultān had to return to Ghazni achieving a partial victory only. He did not think it prudent to pursue his enemy further at the moment.

Siege of Gwālior by Māhmud

"In 413 A.H. (1022 A.D.) he (Māhmud) again invaded the kingdom of Nandā", says Nizāmuddin.[28] Firishtā also records an identical account[29]. But the date, as given in Briggs' translation, is 414 A.H., which is evidently a mistake for 413 A.H., as pointed out by Dr. Ray on the evidence of the Lucknow text[30].

Firishtā, in indicating the purpose of this renewed invasion, states that "the war-like disposition of Māhmud could not long remain at peace". That is to say, the memory of the indecisive campaign of 410 A.H. was too galling for the Sultān, who must have wanted to force a conclusion this time.

As to the incidents of this campaign we find mention firstly of the siege of the fortress of Gwālior, built on a stupendous rock, and reputed to be impregnable. It was included within the Candella dominions and was under the rulers of the Kacchapaghāta dynasty, who were under the Candella hegemony since the occupation of the fortress from the Pratihāras by Vajradāman of the same family.[31] The evidence of Nizāmuddin, as found in his account of the invasion of the Candella dominions by Sultān Māhmud of Ghazni, shows that the Gwālior fort was included within the kingdom of the Candella Vidyādhara, and that it was under a '*hakim*'

[28] *T.A.*, P. 14.
[29] *T.F.*, I., P. 66.
[30] *D.H.N.I.*, II., P. 692., f.n. 1.
[31] *I.H.Q.*, March 1953., Pp. 88-93.

i.e. a governor or a ruler of feudatory status[32]. This '*hakim*' was surely a Kacchpaghāta, and may be identified with Kīrttirāja of the Sās Bahu record.[33] Had he enjoyed the status of an independent ruler, the Muslim historian would certainly not have referred to him only as a '*hakim*'. Dr. Nāzim most probably confused the Kacchwāha ruler of the fort with Arjuna of the Dubkuṇḍ Record.[34]

In spite of strenuous efforts of Māhmud the fortress of Gwālior could not be stormed. "At the end of 4 days the Commandant of the fort sent envoys and offering a tribute of 35 elephants, prayed for protection".[35] The siege was raised and the Sultān proceeded towards Kālañjar. An account of the interview of the Sultān's ambassador with the 'Rājā' of the Gwālior fort, as recorded in the Syriac Chronicle, translated extracts of which have been included in the Appendix of Dr. Nazim's work on 'Sultan Mahmud'[36], seems to be imaginary.

Siege of Kālañjar by Māhmud

The Kālañjar fort, situated on the lofty crag of a precipitous rock of hard stone on an outlying branch of the Vindhyas, was deemed impregnable. This fortress now came under the siege of Māhmud's forces. According to Nizāmuddin, "the siege lasted for a considerable time, when Nandā, the ruler of the fort offered 300 elephants as a tribute and begged for safety"[37]. Evidently like the Gwālior fort, the Kālañjar also could not be stormed by Māhmud in spite of his all-out efforts. It may be remembered that Māhmud set out on this expedition with a specific object of punishing Vidyādhara, but as is evident from the statements

[32] 'Commandant of the Fort' according to the translator of the Tabakāt. F. Johnson's Dictionary, Persian-Arabic-English (P. 461) mentions that a '*hakim*' may be 'a commander, a governor, a judge, a magistrate or a name of God'. But A. N. Wollaston's volume of a Complete English-Persian Dictionary (P. 492) clearly states that '*hakim*' denoted the 'Governor of a city' and not simply of the Fort, the term for which is '*Qalahdar*'. (*I.H.Q.*, March, 1953, P. 91, f.n. 16).

[33] *I.A.*, XV., P. 36., Vv. 9-11.

[34] *S.M.G.*, P. 113.

[35] *T.A.*, P. 14.

[36] *S.M.G.*, Pp. 207-08., App. L.

[37] *T.A.*, P. 14.

of Muslim historians, this was hardly achieved. Both the strongholds of Gwālior and Kālañjar remained unconquered and on both occasions the Sultān raised the siege on receipt of a formal submission, followed by exchange of gifts and presents, which in the hands of the Muslim chroniclers of a later period came to be depicted as 'tribute'. The mode of presentation would also reveal that there was an element of challenge in it. In the words of Firishtā, "the Rājā (*i.e.* Vidyādhara) in order to put the bravery of the Sultān's troops to the test, intoxicated the elephants with drugs, and let them loose without riders, into the camp. Māhmud seeing the animals advance, and perceiving their condition, by the wildness of their manner, ordered a party of his best horses to seize or kill them, or to drive them from the camp. Some of the Tartars, zealous of displaying the bravery in the presence of their king, fearlessly approached and mounted some of the elephants and drove the rest into an adjacent wood, where they were all soon reduced to obedience"[38]. The troops in the fort were astonished at this spectacle, and felt much awe for the prowess of the Turks. Nandā then sent to him a panegyric in the Indian or Hindu tongue (Lughat i Hindui)[39], in praise of the Sultān and the bravery of his troops. The Sultān felt much elated at the compliments, which were very highly spoken of by the learned men of Hindusthān and other poets of Arabia and Persia, who were in attendance on him. In return Māhmud also sent his congratulations to Vidyādhara and conferred on him the government of 15 fortresses and other presents before returning to Ghaznā "with victory and triumph", according to Tabakāt i Ākbari. The Zainul Ākhbār even goes the length of recording payment of 'Jiziyā' by Nandā as one of the conditions for peace. But, as has been mentioned earlier, these statements are to be taken with a grain of salt, as the expedition could by no means be regarded as successful as Māhmud's earlier invasions. Though there was a formal

[38] *T.F.*, Pp. 66 67; Nizāmuddin also records an almost identical account. *T.A.*, P. 14.
[39] *K. Z. A.*, P. 80.

submission by the Candella ruler, the real fact was that both sides retired with honours even.

Browne[40] and Md. Iqbal[41] suggest that this friendship between the ruler of Kāliñjar and the Sultān of Ghazni continued till at least 1029 A.D., when Māhmud sent a Tartar prince as a prisoner to the fort of Kālañjar in India. Dr. Ray rightly feels sceptical about the identification of the fort of Kālañjar as has been suggested by Browne and Iqbal. According to him, it seems more likely that it should be identified with the Kāliñjar of Kalhaṇa or Kāluñjur of Firishtā, situated on the frontiers of Kāshmir.[42]

Relations with the Paramāras and the Kacchapaghātas

Thus we find that Vidyādhara, who came to be regarded as the most powerful ruler of India, devoted himself mainly to the task of resisting the encroachments of Islām in which he proved himself not an unworthy leader. With regard to his achievements in tackling the internal forces, as has already been seen, he is credited with the capture of the last remnants of the Pratihāra power, which practically saddled him on Imperial status. We do not however find any direct mention of his fight with other contemporary powers of North and Central India. But in the Sās Bahu record[43] (v. 10) we are told that the Kacchapaghāta prince Kīrttirāja defeated the countless host of the prince of Mālwā. The Mālwā army received such a terrible shock on the occasion that the spears fell from their hands through fear, and were subsequently collected by the villagers (apparently of Gwālior), and heaped around their houses. The 'Mālava-bhūmipa' has generally been identified with the Paramāra king Bhoja[44], who was by no means a less important ruler. As such it is rather difficult to believe that the Kacchawāha chief accomplished this victory unilaterally, without any help or assistance from Candella Vidyādhara, his overlord. On the

[40] *Literary History of Persia*, P. 170.
[41] *Rahat us Sudur* Ed. by Md. Iqbal, P. 103.
[42] *D.H.N.I.*, II., 693, f.n. 3.
[43] *I.A.*, XV., P. 36.
[44] *ibid.*, P. 824.

other hand, it may be presumed that Bhoja planned an attack on the Candella dominions but was foiled in his attempt by the Kacchapaghāta prince. This is however corroborated by the claim of Candella Vidyādhara that 'Bhojadeva, together with the Moon of the Kalacuris worshipped full of fear like a pupil this master of warfare,' i.e., Vidyādhara[45], which had probably resulted from the defeat of Bhoja at the hands of the Kacchapāghata Kīrttirāja. This incident must have happened prior to Māhmud's attack on Gwālior fort in A.H. 413 (A.D. 1022).

In this connection it may be observed that Dr. D. C. Ganguly holds that Bhoja undertook two separate invasions of the Candella dominions. The earlier one was defeated at the hands of Vidyādhara , and the latter one by Kīrttirāja.[46] Dr. Ganguly also suggests that Kacchapaghāta Abhimanyu, son of Arjuna of the Dubkuṇḍ Record entered into an alliance with Bhoja on the eve of his northern expedition, as is evident from the same inscription (Ll. 17-18)[47] that the skill of Abhimanyu in his management of horses and chariots and in the use of powerful weapons was highly spoken of by Bhojadeva. That is to say, the incident happened at a later period in Vidyādhara's career, as we have already seen that Arjuna was a contemporary of Vidyādhara and a close ally of him.

Dr. H. C. Ray however holds that after Vidyādhara's demise when the Candella throne came to be occupied by rulers of lesser calibre, Bhoja Paramāra, who outlived Vidyādhara, exerted his influence in the northern regions as far as Dubkuṇḍ, when Abhimanyu, the son of Arjuna, now became subservient to him.[48]

Both the theories however have some lacunae. As regards Dr. Ganguly's theory of two separate invasions of the Candella state by the Paramāra ruler it is, however, not borne out by evidence. The verse in the Māu Inscription[49] does not

[45] *E.I.*, I., P. 219., V. 22.
[46] *H.P.*, *Ganguly.*, Pp. 103-06.
[47] *E.I.*, II., Pp. 237-38.
[48] *D.H.N.I.*, II., P. 870.
[49] *E.I.*, I., P. 219.

indicate achievement of any victory over the invading forces of the Paramāras. Rather the Māu record spoke of the net result that was obtained by the victory of the Kacchapaghāta Kīrttirāja recorded in the Sās Bahu Inscription.[50]

Now with regard to the relationship between Abhimanyu of the Dubkuṇḍ grant and Bhoja Paramāra again nothing definite can be stated. It is not understood how the statement of the Dubkuṇḍ grant could be interpreted to mean that "Abhimanyu's assistance was a great asset to the Paramāras in securing the success of their military operations", as done by Dr. D. C. Ganguly[51]. We have also seen that Arjuna was the contemporary of Vidyādhara, and through him the latter executed his plan of inflicting the capital punishment on Rājyapāla of the Pratihāra dynasty in 1018 A.D.[52], leading to renewed attacks by Sultān Māhmud. The Sultān besieged the Gwālior fort in 1022 A.D., when Kīrttirāja was in possession of it. It is indeed difficult to believe (*i*) that between 1018 and 1022 A.D., Arjuna came to be succeeded by Abhimanyu, (*ii*) that the latter reversed the policy of his father and entered into an alliance with the Paramāras, and (*iii*) that Bhoja invaded Gwālior region during this crucial period of Indian history when fresh Turuṣka raids were being apprehended every moment.

Dr. Ray's suggestions, mentioned above, seem to be more plausible, but in the absence of positive data we cannot be sure about it.

Extent of Candella dominion

With regard to the limits of the Candella state during Vidyādhara's regime we are not however in possession of any clear statement as we have for his grandfather, Dhaṅga.[53] But there is no doubt about the fact that the fortresses of Gopādri and Kālañjar were included in it and that there is no evidence of any diminution in territorial possessions since

[50] *I.A.*, XV., P. 36.
[51] *H.P.*, *Ganguly.*, P. 105.
[52] *E.I.*, II., P. 237.
[53] *ibid.*, I., 129. V. 45.

the days of Dhaṅga. Rather the Dubkuṇḍ record testifies to some expansion in the north-western region of the Candella state reaching the banks of the Pārvatī river. But the zone of influence of the Candella power during this period was much greater, it covered practically the whole of Northern India from the Chambal to the Narmadā in the south, and to the Ganges-Jumna valley in the east. There was therefore not much exaggeration in the accounts of the Muslim chroniclers that Vidyādhara was 'the most powerful of the Indian rulers of the time'. A number of inscriptions belonging to the time of his successors make eulogistic references to his personal traits with particular reference to his military leadership, which however in the circumstances do not appear to be mere praśasti. As for example, V. 5 of Māu Stone Insc. of Madanavarman[54] compares him with 'Vāsava' the leader of the Gods against the forces of the Asuras. V. 21 of the Fragmentary Mahobā Inscription refers to Vidyādhara having gathered the flowers of the fame of his enemies. The next verse (V. 22) of the same record describes him as the Master of warfare (Samara-guru) to whom other contemporary rulers were like disciples (śiṣyavad).[55] The Deogaḍh Rock Inscription of Kīrttivarman V.S. 1154 also showers similar praises on Vidyādhara.[56] His achievements in augmenting the territorial boundaries of the Candella State as well as in establishing it as a strong power of the time were sufficient to earn recognition from posterity. But the supreme effort that he made in defending the country against strong foreign invaders made him deserving of grateful remembrance by his successors.

The Māu Inscription of the time of Madanavarman gives us the name of his Chief Minister, Śivanāga, belonging to the same family of ministers who served the Candella dynasty rather hereditarily. As for Śivanāga it is said in V. 23-24 that the Saciva was responsible to a great extent in

[54] *E.I.*, I., Pp. 197, 203.
[55] *ibid.*, P. 219.
[56] *I.A.*, XVIII., P. 237.

making other rulers tributary to him.[57] Such expressions suggest that Vidyādhara's prowess was equally matched with the diplomatic skill of his minister, which enabled him to play such an important role in the history of the time.

[57] *E.I.*, I., P. 199.

CHAPTER VII

FROM VIJAYAPĀLA TO KĪRTTIVARMAN: CEDI-CANDELLA CONFLICTS

Vijayapāla.

Vijayapāla, the son of Vidyādhara, according to the Māu Stone Inscription of the time of Madanavarman[1], succeeded him on the throne sometime after 1022 A.D., the last known date of Vidyādhara. In the absence of any record of his reign-period the length of time he occupied the throne can hardly be determined accurately. But as Nānyaura Plate of V.S. 1107 (1051 A.D.)[2] was issued by his son, Devavarman, it may be presumed that Vijayapāla must have ceased to reign before that date, i.e., 1051 A.D.

Epigraphic evidence that is available about him is derived from the records of his successors, viz.,—(*i*) Māu Stone Inscription, (*ii*) Fragmentary Candella Inscription, from Mahobā,[3] (*iii*) Deogaḍh Rock Inscription of Kīrttivarman dated V.S. 1154,[4] and (*iv*) Nānyaura Plate 'B' of Devavarman dated V.S. 1107. Most of these records however make vague eulogistic references to the king (nṛpo-nṛpendraḥ) who is stated to have exterminated all the wicked and gladdened all good men and put an end to the Kali Age—(v. 6. Māu Stone Inscription).

The only political incident of his reign however finds mention in the fragmentary Mahobā Inscription which refers to his conflict with Gāṅgeyadeva of the Kalacuri dynasty. V. 24 of the Inscription reads—

"When Gāṅgeyadeva, who had conquered the world, perceived before him this terrible one, the lotus of his heart closed his knots of pride in battle."[5]

---

[1] *E.I.*, I., P. 198., Vv. 6-7,
[2] *I.A.*, XVI., Pp. 205-07.
[3] *E.I.*, I., P. 219., Vv. 23-26.
[4] *I.A.*, XVIII., P. 238, Ll. 2-3.
[5] *E.I.*, I., Pp. 219, 222,

This statement no doubt looks like mere praśasti, but a closer examination would reveal that under Gāṅgeyadeva the Kalacuri power had not only recovered itself but was expanding on all directions.

The expansion of the Kalacuris

A study of the Kalacuri records[6] would also show that Gāṅgeyadeva effected extensive conquests and assumed the title, 'Vikramāditya'. He is credited with achieving victory over the kings of Kīra, Aṅga, Kuntala and Utkala[7]. Even it is claimed in the Piāwān Rock Inscription[8], issued during the time of Gāṅgeyadeva, and Jabalpur Copper Plate of Yaśaḥkarṇa (v. 12)[9] that he took up his residence at the feet of the holy fig tree at Prayāga. It may be remembered that the Doab region was under the influence of the Candellas till the time of Vidyādhara. So the expansion of the Kalacuris in that region could only be achieved at the cost of the Candellas. It is generally held that the successors of Vidyādhara lacked the ability of their illustrious predecessor. But an analysis of the situation would show that Vijayapāla, the son of Vidyādhara, was only a child of the circumstances. The rot set in from the time of Vidyādhara himself. It has already been discussed how in spite of possessing undoubted military ability Vidyādhara failed to achieve any practical result in resisting the vandalism of the Turks. Though Kālañjar of course did not fall to the Sultān, still it cannot be denied that the invasions of the Turks seriously undermined the prestige and position of the Candellas and damaged the integrity of the Candella organisation. So long Vidyādhara was alive the outer structure of it was however maintained, but with his death it was no longer possible for his successor to stem the tide. To this may be added another menacing factor, the rise of an ambitious ruler, imbued with the vision of empire-building, among the Kalacuris, viz., Gāṅgeyadeva.

---

[6] *ibid.*, II., P. 3., V. 11; *ibid.*, XII., P. 211. V. 11.
[7] *ibid.*, XI., P. 143., V. 17.
[8] *A.S.R.*, XXI., Pp. 112-13.
[9] *E.I.*, XII., P. 211.

These brought about an inevitable diminution of the Candella dominion. Even these states which during the heyday of the Candella power came within the orbit of its political influence, now felt the impact of the rising Cedis. This has further been confirmed by the statement of Baihāqui, who records that when Āhmad Niyāltigin, the general of the Yāmini King Māsud I invaded Banaras in c. 1034 A.D., that city was included within the dominion of 'Gāṅg[10], (Gāṅgeya). It may be noticed that even the Mahobā record admits Gāṅgeyadeva to be 'jitaviśva' (conqueror of the world)[11]. Therefore it appears that during the reign of Vijayapāla, the Candella dominion lost some territory in the eastern region. The western side was however not disturbed, as the Paramāras of Mālwā, their neighbour in the west, maintained status quo with them, and there is no clear evidence of any conflict between the two powers. So long the Kacchapaghātas held the Gwālior Fort and its environs as vassals of the Candellas. But the use of expressions indicative of a higher political status in respect of Kacchapaghāta King Mūladeva in the Sās Bahu Record[11a], led scholars to think that the Kacchapaghātas might now have disowned their allegiance to the Candellas and have become independent[11b], which, however, is not impossible.

As regards the personal life of Candella Vijayapāla, it may be observed from the records that he has generally been praised for his virtuous conduct (Subhacarita pavitra) and that he has been endowed with such imperial titles as "Parama-bhaṭṭāraka Mahārājādhirāja and Parameśvara". The name of his queen, Bhuvanadevī, the mother of Devavarman, his son and successor, is found in the Nānyaura Plate 'B' of the latter's reign[12]. The illustrious Kīrttivarman was his another son, who also claims to be the successor of

[10] *Tārikh i Baihāqui* Ed. Morley., P. 497; *Elliot.*, II., P. 123.; *C.H.I.*, III., Pp. 29-30. The Sārnāth Inscription of V.S. 1083 (1026 AD.) may indicate that the Pāla King Mahīpāla I held Banaras for sometime.

[11] *E.I.*, I., P. 219., V. 24.

[11a] *I.A.*, XV., Pp. 36-42., Vv. 12-13.

[11b] *D.H.N.I.*, II., P. 825.

[12] *I.A.*, XVI., P. 205.

Vijayapāla in a number of Candella records viz., Māu Stone Inscription of Madanavarman, Fragmentary Candella Inscription from Mahobā and Deogaḍh Rock Inscription, which make no mention of his brother, Devavarman. As there is no evidence of any dynastic conflict it has been held that Devavarman succeeded Vijayapāla, but after a short spell of reign the throne passed to his brother, Kīrttivarman.

In the sphere of internal administration of the Candella state under Vijayapāla it is highly interesting to note that the office of the Chief Minister continued in the same family and Mahīpāla, the son of Śivanāga the Mantrīmukhya of Vidyādhara, now carried on the affairs of the state in a most efficient manner. It is claimed in V. 26 of the Māu Inscription that Mahīpāla became the standard of comparison among good ministers (susaciveṣu babhūva nidarśanaṁ)[13].

Devavarman

Devavarman is known to us only from two of his own records, one dated in V.S. 1107 (1051 A.D.),[14] found at Nānyaura in the Hamirpur district of U.P., and the other dated in V.S. 1108 (1052 A.D.), found from the Chārkhāri Darbār in Central India[15]. He claims in these records to be the son and successor of Vijayapāla (Paramabhaṭṭāraka Mahārājādhirāja Parameśvara Vijayapāladeva-pādānudhyāta) and assumes the epithet of 'Kālañjarādhipati' (Lord of the Kālañjara fortress). In most other Candella records Devavarman is omitted and Kīrttivarman is stated to have been 'meditating on the feet of Vijayapāla.' Such an exclusion from the genealogy naturally arouses suspicion that there might have been dynastic quarrels, which resulted in the overthrow of one by the other prince. In the absence of any evidence it is however not possible to be definite about it.

A review of the political condition would show that already during the last lap of Vidyādhara's reign the Candellas

---

[13] *E.I.*, I., P. 200.
[14] *I.A.*, XVI., Pp. 205-07.
[15] *E.I.*, XX., Pp. 125-28.

were facing a critical position, which was further endangered by the rise of the Cedis, who for sometime even suppressed the former. The literary work, 'Prabodhacandrodaya' distinctly mentions that the race of the Moon (the Candellas) was dethroned by the lord of Cedi (Cedipatinā samunmūlitaṁ Candrānvaya-pārthivānāṁ....)[16]. Another such work, 'Vikramāṅkadevacarita' describes Lakṣmīkarṇa of the Kalacuri family as "Kālaḥ Kālāñjara-giripater-yaḥ...." (death to the lord of the Kālañjara fortress)[17], which appears to be corroborated by the evidence of the Candella records in which Kīrttivarman is credited with recreating Candella power like the Creator.[18] Therefore the reign period of Devavarman particularly may be regarded to have proved to be a dark period for the Candellas. It was most probably due to this that the Candellas did not like to recount the condition obtaining during this period in the records of the later rulers. In the process the unfortunate prince Devavarman also stands excluded even from the genealogical accounts of later period.

He had practically nothing to his credit and that is why no political incident could be mentioned even in the inscriptions of his own time. But the fact that he uses the title of 'Kālañjarādhipati' shows that though the Candella ruler might have suffered defeat at the hands of Kalacuri Karṇa, yet he retained his hold on the strategic fortress of Kālañjara. The mention of the Yamunā on the banks of which the village Bhūtapallikā was situated, as mentioned in the Chārkhāri Plate (V.S. 1108), indicates that Candella Devavarman maintained his hold on the territory extending upto the Yamunā in the north east, though Banaras might have been under the Cedis. Thus the sovereignty of the Candella rulers was not suppressed nor were their kingdom wholly occupied by the Kalacuris as a result of their victory. The Chārkhāri Plate alludes to the existence of feudatories of

---

[16] *P.C.*, L. 6., P. 19.
[17] *Vik. C.*, XVIII., 93.
[18] *E.I.*, I., P. 327., V. 3.

Devavarman while describing him as "Mahāsāmanta-rāja-putra-vandita-pādaḥ"[19].

A description of the qualities of his head and heart is available in both the inscriptions mentioned above. But the statement in the Nānyaura Plate (V.S. 1106) that 'by the fire of his prowess he has devoured the whole circle of the regions, and became the spiritual guide to initiate into widowhood the wives of the enemies slain by him on the field of battle,[20] is no doubt a conventional praśasti of a court panegyric.

The use of the title 'Parama-Māheśvara' by the king is also not without any significance. It reflects to the fact that the King was a strong Saivite himself. His great regard for his mother, Bhuvanadevī, is evident from the Nānyaura Grant, which records the gift of the village of Kaṭhahau in the Raṇamaua situated in Rājapura-avasthā to the Brahmin to mark the occasion of the death anniversary (sāṁvatsarika).[21]

Kīrttivarman

By the middle of the 11th century A.D., Kalacuri Lakṣmī-Karṇa secured a predominant position in the political set-up of Northern India, mainly by virtue of his military achievements over the neighbouring states. It has already been mentioned that the Candellas suffered terribly at his hands, and the reign of the Candella prince, Devavarman, son of Vijayapāla, was most probably cut short during this Cedi-Candella encounter.

Devavarman, it appears, died without any lineal descendant, and the throne passed laterally to his younger brother Kīrttivarman. It was indeed a happy augury for the Candella state which gained a fresh lease of glorious existence mainly through the efforts of the latter. Both literary and inscriptional evidence vie with each other in extolling the achievements of King Kīrttivarman.

---

[19] *E.I.*, XX., P. 127.

[20] *I.A.*, XVI., P. 205., L. 3, "pratāpānala-kavalit-ākhila-dik-cakravālaḥ/Saṁgrā-māṁganā nihatārāti-vaṇitā-vaidhavyadāna-dīkṣā-guruḥ//".

[21] *ibid.*, Ll. 8-9.

Revival of the Candella power

The available Candella records clearly indicate that their fortune was at a low ebb prior to the accession of Kīrttivarman, and that Kalacuri Lakṣmī-Karṇa was mainly instrumental in effecting a temporary eclipse of the Candella power. Bilhaṇa, the court poet of Cālukya Someśvara I (1044-68 A.D.) seems to have referred to this event in his 'Vikramāṅkadeva-carita', wherein Karṇa has been described as 'Kālaḥ Kālañjara-giripater-yaḥ', death to the lords of the Kālañjara mountain[1]. The eloquence of the Candella records[2] in describing the glorious recovery of the Candella state by Kīrttivarman, testifies to the importance attached to the victory of the Candella king over the Cedis. It may however be construed to indicate an indirect admission of the defeat suffered by the Candellas at the hands of the Cedi prince previously.

Ajaygaḍh Rock Inscription of Vīravarman (V. S. 1317) refers to the victory of Kīrttivarman over the forces of Karṇa in V. 3 as follows—

Kumbhodbhavaḥ Karṇa payodhipāṇe prajeśvaro nūtana-rājyasṛṣṭau/
Tatrāsa vidyādhara-gīta-kīrtteḥ Śrī Kīrttivarmma-kṣitipo jagatyāṁ//

"In that race there was a ruler over the earth whose fame is sung by the vidyādharas, who was a pitcher-born (i.e., Agastya), in swallowing that ocean, Karṇa, and the lord of creatures in creating anew the kingdom, the illustrious Kīrttivarman[3]".

The expression '*nūtana-rājya-sṛṣṭau*' is highly significant. It indicates that the kingdom which was engulfed in the surging tide of the Cedi invasion, has now been created anew, after the enemy had been completely defeated.

Another inscription from Mahobā also refers to the achievements of Kīrttivarman in the following words—

[1] *Buhler's Edn.*, XVIII., 93.

[2] Fragmentary Mahobā Insc. (*E.I.*, I., P. 217, V. 26); Ajaygaḍh Rock Insc. of Vīravarman (*ibid.*, Pp. 327, 329,V. 3); Fragmentary Kālañjar Insc. (*J.A.S.B.*, XVII, 1848, P. 317).

[3] *E.I.*, I., Pp. 327, 329.

"Just as Puruṣottama having produced the nectar by churning with the mountain (Mandāra) the rolling milk-ocean, whose high waves swallowed many mountains, obtained the Goddess of Lakṣmī, together with the elephants (of the 8 regions), he (Kīrttivarman) acquired fame by crushing with his strong arms the haughty Lakṣmī-Karṇa, whose army had destroyed many princes, obtained splendour in this world together with elephants[4]".

This glorious episode in the history of the Candella dynasty has also been related in the prologue of the 'Prabodhacandrodayaṁ', an allegorical drama, written by Śrī Kṛṣṇa Miśra[5]. It will be noticed that just as both the inscriptions mentioned above, compare the forces of Karṇa with the rolling waves of the sea (Karṇapayodhi; Laksmī-Karṇaṁ mahārṇavaṁ), probably to indicate the magnitude of the invasion, so also in the drama we find the use of the expression 'Karṇasenā-sāgaraṁ[6]'. Then again in the Mahobā record, Kīrttivarman is compared with Puruṣottama (Viṣṇu) in recovering his Lakṣmī (the Goddess of Fortune, i.e., the kingdom or Rājya-Lakṣmī)[7]. In the drama also an almost similar expression has been used, where the army of Karṇa is compared to the Milk-Ocean, and Gopāla, who defeated the Cedi ruler on behalf of Kīrttivarman, is likened to Madhumathana, i.e., Viṣṇu[8]. This coincidence, suggests Hultzsch, who edited the Mahobā Inscription, is probably due to the fact that the composer of the inscription knew the drama Prabodhacandrodaya and borrowed the description from it[9].

One cannot however fail to notice a serious discrepancy which exists between the account furnished by epigraphic sources and the one contained in the drama. In the former the credit for defeating the Cedi ruler Karṇa has been given

---

[4]*E.I.*, I., P. 219. V. 26.
[5]*Nirṇaya Sāgar Press Edn.*, Bombay, 1924.
[6]*P.C.*, L. 6.
[7]*E.I.*, I., 219.
[8]*P.C.*, L. 6.
[9]*E.I.*, I., P. 220.

to Kīrttivarman, but in the drama both the Sūtradhāra[10] and the Naṭī[11] state that it was Śrī Gopāla who inflicted a crushing defeat on Lakṣmī Karṇa and re-installed the Candella prince Kīrttivarman on the throne. As the play was staged before Kīrttivarman, the reigning monarch, it may be presumed, as has been done by Dr. H. C. Ray,[12] that the story given in the drama could not have offended the king, as it was true.

The question therefore arises, who was this Gopāla, and what was his relationship with the Candella king ? From the drama it appears that Śrī Gopāla was held in high esteem at the court of Kīrttivarman, particularly by the feudatory princes. The Sūtradhāra says, "Adiṣṭo'smi sakala-sāmanta-cakra-cūḍāmaṇi marīci-mañjarīnirājita-caraṇa-kamalena ... Śrīmatā Gopālena."[13] This means that he was ordered to stage the drama by Śrī Gopāla, on whose lotus-like feet were reflected the crest-jewels of the circle of the feudatory princes.

This passage is very important. But it is found that it has not been correctly interpreted by some scholars. They have relied upon this passage in inferring that Gopāla served as the Chief Sāmanta or feudatory under Kīrttivarman. The relevant portion of the text which I have quoted does not lend any support to this view, which is based on '*sakala-sāmantacakra-cūḍāmaṇi*' being taken as an epithet of Gopāla.[14] But it is not so, as it is a part of the compound, which includes '*marīci-mañjarī-nirājita-caraṇa kamalena*' to indicate the complete epithet of Gopāla. There is no definite proof in support of of this view afforded by the passage quoted. It would therefore be a mere guess if Gopāla is taken as a chief sāmanta. It is noteworthy that the commentator Nāṇḍillagopaprabhu in explaining '*Śrimatā Gopālena*' applies the designation '*rājan*' to him,—"*Śrimatā mahānubhavena Gopālena rājñā.*"[15]

---

[10]L. 6 & 9., Pp. 19, 21-22.

[11]L. 6 ".....Kṛṇṇasenāsāaram nimmahia Mahumahaneneva khīrasamuddamāsāditā samara vijaalacchī/". (Sanskrit rendering—Karṇasenāsāgaraṁ nirmathya Madhumathaneneva Kṣīrasamudram-āsāditā samara vijayalakṣmīh/).

[12]*D.H.N.I.*, II. P. 697, f.n. 3.

[13]*P.C.*, L. 3.

[14]*D.H.N.I.*, II., P. 695.

[15]*P.C.*, P. 12, f.n.

Hultzsch,[16] and following him V. Smith,[17] took Gopāla to be a Brāhmaṇa General of Kīrttivarman. It is not known why Hultzsch took him to belong to the Brāhmaṇa caste.

We may next refer to the information supplied by the drama with regard to Gopāla's activities. He was the main architect of the '*digvijaya*' of the ruler Kīrttivarman. With sword as his only friend (asilatāmātra-mitrena),[18] Gopāla extirpated the enemies not sparing even the women, the aged and the children (yasya strī-bāla-vṛddhāvadhi nidhana-vidhau viśruto'sau).[19] With great passion he desired, as the Sūtradhāra says, to re-establish the sovereigns of the race of the Moon, dethroned by the lord of the Cedis, who has been compared to Rudra, the fire of destruction of all other royal families (yataḥ sakala-bhūpāla-kula pralaya-kālāgni-rudrena Cedipatinā samunmūlitaṁ Candrānvaya-pārthivānāṁ pṛthivyām-ādhipatyāṁ sthirīkartuṁ ayamasya saṁrambhaḥ/).[20] Gopāla having overcome Karṇa caused the rise of the illustrious Kīrttivarman, just as conscience overcoming delusion gives rise to knowledge (Vivekeneva nirjjitya Karṇaṁ-mohamivorjitaṁ/ Śrī Kīrttivarma-narapater bodhasyevodayah kṛtaḥ//9). Gopāla having acted as the saviour of the Candella sovereignty, and having re-installed Kīrttivarman there (sāmrājye Kīrttivarma-narapati-tilako yena bhyuyo' bhyaṣeci//4), is regarded by the author to be as great as Viṣṇu, represented in the Man-Lion (Nṛsiṁha), the Primeval Boar (Mahā-Varāha) and Paraśurāma incarnations.

These references taken together indicate that Gopāla must have shown exceptional skill as a military leader or a general in organising the campaigns of Kīrttivarman and winning victories for him. This is particularly supported by the passage in which Gopāla's part in Kīrttivarman's *digvijaya*

[16] *E.I.*, I., P. 220.
[17] *I.A.*, XVIII., P. 143.
[18] *P.C.*, L. 4., P. 15.
[19] *ibid.*, L. 7., P. 20.
[20] *ibid.*, L. 6., P. 19.

is definitely mentioned.[21] As this natural friend of king Kīrttivarman was engaged in the '*digvijaya-vyāpāra*' of the king, the enjoyment of the supreme bliss (witnessing the drama) was kept suspended, and the days were vitiated with various kinds of material pleasures.[22] Thus his important role in the victorious expeditions of the king is clearly indicated in the passage.

Gopāla's services to the Candellas as Kīrttivarman's '*Sahaja-suhṛt*' cannot be over-estimated. We do not gain very much by simply taking this expression to mean a natural friend. It may be pointed out that the term '*sahaja-suhṛt*' or '*sahaja-mitra*' has some special significance in Hindu political philosophy. Kauṭilya applies the expression to denote the territory beyond that of the immediate neighbour, the latter being called an enemy (ari)[22a]. "He, whose friendship is derived from father to grand-father, and who is situated close to the territory of the immediate enemy of the conqueror, is a natural friend, while he, whose friendship is courted for self-maintenance is an acquired friend."[22b] Mm. Gaṇapati Śāstri in commenting on this expression observes that one kind of '*Sahaja-mitra*' is, as already stated, the friendly state situated beyond the immediate neighbour state ("svabhūmyeka-vyavahitaṁ prakṛti-mitraṁ ekaṁ sahaja-mitraṁ").[23] But there is apparent difficulty in accepting Gopāla as an ally of the Sahaja-mitra-type in the absence of any royal titles in the text, which does not assign to him any specified territory.

The other type of sahaja-mitra, mentioned by Kauṭilya, as explained by Mm. Śāstri, is represented by one's cousins, sons of maternal uncles and paternal aunts ("Mātula-paitṛ-

---

[21]*ibid.*, L. 9., P. 12. "(yathā khalvasya sahaja-suhṛdo rājñah Śrī Kīrttivarma-devasya digvijaya-vyāpar-āntarita para-brahmānanda-rasair-ąsmābḥih samunmīlita-vividha-viṣayarasāsvāda-duṣita-iv-ātivāhita -divasāh/)".

[22]The inference that Gopāla himself became '*viṣaya-rasäsvädaduṣita*', as found in *D.H.N.I.*, II., P. 696., Ll. 14-15, is evidently unacceptable.

[22a]"Bhūmyekāntaraṁ prakṛti-mitraṁ māta-pitṛ-sambandhaṁ sahajaṁ, dhana-jīvita-hetor-āśṛitaṁ kṛtṛima-mitraṁ" (Kauṭilya Arthaśāstra, Maṇḍalayoṇih, ṣaṣṭhaṁ-ādhikaranaṁ, Samavyāyāmikaṁ prakaraṇaṁ).

[22b]Shamashastry's Edn. P. 290.

[23]*K.A.*, Gaṇapati Śāstri's Edn., P. 233.

svaseyādirūpaṁ aparaṁ sahaja-mitraṁ")[24]. In the 'Śiśupāla-vadha kāvya'[25] also a similar expression is used to explain the relationship between Śrī Kṛṣṇa and Śiśupāla.

In the circumstances it may not be wrong to presume that the expression '*sahaja-suhṛt*', as used in the Prabodhacandrodaya nāṭaka, bears the meaning given to it by Kauṭilya, as commented on by Mm. G. Śāstri. In that case Gopāla may be taken to have been a cousin of King Kīrttivarman. It was Gopāla who organised the armies of the sāmanta chiefs and defeated the Cedi prince Karṇa, and it was he, who was mainly instrumental in reviving the Candella power. This was admitted by king Kīrttivarman in permitting the drama to be staged in his own presence, and it is further proved by the interest he took in the performance of it, as mentioned by the Sūtradhāra in the passage

> "Rājñaḥ Śrī Kīrttivarmanaḥ purastād abhinetavyaṁ bhavatā/Asti-cāsya bhūpateh sapāriṣadas-tad avalokena kutuhalaṁ-iti//"

i.e., The drama is to be enacted before the king Kīttivarman, who expressed particular curiosity to witness the show along with his courtiers.

There is therefore no real discrepancy between the literary and inscriptional accounts, as both mention the restoration of Candella power to have taken place during the time of Kīrttivarman. The '*digvijaya*' referred to by Śrī Kṛṣṇa Miśra is also attributed by him to Kīrttivarman. Kṛṣṇa Miśra's drama only furnishes some necessary details about the leadership in the battle which resulted in the Candella victory. The leadership was in the hands of Gopāla, Kīrttivarman's '*sahaja-suhṛt*' or cousin, who must have also made himself conspicuous by organising a confederacy of the sāmantas of the Candella state.

As to the date of this glorious victory of the Candellas over Karṇa there is no definite evidence. The dated records of Candella Kīrttivarman are Deogaḍh Rock Ins-

---

[24]*K.A.*, Gaṇapati Śāstri's Edn., P. 233.

[25]Canto II., V. 36-37. Mallinātha's commentary—'Saha jātaḥ sahajaḥ/ Ekaśarīrāvayavatvāt tatra·sahajaṁ mitraṁ mātṛsvase-pitṛsvaseyādi.'

cription of V.S. 1154 (1098 A.D.)[26] and Kālañjar Inscription of V. S. 1147 (1090 A.D.)[27]. But, as Karṇa abdicated his throne sometime before 1073 A.D., when Yaśahkarṇa had already succeeded to him, it may be presumed that this incident happened in about 1070 A.D., i.e., at least 20 years earlier than the date of Kālañjar Inscriptīon. Dr. D. C. Sircar has recently drawn our attention to an image Inscription[28], which Dr. N. P. Chakravarti ascribed to the time of Kacchapaghāta Vijayapāla of the Dubkuṇḍ branch. It has been re-edited by Dr. Sircar as belonging to the time of Candella Kīrttivarman, son of Vijayapāla, which goes in favour of the suggestion referred to above.

Besides this all-important Cedi-Candella encounter no other incident of political importance is indicated in the Candella records. The Deogaḍh record, dated in A.D. 1098 incised on a rock near the river-gate of the Deogaḍh fort, overlooking the Betwā. It records the construction of a flight of steps on the bank of the river by Vatsarāja, the Chief minister of Kīrttivarman, who is also credited with having constructed the '*Kīrttigiri-durga*' (in honour of his master) defeating the enemies. Verse 6 of the record reads-

"Khyāto babhūva khila mantripadaikamātre Vācaspati tadiha mantra supauruṣābhyāṁ/

Yo yaṁ samastaṁ-api-maṇḍalaṁ āśu śatror-ācchidya Kīrttigiri-durgaṁ idaṁ vyādhatta//6"[29].

The expression "*samastaṁ api mandalaṁ āśu śatror-ācchidya*" in the above verse has been translated by Kielhorn as 'having quickly wrested from the enemy the whole district (maṇḍala)'. Vincent Smith[30] and Dr. Ray[31] on the basis of this interpretation concluded that Vatsarāja appears to have conquered the Deogaḍh district in the Betwā valley for his master. But it may be pointed out that the inscrip-

[26] *I.A.*, XVIII., Pp. 237-39.

[27] Noticed by Dr. N. P. Chakravarti. *An. Rep. A.S.I.*, 1936-37, P. 93.

[28] Darbāt Śāntinātha Image Insc. of V. S. 1132 (1075 A.D.). The name of the king, which was earlier read as Kīrttidhara by Dr. N. P. Chakravarti, has been recently read as Kīrttivarman by Dr. D. C. Sircar in *I.H.Q.*, XXX., Pp. 183-85.

[29] *I.A.*, XVIII., P. 238.

[30] *ibid.*, XXXVII., P. 143.

[31] *D.H.N.I.*, II. P. 700.

tion does not specify the name of the 'maṇḍala' liberated by the minister, nor does it refer to any particular enemy of the Candellas defeated by him. Further, there is no evidence to conclude that the Betwā valley was lost to the Candellas prior to the date of the record (1098 A.D.). It is quite possible therefore that the achievements of the minister appear to have been recorded in the inscription concerned in a figurative sense. The term 'maṇḍala' in the particular context may mean the cardinal regions and not a particular district. It is not unlikely to presume that the minister by his wise policy stamped out some anti-social elements or internal enemies of the kingdom, who might have raised their heads during the weakness of the Candella power prior to the time of Kīrttivarman.

In the administration of the kingdom it appears that Kīrttivarman was aided by a group of very capable ministers and officials.

The services of Śrī Gopāla, the cousin (sahajasuhṛt) of the king, who was in charge of the feudatory chiefs and their forces, has already been mentioned. He directed the military operations of the king and achieved unique successes against the Cedi prince, Karṇa, the chief enemy of the Candellas.

Reference has also been made to Vatsarāja, who claims to have enjoyed the position of the Chief Counsellor (amātyamantrīndra) of the King. He has been compared to Vācaspati in counselling.[32]

Another important minister was Ananta, belonging to the hereditary line of ministers mentioned in the Māu Record.[33] His father, Mahīpāla, it may be remembered, served as the minister of Vijayapāla, the father of Kīrttivarman. Ananta, during his service career earned the distinction of acting in different capacities, viz., Hastyaśvanetā (leader of horses and elephants) in leading successful expeditions against the enemy forces; Purabalādhyaksa (Superin tendent of the forces of towns, i.e., the pivot of organising

[32] *I.A.*, XVIII., P. 238 L. 6.
[33] *E.I.*, I., Pp. 200, 205.

the defence of the capital, and as such acting as an unrivalled protector of property (Ekasvagoptā), and 'Adhimata saciva' (the approved minister) of the king. With his mature knowledge and experiences in different branches of administration, both civil and military, he was later appointed by king Kīrttivarman to act as a Privy-Counsellor, counselling the king in confidential matters (Mantri-mantraṇādhikāre sumahati hṛdayam gūḍha viśraṁbha kṛtye).[34] It is claimed on his behalf in the Māu Candella Inscription that, 'when a king has for his guide a minister of noble birth, endowed with understanding, uprightness and similar qualities, then there is nothing so high as it would be more difficult for him to attain. No wonder then that the lord Kīrttivarman by his fame, good acts, and prosperity surpassed the son of Dharma, even when that best of guides was governing the earth'.[35]

Besides these ministers there is mention in the Ajaygaḍh Rock Inscription of the time of Bhojavarman[36] of another officer of Kīrttivarman, named Maheśvara, belonging to the Vāstavya Kāyastha family of Tarkārika, whose father, Ṭhakkura Jājuka was granted the village of Duguaḍa by the Candella king Gaṇḍa. For his distinctive services to the king, Maheśvara was awarded the title of '*Viśiṣa*' of Kālañjara along with the grant of a village named Pipalāhika.[37] Viśiṣa is a new designation not met with in any other record, but in all probability it refers to an administrative post associated with the fort of Kālañjar. Alternatively the term '*Viśiṣa*' may indicate the introduction of a system of awarding honours and titles to officials in recognition of their meritorious services. It is no doubt a feature which indicates that the internal administration of the kingdom was in an well-ordered state under careful sup ervision of the monarch.

That works of public interest received close attention of King Kīrttivarman is alluded to in local traditions. It had been observed by V. Smith that 'the Kirāt Sāgar Lake, 11

---

[34]*ibid.*, V. 30.
[35]*ibid.*, V. 31.
[36]*E.I.*, I., P. 330.
[37]*ibid.*, Pp. 333, 336., V. 9.

miles in circumference, to the west of Mahobā, was the work of Kīrttivarman'. Another Kirāt Sāgar, no doubt contemporary, exists at Chanderi, in Lalitpur District.[38] A third tank, named 'Buḍhiyā-Tāl' in Kālañjar fort, according to Cunningham, is associated by tradition with the name of Kīrttivarman.[39] The name of this ruler is also connected with some buildings at Ajaygaḍh and Kālañjar.

Kīrttivarman was also a great patron of arts and letters. It has already been mentioned how under the patronage of Kīrttivarman a highly philosophical drama like 'Prabodhacandrodayam' was composed and staged in his presence. It has expressly been mentioned in the preamble of the drama that the king evinced a keen interest in the drama by being present with all his court at its performance. This however reveals an aspect of king's life, who spent his leisure hours in intellectual and cultural entertainments in the company of his courtiers.

As for his religious inclination it may be stated that he was defnitely a Śaiva, as is evidenced from inscriptional references. Kīrttivarman, however, following the tradition of his ancestors, was not only tolerant to other sects but even patronised them occasionally. The Deogaḍh Inscription unhesitatingly describes him as 'agadam nūtanam Viṣṇuṁ' or a new Viṣṇu without his club (gadā).[40] The expression 'agadam' has been interpreted by some to mean 'free from disease' which reminds us of the local tradition current in Kālañjar, which believes that King Kīrttivarman was a leper, and is said to have recovered his health by bathing in the Buḍhiyā Tāl within the fort.[41] The Mahobā Inscription also in referring to the achievements of Kīrttivarman against Kalacuri Lakṣmī-Karṇa calls him a 'Puruṣottama'.[42] All these go to show that he had no bitterness against Vaiṣṇavism.

---

[38] *I.A.,* XXXVII., P. 134.
[39] *ibid.,* P. 135.
[40] *ibid.,* XVIII., P. 238.
[41] *ibid.,* XXXVII., P. 135.
[42] *E.I.,* I., P. 219., V. 26.

The Darbāt Śāntināth image inscription of V.S. 1132 (1075 A.D.), which has been ascribed by Dr. D. C. Sircar[43] to the reign of Candella Kīrttivarman reveals the patronage of the ruler to the followers of the Jaina faith. If the reading of '*Kulāmātyavṛnda*' (the group of hereditary ministers) is admitted, then firstly we get the names of two Jaina officers of Kīrttivarman, Pāhila and Jāju, and secondly we learn that a śreṣṭhin, a representative of the merchant community graced the court of the Candella ruler. Pāhila of the Darbāt record, according to Dr. Sircar, is identical with Pāhilla of the Grahapati family,[44] mentioned in another Jain image inscription of Khajurāho of V.S. 1215 (1158 A.D.).[45] So even adherence to a different religious community constituted no bar to administrative appointments under the Candella king.

[43] *I.H.Q.*, XXX., Pp. 183-85.
[44] *ibid.*, P. 185.
[45] *E.I.*, I., P. 151.

CHAPTER VIII

FROM SALLAKSAṆAVARMAN TO MADANAVARMAN

Sallakṣaṇavarman.

After having restored the Candella power to its former glory, Kīrttivarman passed away sometime towards the close of the 11th century A.D. He was then succeeded on the throne by his son, Sallakṣaṇavarman, also mentioned as Hallakṣaṇavarman in the coins issued by him.[1] Unfortunately he has no inscription to his credit, but records of the later Candella rulers contain references to him, which enable us to make a somewhat fair estimate of his character and attainments.

The Māu Stone Inscription of Madanavarman, in verses 9 and 10,[2] is eloquent about Sallakṣaṇa's qualities of head and heart. He is described as 'a leader of those versed in the sacred lore, a kinsman of the virtuous, a store of arts and an abode of good conduct, and a tree of paradise to all suppliants for support'. These are no doubt conventional praises of a court poet, but may be taken to indicate that due to the continuance of an well-ordered system of government in the country, Sallakṣaṇa the ruler, could devote himself to these peaceful pursuits. The Māu record informs us that with the help of efficient ministers Sallakṣaṇa effectively carried out the work of '*kaṇṭaka-śodhana*',[3] clearing of thorns, (i.e., anti-corruption drive) within his realm, and dissipated fears of his subjects. Thus Sallakṣaṇa was able not only to establish peace and order in the state, but also to upgrade the standard of living of the people and augment the strength of the royal treasury.

It need not, however, be presumed that Sallakṣaṇa was a man of passive disposition. The same record (Māu Stone Inscription) refers to the presence in the court of Sallakṣaṇa,

---

[1] *C.M.I.*, P. 79.; *A.S.R.*, II., Pp. 458-59; *ibid.*, X., P. 26.

[2] *E.I.*, I., Pp. 198, 203. (Dhaureyaḥ śrutaśālināṁ-guṇavatāṁ vandhuḥ kalānāṁ nidhiḥ sad-vṛttasya ca sadma Kalpa-viṭapī niḥśeṣa-puṣṭyarthināṁ//9).

[3] *ibid.*, Pp. 201, 206,. V. 39.

kings doing homage to him as well as his other dependents,[4] which reminds us of the 'sāmanta-cakra' (circle of feudatory princes) organised by Śri Gopāla, as mentioned in the drama, Prabodhacandrodaya, to defeat the Cedi prince Lakṣmī Karṇa.[5] It is quite likely that Sallakṣaṇa, the son and successor of Kīrttivarman, enjoyed almost the same allegiance from the sāmantas as did his father.

As for the military achievements of Sallakṣaṇa we have no definite evidence in the records. But the Māu record refers to his prowess which kept his enemies always awake.[6] According to the evidence of the Ajaygaḍh Rock Inscription of Vīravarman (V.S. 1317), Sallakṣaṇa is said to have taken away the fortunes of the Mālavas and the Cedis. (Sallakṣaṇa Mālava-Cedi-lakṣmīḥ luṇṭhaka-khaḍgaḥ).[7] Though no direct reference is made to any particular battle between the Candellas and the Cedis or the Paramāras during the reign of Sallakṣaṇa, yet a study of the history of these dynasties may throw some leading light on the matter.

The Kalacuris, it may be noticed, were passing through a very critical time after the fall of Lakṣmī Karṇa. Yaśah-Karṇa, who suceeded him had to face a strong neighbour on the west, the Paramāras, as well as another rising power beyond the Vindhyas, the Cālukyas. According to the Nagpur Praśasti of Paramāra Naravarman (1097-1111 A.D.), his elder brother, Lakṣmadeva, in course of an unchecked expedition 'attacked Tripuri, and annihilated his warlike and spirited adversaries'.[8] The Cedi prince, who suffered the reverse at the hands of the Paramāras, could not have been any one else than Yaśahkarṇa (1073-1125 A.D.).[9] Belgāmi inscription of Vikramāditya VI dated in 1081 A.D. also refers to the Cālukya ruler's victory over Yaśahkarṇa.[10] In the circumstances it might not have been very difficult for the

---

[4] "rājñām sevāgatānāṁ.....cāśritānāṁ" *ibid.*, V. 10., P. 198.
[5] *P.C.*, L. 3.
[6] *E.I.*, I., P. 198., V. 9.
[7] *ibid.*, P. 327., V. 4.
[8] *ibid.*, II., P. 186., V. 39.
[9] *D.H.N.I.*, II., P. 880.
[10] *An. Rep. Arch. Survey Mysore* 1929., Pp. 133, 137, L. 33.

Candella prince, Sallakṣaṇa, succeeding to Kīrttivarman's effective orgnisation, to launch attacks on the Cedi country, particularly when the situation there was so favourable for the Candella ruler. But it must be admitted at the same time that such expeditions could hardly be of any permanent political value.

Since Bhoja's tragic end the Paramāra power was on the wane. Jayasiṁha I, the son and successor of Bhoja, was also compelled to acknowledge the suzerainty of Kalacuri Lakṣmī Karṇa. But there was an attempt at revival by Lakṣmadeva, a son of Udayāditya, as has already been mentioned. His successes, however, were shortlived due to the growing power of the Cālukyas, which culminated in the defeat and death of Naravarman, the brother of Lakṣmadeva, as described in the Kumārapālacarita,[11] and corroborated by epigraphic evidences.[12] During this period of turmoil in the Paramāra kingdom it might have been possible for the Candella ruler to take out an expeditionary raid, referred to in the Ajaygaḍh record.[13] It may be remembered that the Candellas were already well-settled in the Betwā valley by the establishment of a 'Kīrttigiri-durga' on the bank of the river during the time of Kīrttivarman,[14] which probably marked the boundary between the Candella and the Paramāra dominions. Therefore it may not be wrong to presume that Sallakṣaṇa maintained the integrity of the Candella state as revived by his father, Kīrttivarman. As for his personal achievement, we have only a vague reference to his success against some unknown enemies in the Doab between the Ganges and the Jumna (antarvedi viṣaya).[15] It may be remembered that since the defeat of the Gurjara Pratihāra ruler, Rājyapāla, Candella Vidyādhara extended his influence over the Doab region. But, as is evidenced by the Set Māhet Stone Inscrip-

[11] V. 41; The 'Vasanta vilāsa' also refers to imprisonment of 'the lord of Dhārā' like a śuka bird in a cage.

[12] The Vaḍnagar praśasti of Kumārapāla. *E.I.*, I., P. 293, V. 11.; The Talwāra Insc. (*Rajputana Museum Report* 1915., P. 2).

[13] *E.I.*, I. P. 327, V. 4.

[14] *I.A.*, XVIII., P. 238.

[15] *E.I.*, I., P. 201, P. 38.

tion of Vidyādhara (V.S. 1176),[16] and the Budāun Inscription of Lakhaṇapāla,[17] the area was ruled over by a Rāṣṭrakūṭa, who was probably a feudatory of the Candellas. The Jhansi fragmentary stone inscription of Sallakṣaṇa-siṁha[18] also refers to a line of Kānyakubja rulers of the lunar family. The identification of Sallakṣaṇa-siṁha with Candella Sallakṣaṇavarman has not, however, been established beyond doubt. During the period of confusion prevailing in the country as a sequel to Māhmud's invasion and the eclipse of the Candella power, these local rulers of Kanauj might have assumed sovereign status. So, for Sallakṣaṇa it might not have been impossible to make a bold bid for the recapture of the Kanauj region, as referred to in the Māu record. But it is quite well known that Candradeva of the Gāhaḍavāla dynasty acquired sovereignty over Kānyakubja or Gādhipura by the prowess of his own arms (nija-bhujopārjjitaṁ) in about 1070 A.D.[19] So it is doubtful whether Sallakṣaṇa was really victorious in the 'antarvedi' region.

In the administration of the state Sallakṣaṇa was aided by a group of very able ministers and officials, the chief of whom was, according to the evidence of the Māu Stone Inscription of Madanavarman, Ananta, who was a tower of strength to Kīrttivarman.[20] The success in the Antarvedi region, that is claimed in the record, is attributed to the policy of this very minister, or his son Gadādhara.[21] Again, it was the latter who is believed to have been mainly instrumental in clearing the country of anti-social elements (kaṇṭaka-śodhana), and strengthening both financial as well as law and order position of the state (koṣasya daṇḍasya ca). Other sons of Ananta were also appointed by Sallakṣaṇa to very important posts in the administration. But it is interesting to note that the criterion of their selection was not that they were sons of the Chief Minister, but that they had

---

[16] *R.A.S.B.*, LXI. Pt. I. Extra No., Pp. 57-64.
[17] *E.I.*, I., Pp. 61-66.
[18] *ibid.*, Pp. 214-15.
[19] *D.H.N.I.*, I., Pp. 506-07.
[20] *E.I.*, I., P. 200., V. 30-31.
[21] *ibid.*, V. 38-39.. P. 201.

been found suitable after proper tests conducted by the king (parīkṣya-samyak), and appointed to high offices requiring the services of wise, upright and valiant men (niyuktah-kāryeṣu-sūkṣma-śuci-śūrajanociteṣu).[22]

Jayavarman.

Māu Stone Inscription[23] and Ajaygaḍh Rock Inscription of Vīravarman[24] bear evidence to the fact that Jayavarman, the son of Sallakṣaṇa succeeded him on the Candella throne. It is however curious that Nānyaura Plate of Madanavarman[25] omits the names of both Jayavarman and his father, Sallakṣaṇa from the Candella genealogy. It may be that the Nānyaura record only referred to the highlights of the family, whereas the Māu inscription of the same time, issued by one of the ministers of king Madanavarman, had no such obsession, and hence may be taken as more reliable. The former one was issued by Madanavarman himself, and as such contain references to his father, Pṛthvīvarman and grandfather, Kīrttivarman, omitting the collateral branch of Sallakṣaṇa and his son, Jayavarman.

A direct epigraphic evidence for this prince is, however, contained in the Khajurāho stone inscription of V.S. 1059 of the time of Dhaṅga, which had been "re-written in clear letters by Jayavarmmadeva-nṛpati" in V.S. 1173 (1117 A.D.).[26] It appears therefore that he came to the throne sometime before that date. If it is admitted that Sallakṣaṇa came to the throne in about 1100 A.D., it may be presumed that those two generations had an average-period of about 10 years each.

Both the records, referred to above, mention Jayavarman as a valiant hero. The Māu record describes him as 'a dwelling place of generosity, truth, policy and heroism, whose

[22] *ibid.,* V. 37.
[23] *ibid.,* P. 206., V. 40.
[24] *ibid.,* P. 327., V. 4.
[25] *I.A.,* XVI., P. 202, 207-10.
[26] *E.I.,* I., P. 147., Ll. 33-34.

majesty,like the rising sun, deprived other princes of their lustre.'[27]

The administrative structure of the state during the time of Jayavarman continued in the same way as previously. The most influential minister of the last two generations, Ananta, however, died by abandoning his body in the waters at the confluence of the Ganges and the Jumna, following the custom adopted by an earlier Candella ruler, viz., Dhaṅgadeva. In the ministerial office Ananta, the chief minister of Kīrttivarman and Sallakṣaṇa, was succeeded by his son, Gadādhara, whom Jayavarman appointed near his own person as Pratihāra.[28] The revised Khajurāho Inscription refers to another official of Jayavarman. He was a learned kāyastha, Gauḍa Jayapāla by name.

Pṛthvīvarman.

Nānyaura Plate 'C' of Madanavarman[29] suggests that Kīrttivarman was succeeded by Pṛthvīvarman. But it is clearly indicated in the Ajaygaḍh Rock Inscription of Vīravarman[30] that Pṛthvīvarman came to the throne succeeding Jayavarman, whom the Nānyaura record omitted altogether. The evidence of another record of the time of Madanavarman (Māu Stone Insc.) proves very helpful in the matter. It states that after Jayavarman, the Candella sovereignty passed on to Pṛthvīvaram, the co-uterine younger brother of the illustrious king Sallakṣaṇavarman.[31] It was however an unusual succession, an uncle succeeding a nephew. In the absence of any reference to the circumstances leading to this abrupt change in the line of succession we may presume that Jayavarman must have died childless or there was a rising engineered by Pṛthvīvarman, who usurped the throne. It is learnt however from the fragmentary

[27] *ibid.*, P. 198., V. 11. "yasya pratāpa-tapanābhyudayena bhūpa dīpa iva kṣata."
[28] *ibid.*, P. 201. V. 40.
[29] *I.A.*, XVI., 208., Ll. 3-4.
[30] *E.I.*, I., P. 327., V. 4-5.
[31] *ibid.*, 198, 203,,V. 12. "Śrī Sallakṣaṇavarmma-kṣoṇināthasya sodaravarājah/ Atha Pṛthvīvarma-nṛpah."

Kālañjar inscription that Jayavarman was devoted to Nārāyaṇa and being wearied of government the king made it over to '...... varman'[32] (this portion being broken, the earlier part of the name cannot be recovered, but evidently it must have referred to Pṛthvīvarman). Jayavarman, it is stated, then proceeded to wash away his sins in the divine river, probably in the same manner as had been adopted by Dhaṅga[33]. It may not be unlikely that this was a voluntary abdication, as is evident from the expression 'made it over', and not a case of disputed succession culminating in a *coup-de-etat* by Pṛthvīvarman, of which there is no evidence.

Candella records are curiously silent about any achievement of Pṛthvīvarman as well as of any political incident of his reign period. This may lead to the natural presumption that it was not a particularly brilliant period of the Candella history, and that the reference to Pṛthvīvarman's devotion to Nārāyaṇa might also suggest that he was a man of passive disposition. But a study of the contemporary history of Northern India would reveal that in the second quarter of the 12th cent. A.D., besides the Candellas there were other equally potential powers on the field, viz., the Paramāras, the Cedis, and the Caulukyas. It has already been seen that in the absence of any imperial power all of them were vieing with one another in a contest for supremacy. In the circumstances when we find in the Māu Record that Pṛthvīvarman is described to have been equal to the task in bearing the burden of the hereditary government, and was able to maintain the integrity of the boundaries of the state, it is hardly possible to believe that Pṛthvīvarman was a weak ruler. It may be that he did not adopt an aggressive policy against other powers.

The same principles of administration were maintained during the regime of Pṛthvīvarman. V. 13 of the Māu Record states that he used to take lawful wealth and then expand

[32] *J.A.S.B.*, 1848., P. 318-19., L. 10-11.
[33] *E.I.*, I., 146., V. 55.

the same according to the prescripts on the sacred objects, carefully protecting all being and wholly intent on securing propriety of conduct.[34] Gadādhara, the son of a former minister, Ananta, who had been appointed by Jayavarman in the office of Pratihāra, was now in the present regime elevated to the high office of 'Mantrimukhya' (Chief Minister), in which capacity he claims to have made the government of the king prosper in all its constituent parts.[35]

Madanavarman.

Pṛthvīvarman's son, Madanavarman came to the throne in the first quarter of the 12th cent. A.D., and enjoyed a rather long period of reign from c. 1129-1163 A.D. During this period the Candellas flourished once again in the political scene of Northern India as an important power, for which we have evidences inscriptional and numismatic as well as traditional and literary.

It has already been pointed out that since the demise of Kīrttivarman till the accession of Madanavarman, the intervening Candella rulers could hardly achieve any spectacular success, though of course the state might not have suffered any territorial diminution. With the accession of Madanavarman it will be evident that the non-aggressive policy so long followed was totally reversed and King Madanavarman from the very start of his career launched a vigorous policy in reviving the strength and organisation of the Candella power and restoring respect for it among other contemporary powers of the adjacent regions, viz., the Cedis, the Paramāras, the Gāhaḍavālas and the Caulukyas. This is best evidenced in V. 15 of the Māu stone inscription, which reads as follows :—

'Before whose name even ever quickly flees the Cedi king, vanquished in fierce fight, and through the dread of whom the king of Kāśī always passes his time in friendly behaviour; by whom moreover the ruler of Mālava, full of arrogance

[34] *ibid.*, I., P. 198.
[35] *ibid.,* P. 201., V. 41.

was quickly exterminated, while other monarchs paying homage to him have enjoyed supreme comfort."[36]

The account of the Candella ruler, as provided in the verse quoted above, is undoubtedly an exaggerated description of the court poet. But the study of the history of the period would reveal that the condition of the powers mentioned in the verse, viz., the Kāśirāja, the Mālaveśa and the Cedis, particularly during this period (i.e., the first quarter of the 12th cent. A.D.), was not quite strong to withstand the onslaught of a vigorous ruler of the Candella family. As such, it may not be a mere praśasti to describe that the Candella king Madanavarman was able to exert his political influence over those powers. There was no question of any expansion of the Candella dominion at the cost of any of these powers, but they might have had to submit before the military might of the Candella ruler, Madavarmmadeva.

The Cedis, it may be remembered, suffered a defeat at the hands of the Candella king, Sallakṣaṇa towards the close of the 11th cent. A.D., and since then they could not gain sufficient strength to effect a recovery. The discovery of the hoard of coins,[37] which included some of Madanavarman, in the village named Pānwār in the Teonthār Tehsil of the former Rewā state, has been taken by some scholars to indicate that the Candella kingdom extended in the south-east upto the Kāimur Range of the Vindhyas, beyond which lay the dominion of the Ḍāhala Kalacuris. The situation of an expanding power as an immediate neighbour is by itself dangerous which becomes more acute when the other power is weaker. Though the name of the Cedi king who might have clashed with Madanavarman is not mentioned in any record, yet there is every probability of his being identified with Gayākarṇa, of whom we have a record, viz., Tewār stone inscription, dated 1151 A.D.[38] The Kalacuris had already lost some of their territories in the Ganges valley to the

---

[36] *ibid.*, I., P. 198, 204.
[37] *J.A.S.B.*, X (N.S.), P. 199-200.
[38] *I.A.*, XVIII., P. 209-11.

Gāhaḍavālas during the time of his father, Yaśahkarṇa (1073-1125 A.D.). Naturally their hold in this region must have been weaker after this adverse development. For the Candellas too, an expansion of the Gāhaḍavālas was fraught with dangerous potentialities, and as such they might have under Madanavarman annexed the region into their own dominion lest it might fall to the Gāhaḍavālas. The claim that 'ever quickly flees the Cedi king vanquished in fierce fight' may not therefore be an idle boast. The incident hinted at in this verse might have referred to the Candella victory over the Kalacuris in the North Bāghelkhaṇḍ region. Increasing danger from the Candellas must have compelled the Cedis to sink their feeling of enmity with their eastern neighbour, the Paramāras, with whom now they enter into a marriage alliance, Gayākarṇa having married Ālhaṇadevī, a Guhila princess, who was a grand-daughter of Paramāra Udayāditya, as stated in the Bherāghāṭ stone inscription.[39]

The Paramāras themselves were also hardly better off. As early as the time of Kīrttivarman, it has been seen, that in 1093 A.D. the Candella kingdom stretched upto Lalitpur district in the Betwā valley with the establishment of a fortress named Kīrttigiridurga.[40] Further expansion of the Candella dominion in the same direction was quite possible during the time of Madanavarman, as evidenced by the Māu stone inscription (Jhansi district)[41] and the Augāsi grant (Banda district).[42] The latter record, it will appear, was issued when the king was in residence near Bhaillasvāmin (mod. Bhilsā). This is further corroborated by the evidence of the Semrā grant of Paramarddideva, grandson of Madanavarman. The Semrā Plates[43] indicate that in 1162 A.D., Madanavarman was in residence at Vāridurga (mod. Bārigār) and granted the villages of Madanapura in the Jhansi district, Vaḍavāri (Berwārā) and Dudāhi in Lalitpur. All these go to show that the Candella dominion not only crossed the

---

[39] *E.I.*, II., P. 12, V. 17-25.
[40] *I.A.*, XVIII., P. 237-39.
[41] *E.I.*, I., P. 198.
[42] *I.A.*, XVI., P. 202, 207-10.
[43] *E.I.*, IV., P. 158.

Betwā, in the south-west but also absorbed a considerable portion of the Mālwā territory.

As to how did the Candella power advanced or which particular Mālava prince had been defeated by Madanavarman is however nowhere indicated in any of these records. It is only vaguely mentioned in the Māu inscription that 'the ruler of Mālwā, full of arrogance, was quickly exterminated'. The history of the Paramāras would show that during the reign periods of Naravarman (1097-1111 A.D.) and Yaśovarman (1134-42 A.D.) the military resources of the Paramāra state were exhausted by protracted warfare with the Caulukyas of Gujarat. The Paramāra records are rather reticent about any incident of the reign of these two princes. But the Caulukya records, both literary and epigraphic, clearly indicate how the rulers of Mālwā sufferred terrible defeats at the hands of the rulers of Gujarat. Merutuṅga in his Prabandhacintāmaṇi[44] tells us that when Siddharāja was away from his capital on a pilgrimage, the Mālava king Yaśovarman overran Gujarat and exacted submission from the minister of Siddharāja. The latter, on his return to his capital, felt very much humiliated and made preparations for an invasion of the Mālava kingdom. This led to a war of 12 years' duration ending with the defeat and capture of Yaśovarman before 1137 A.D., i.e., in about three years' time since his accession. As such it is quite probable that Yaśovarman led the invasion of Gujarat during the reign of his father, Naravarman. Hemacandra, a contemporary of both Siddrāja and Yaśovarman, in his Dvāśrayakāvya[45] corroborates the statement of Merutuṅga though the details may somewhat differ.[46] Other literary works like the Sukṛtasankīrtana, Surathotsaba, Kīrttikaumudi and Vasantavilāsa also refer to the storming of Dhārā by the Gujarat prince and annexation of the whole Avantideśa to the Gujarat Empire.

It is therefore highly probable that during the early years of the reign of Yaśovarman, when he was grappling

---

[44] Pp. 85 ff.
[45] *I.A.*, IV., P. 266.
[46] *H. P., Ganguly.*, Pp. 167-68.

with the Caulukyas in a deadly struggle, the Candella ruler Madanavarman exploited the opportunity by acquiring some portions of the Mālava country adjacent to his dominions. The Paramāras, being too busy with their enemy on the west, could hardly put up adequate defence against their eastern neighbour, the Candellas. The Candella claim of having exterminated the ruler of Mālava may not be unjustifiable, as their defeat at the hands of the Gujarat chief and loss of territory to the Candellas left with them only a short strip of territory in the lower valley of the river Kāli Sindhu upto V.S. 1199 (A.D. 1142).

Therefore it must be admitted that Siddharāja's victory over the king of Mālwā was more than a mere military raid. A number of Caulukya Grants of different dates designate Siddharāja as "Avantinātha"[47]. The annexation of Mālwā brought Caulukya Jayasiṁha closer to the Candella dominions, which also by now stretched upto the eastern Mālwā, and ultimately a clash between the two powers became inevitable. The Gujarat chronicles including the Kīrttikaumudi refer to the invasion of Kālañjara by Jayasiṁha. The Kumārapāla-carita claims that Jayasiṁha defeated Madanavarman, the lord of Mahobā, but came to terms with the latter and made peace. Evidently the Caulukya ruler could not gain much from his wars with the Candellas and was compelled to withdraw his forces from Kālañjara. The Kālañjara stone inscription claims that Madanavarman in an instant defeated the king of Gurjara, (identified with the king of Gujarat, i.e., Jayasiṁha), as Kṛṣṇa defeated Kaṁsa[48]. There may be some exaggeration in the evidence of Candella epigraphy but it cannot be denied that the Candellas threw back the Gujarat invasion completely and this by itself may well justify the claim of Madanavarman, as recorded in the Kālañjar record.

To the north-west of the Candella state the rising power of the Gāhaḍavālas might have constituted a threat to their security, but as is evident from the Māu record, there

[47] Gala Stone Insc. of V.S. 1193. *J.B.R.A.S.*, XXV., Pp. 322-24; Ujjain Frag. Stone Insc. of V.S. 1195. *A.S.I., W.C.*, 1921, Pp. 54-55.

[48] *J.A.S.B.*, 1848, XVII, Pt. I., P. 318., L. 14.

was continued good relationship between these two powers. The statement of the Māu inscription that through the dread of the Candella ruler, Madanavarman, 'the King of Kāśi always passes his time in friendly behaviour', should of course be taken with some reservation. The real state of affairs most probably was that both these powers realised each other's potentiality and formed a sort of alliance which enabled them to play significant roles in contemporary politics.

A study of the distribution of the records of the time of Madanavarman indicates that he enjoyed rather a long span of life occupying the Candella throne for a period of at least 34 years. The earliest of his records is dated in A.D. 1129[49], and the latest one dated A.D. 1163[50]. During his regime not only do we witness a revival of the Candella power in the political theatre of Northern India, but also the establishment of a strong and consolidated state with enlarged boundaries, which was possible, it must be admitted, by the steady application of Kauṭilyan principles of diplomacy by some efficient ministers of Madanavarman. The findspots of his inscriptions and coins suggest that in the south the Candella state verged on the Vindhyas from the Kāimur range in the west to the Bhānrer range in the east. The eastern boundary ran along the course of the Jumna beyond which lay the Gāhaḍavāla kingdom, while in the west the Betwā course divided the Candella dominions from the Mālava country, then annexed to the Caulukya state. Thus the whole of the central Indian triangle including the important fortresses of Kālañjar and Ajaygaḍḥ and the cities of Khajurāho and Mahobā, was firmly held by Madanavarman.

Bhārat Kalā Bhavan Plates of Madanavarman (V.S. 1192) give names of three queens of the King, viz., Lakhamā-devī, Vālhana-devī and Cāndala (or Candela)-devī. Of these Vālhana-devī was the Chief Queen being described as 'Mahārājñī,' and the two others simply as 'Rājñī'[51].

---

49 Kālañjar Pillar Insc. *A.S.R.*, XXI., P. 34.
50 Mahobā Jain image Insc. *ibid.*, II., P. 448, No. 25.
51 *E.I.*, XXXI.

CHAPTER IX

CĀHAMĀNA—CANDELLA RIVALRY: *FALL OF MAHOBĀ.*

Yaśovarman II.

Baṭeśvar Inscription of Paramardideva is the only record which reveals the existence of a prince named Yaśovarman intervening between the rulers, Madanavarman and Paramardideva. Before the discovery of this record it was generally believed that Paramardi, the grandson of Madanavarman, succeeded the latter on the throne due probably to the death of his (Madana's) son in his own lifetime. But the evidence of the Baṭeśvar record clearly indicates that Yaśovarman, the father of Paramardi, ascended the throne after Madanavarman for however short a time it might have been. Verses 8 & 9 of the inscription state as follows :—

"As the Moon, the crest jewel of Maheśvara arise from the ocean, so was born from him Yaśovarman, who was an ornament of great rulers causing joy to the people, whose fame spreading in three worlds with the loveliness of jasmine and the moon, made the hair of men appear white and thus caused the unprecedented notion, that people before they had attained old age had, alas, turned grey."[1]

The earliest recorded date of Paramardi being V.S. 1223 (1165-66 A.D.),[2] Yaśovarman must have had a very short tenure on the throne. Dr. Ray suggests that v. 9 of the Baṭeśvar record hints at the untimely end of his career.[3] But the idea that there might have been some sort of dynastic troubles, and that Paramardi achieved the throne at the cost of his father, cannot be upheld with the materials at our disposal. It is easier to presume that Yaśovarman died normally shortly after his accession. As nothing remarkable could have been achieved during the brief spell of Yaśovarman's reign, for which the ministerial family could

---

[1]*E.I.*, I., P. 212.
[2]The Semrā Grant. *E.I.*, IV., P. 153-70.
[3]*D.H.N.I.*, II., P. 712-13.

boast of, the name of this ruler may have been omitted from their record (Māu Inscription) altogether.

Paramardi.

Paramardideva, the grandson of Madanavarman, was the last Candella ruler of eminence. He came to the throne early in life in c. 1166 A.D., at the age of five, according to the Parmāl Rāso,[4] within a couple of years of the date of his grand-father's last dated record, c. 1163 A.D.,[5] his father Yaśovarman II having died after a short reign. Verse 6 of the Ajaygaḍh Inscription of Vīravarman (V.S. 1317) refers to Paramardi as "a leader even in his youth, who struck down the opposing heroes, and to whom the fortune of universal sovereignty quickly came, like an enamoured damsel, choosing him of her own free will."[6] The verse indirectly hints at the suddenness of Paramardi's accession necessitated most probably by the untimely passing away of his father.

The records attributed to the reign of Paramardi indicate that he enjoyed a fairly long reign extending over 35 years, the earliest of his records being dated in 1165-66 A.D.,[7] and the latest in 1201-02 A.D.[8] The period may be divided under three broad sections, of which the first was concerned with the accession and the early career, the second with the hostility between the Candellas and the Cāhamānas, leading to the fall of Mahobā, and the third with the Muslim invasions.

For the first part of his reign we have the following records, viz., the Semrā Plates (1165-66 A.D.),[9] the Mahobā image inscription (1166-67 A.D.),[10] the Icchāwār Plate (1171 A.D.),[11] the Mahobā Plate (1173 A.D.),[12] the Pachār Plate (1176 A.D.),[13] and the Chārkhāri Plate (1178 A.D.).[14] In

---

[4]P. 28., V. 102.

[5]Mahobā Jain image Insc. *A.S.R.*, II., P. 448, No. 25.

[6]*E.I.*, I., P. 325-30. "Athābhavad-Śrī Paramardirājo bālopi-netā ripu-vīra-hantā Sāmrājyalakṣmīr yaṁ-ihānuraktā patiṁ varevāsu samājagāma"//6.

[7]*E.I.*, IV., P. 153-70.

[8]*J.A.S.B.*, XVIII., P. 313-17.

[9]*E.I.*, IV., P. 153-70.

[10]*A.S.R.*, XXI., P. 74.

[11]*I.A.*, XXV., P. 205-08.

[12]*E.I.*, XVI., P. 9-15.

[13]*ibid.*, X., P. 44-49.

[14]*ibid.*, XX. P. 128-31.

all these inscriptions full imperial titles are used by Paramardi, viz., "Paramabhaṭṭāraka-Mahārājādhirāja-Parameśvara-Parama-Māheśvara-Śrī-Kālāñjarādhipati-Śrīmanmat-Paramardideva". These show that Paramardi well maintained the dignity of the Candellas, whose power had revived under his illustrious grand-father, Madanavarman.

The findspots of the records belonging to the reign of Paramardi indicate that he administered the entire dominion inherited by him quite efficiently and peacefully. His early years were not marred by any military reverses or anything of the sort. The Candella records do not refer to any brilliant success either during the first fifteen years of his reign (1166-1182 A. D.).

It was the second phase of his reign that was marked by protracted conflicts with the Cāhamānas of Delhi, which culminated in the fall of Mahobā and the defeat of Paramardi. Strangely enough, the epigraphic documents of the Candellas are conspicuouly silent over this vital issue. The only explanation that may be offered for this deliberate reticence of the Candella *praśastikāras* is probably their unwillingness to refer to the ignominions defeat of their master. We have naturally, therefore, to rely on the popular bardic accounts still current in Central India, known as the Pṛthvīrāj Rāso by Cānd Bardāi,[15] the Mahobā Khaṇḍ (Parmāl Rāso)[16] and the Ālhā Rāso by Jagnaik Rāo.[17] These Raso accounts refer to the serious hostilities between Pṛthvīraj Cauhān and Parmāl Candel in some details. Much of these is later fabrication by different popular bards, who were either interested in glorifying Pṛthvīrāj or Parmāl. It cannot but be admitted that there is a kernel of truth in these accounts, as is borne out by the evidence of the two Madanpur Stone Inscriptions, which record the defeat of Paramardi at the hands of Pṛthvīrāj, and the plunder of Jejābhukti by the latter in Saṁ 1239 (A. D. 1182-83.)[18].

[15]Ed. by M. V. Pandia & S. S. Das, Benares, 1913.
[16]Ed. by S. S. Das, Benares, 1920.
[17]*Lays of Alha* (Trans. by W. Waterfield).
[18]*A.S.R.*, X., P. 98-99; *ibid.*, XXI., P. 173-74; *A.S.I.* (*W.C.*) 1904, P. 55.

The circumstances leading to the outbreak of hostilities between the Candellas and the Cāhamānas, as can be reconstructed from the bardic ballads, may be briefly described here.

Pṛthvīrāj Cauhān, while returning to Delhi after marrying the daughter of Padamsen, was attacked on the way by the Turkish hordes, who were, however, beaten back. Pṛthvīrāja's forces also suffered some casualties. Unfortunately the party, including the wounded soldiers, having lost direction came to Mahobā, the capital of the Candellas, when it was raining. They camped in the royal garden without knowing that it was so. The keeper of the garden strongly objected to this intrusion, and in course of an altercation that followed, he was struck down. When the report reached Parmāl Candel (Paramardideva), he felt offended and sent his soldiers to take action. In the battle that followed the Candels suffered serious losses, and of the Cauhāns some 30 men were killed and 17 injured. Parmāl, then in strong indignation, summoned one of his generals, Udal, a leader of the Banāphar clan, and asked him to attack the soldiers already wounded. In vain did Udal try to impress upon the Candella king that it would not only be unchivalrous to attack the wounded soldiers, but would also unnecessarily antagonise a powerful ruler like Pṛthvīrāja. But Parmāl was under the evil influence of Māhil Parihār (Pratihāra), his brother-in-law, who, though a Sāmanta, nourished a secret feeling of revenge against the Candellas, and whenever there was an opportunity, either he gave wrong advice to the Candellas or helped the enemy with secret messages. In this case also at his instigation Parmāl prevailed upon the Banāphar to lead the unfair attack, but the result was no better than the previous one. The seige, however, was raised by Pṛthvīrāj, who returned to Delhi.

In the meantime the Banāphar chiefs, Udal and his brother Ālhā, finding Mahobā too hot for them due to the machinations of Māhil Parihār, left the Candella court and sought refuge with King Jaicānd of Kanauj.

Māhil, now secretly communicated the news about the

desertion of the best warriors of the Candellas to Pṛthvīrāj, and advised him to avail himself of this opportunity of subjugating the Candellas. Pṛthvirāj took counsel with all his chiefs and set out with a strong army to attack Mahobā. The Mahobā Khaṇḍ describes in detail the route followed by Pṛthvīrāj and the different stages of his march to Mahobā.

Starting from Delhi in Saṁ 1240 (1182 A.D.)[19] on a Wednesday, as stated in the Parmāl Rāso, Pṛthvīrāj marched to Gaḍh Gopācal (Gwālior) and encamped there for seven days. Then his army trekked eastwards to Baṭeśvar (near Agra) and worshipped Śiva there. Then they proceeded towards the Candella kingdom. Next halt was on the banks of the Pahuj at a place called Bāsavgaḍh or Indragaḍh, near Sirsā or Sisargaḍh (Sisarwāgarh). The fortress of Sisargaḍh was held by Malkhān, a valiant sāmanta of Parmāl. He was a Banāphar, and the famous heroes, Ālhā and Udal, were his cousins. Malkhān stoutly defended the fort for about eight days. Pṛthvīrāj at the outset tried to win him over, but Malkhān stuck to his *svāmidharma* (allegiance to his master) and fought bravely with all the resources at his command, killing as many as eight strong generals of the Cauhān army in eight consecutive days. Pṛthvīrāj at last personally took the field and Malkhān bravely laid down his life in the battle along with his noble associates.

After the fall of Sirsā, Pṛthvīrāj marched towards Mahobā and camped on the banks of the Betwā (Vetravatī). Realising the imminent danger which it would be rather impossible to forestall, Parmāl and his Sāmantas, on the suggestion of the Chief Queen Malhān Devi, decided to seek for a temporary truce for a couple of months, and to send an envoy to Kanauj recalling the Banāphar brothers, Ālhā and Udal.

Pṛthvīrāj agreed to the proposal, but remained camping on the banks of the river, practically besieging the town. Ālhā and Udal, on receipt of this message, were at first reluctant to come, as they had been unfairly treated by the

[19]The date is Saṁ 1140 according to some Mss. of the Mahobā Khand. Sri Shyamsundar Das, the Editor of the Parmāl Rāso, believes, it was a calligraphist's mistake for Saṁ 1240. *P. R.*, P. 60., f.n. 1.

Candel ruler. But their mother prevailed upon them that '*svāmidharma*' should not be violated. Jaicānd, the ruler of Kanauj, sent along with them some of his best generals, including two of his sons and a strong contingent of soldiers. The reference to this friendly assistance of the Gāhaḍavāla ruler to Parmāl, in the latter's conflict with Pṛthvīrāj, may not have been a mere fabrication by the popular bards. The Māu record refers to the existence of friendly relations between the Candella king Madanavarman, the grandfather of Parmāl, and the Gāhaḍavālas. The recent find of the Bhārat Kalā Bhavan plate of Paramardideva (V.S. 1247)[20a] is a further proof on the point. It was issued when the Candella King Paramardi was at the "*Manikarṇikā Ghaṭṭa* at *Śrī Vārāṇasī*" (Mod. Banaras). Evidently the Candella King visited this holy city in the Gāhaḍavāla dominion on a pilgrimage.

On the arrival of the Banāphar chiefs at Mahobā at the head of the Kanauj army the Candellas felt greatly inspired and they made necessary preparations for the final battle. Pṛthvīrāj now demanded reopening of the operations held in abeyance under the terms of the truce, or surrender of the capital city, Mahobā. The battle started in full fury, the Candel troops advancing within a range of two 'krośas' (i.e., about 4 miles) from the Cauhān encampments.

Realising the fury and intensity of the impending battle, Parmāl, it is said, became nervous and left for Kālañjar along with some of his troops. Brahmajit, a son of Parmāl, however, along with the Banāphar heroes, Ālhā and Udal, led the Candel army. In this great armageddon of Mahobā, both sides suffered serious losses and numerous casualties, which included Brahmajit, Udal, the sons of Jaicānd and almost all the valiant generals on the Candella side. Ālhā was wounded, but survived the battle. Pṛthvirāj celebrated his victory by sacking the Candella capital, Mahobā, which is corroborated by the evidence of the Madanpur Stone Inscriptions, already quoted.[20]

A Cauhān general, Cāvand Rai, now proceeded to

20a *E.I.* XXXI.

20 *A.S.R.*, XXI., Pp. 173-74.

Kāliñjar, where Parmāl took refuge. The Cauhān army occupied the fort and plundered it, and started back with their most important trophy, Parmāl, to present him before their master, Pṛthvīrāj. The Pṛthvīrāj Rāso stops abruptly here, and states that Pṛthvīrāj raising the seige of Mahobā,[21] proceeded towards his own capital, Delhi, after appointing Pajjun Rāi, one of his generals as the Governor of Mahobā. But what was the fate of Parmāl? How long did the Cauhān occupation of Mahobā continue?

Some light is thrown on these points by the Parmāl Rāso.[22] It states that when after plundering the fortress of Kālañjar, the Cauhāns were returning along with Parmāl, the Candel king, as their prisoner of war, Indal Kumār, son of Ālhā, attacked them without any warning. This sudden attack of the Banāphar soldiers completely outmanouvred the Cauhāns, and the Candel king was freed from their clutches. Parmāl then returned to Kālañjar; but, according to the Rāso accounts, out of a sense of shame for his captivity at the hands of the enemies, he voluntarily put an end to his life at the Gajrāj temple. He was followed by the Chief Queen, Malhān Devi and other queens. Cānd Bardāi, however, mentions that Parmāl retired to Gayā and died there.

These bardic accounts being full of unhistorical material, which was added in course of time, it is extremely difficult to trace the historical kernel in them. That Parmāl died immediately after his defeat at the hands of Pṛthvīrāj is disproved by the find of a number of dated Candella records, some of which were issued directly by Paramardideva. Those are, the Kālañjar Rock Inscription[23] and the Mahobā Stone Inscription of Saṁvat 1240 (A.D. 1184),[24] the Ajaigaḍh Stone Inscription of V.S. 1243 (A.D. 1187),[25] the Baghāri (Baṭeśvar) Stone Inscription of Saṁ 1252 (A.D. 1195),[26] and the Kālañjar Stone Inscription of V.S. 1258

[21] *Pr.R.*, Mahobā Samaya., P. 2614-15.
[22] *P.R.*, Antima Khaṇḍa., Pp. 532-53.
[23] *E.I.*, XIX-XXI. App. No. 400.
[24] *A.S.R.*, XXI., P. 72.
[25] *ibid.*, P. 50.
[26] *E.I.*, I., P. 207.

(A.D. 1201).[27] That is to say, Paramardi lived for about 20 years after the Cauhān-Candel battle of 1182 A.D. This is also corroborated by the Muslim historians, Hāsān Nizāmi[28] and Firishtā.[29]

The occupation of Mahobā by the Cauhāns and the appointment of Pajjun Rāi as the governor of Mahobā, as mentioned in these accounts, are statements hardly corroborated by any other evidence. That the city fell to the Cauhāns in 1182 A.D., and that it was plundered, is borne out by the Madanpur records; but it is difficult to prove that the Cauhāns retained their hold on it for any length of time. The capture of Kālañjar by Pṛthvīrāja's forces is also more than can be admitted. Inscriptions are found to have been issued by Paramardideva both from Kālañjar and Mahobā within two years of its fall to the Cauhāns, i.e., 1184 A.D., as quoted above.

It may be quite probable that the fortress never passed out of the hands of the Candellas. It was there that the seat of the government was shifted during the seige of Mahobā. The account of the Parmāl Rāso about the rise of the Banāphars under Indal Kumār, son of Ālhā, and liberation of Parmāl, appears easier to believe. The Banāphars thus might have been instrumental in compelling the Cauhāns to raise the seige and leave for Delhi, before they had time to consolidate their position.

According to the Pṛthvīrāj Rāso, Samarjit, a son of Parmāl, with the help of Narasiṁha, an officer of Rājā Jaicānd of Kanauj, captured Mahobā from Pajjun Rāi, the Thānāpati of Pṛthvīrāj, and ruled over the whole territory between Kālañjar and Gayā. He is, however, not mentioned in any of the Candella records.

So the story of the Cauhān occupation of the Candella dominions was either a fabrication by the bardic authors, or, if there is any truth in it, the occupation may have lasted for a very short period. In fact, the Candella records issued

---

[27] *A.S.R.*, XXI., Pp. 37-38.
[28] *Elliot.*, II., 231-32.
[29] *T.F.*, I., P. 197.

from 1184 A.D. onwards, which describe Paramardi with the usual imperial titles, do not indicate that his position was relegated to a petty local chiefship. The Baṭeśvar Inscription of 1195 A.D. mentions that 'the foot-stool of Paramardi was pale red with the lustre of the crest-jewels of kings i.e., the Sāmantas, bowing down before him'.[30] Besides, the Kālañjar record of 1201 A.D. mentions him as '*Daśārṇādhināthā*' (Lord of the Daśārṇa country),[31] which has been taken by Dr. H. C. Ray as indicative of his recovery of a substantial portion of his territory.[32] But from whom did he recover, and in which particular encounter? It is not mentioned in any of the documents how and from whom it was recovered. Secondly, if it was a case of recovery, it would have been usual for the *praśastikāras* to refer to it. In the absence of any such evidence it may be presumed that the Cauhāns after plundering the city of Mahobā raised the seige and left for Delhi. The Cauhāns probably intended only to cripple the Candellas. They had no intention of annexing any part of the Candella dominion to their own kingdom. Paramardi repaired the damages caused by the enemy, and stabilised his hold over Mahobā in a short time.

But Paramardi was really an unfortunate king. Hardly could be recover from the shattering blows of the Cauhāns, when his territories came to be invaded by a more formidable foe, the Muslims. Kutubuddin, according to the Tāj-ul-Māthir, accompained by Sāhib Kiran, Shāmsuddin Altāmāsh, and others, proceeded to invade Kālañjar in 599 A.H. (1202 A.D.).[33] 'The accursed Parmār, the *Rāi* of Kālañjar', offered stiff resistance, but could not stand the onslaught of the Muslim invaders, and agreed to surrender. As described by Hāsān Nizāmi, on promise of allegiance he was admitted to the same favours as his ancestors had experienced from Māhmud Sabuktigin. But while he was preparing for the payment of tribute and elephants, he died a

[30] "Āsīt-tato namra-narendra-mauli-ratnaprabhā-pāṭala-pādapīṭhah." *E.I.*, I., P. 209., V. 10.

[31] *A.S.R.*, XXI., P. 37-38.

[32] *D.H.N.I.*, II., P. 720.

[33] *Elliott*, II., Pp. 231-32.

natural death whereupon his minister (Diwān or Māhliā), Āj Deo, reorganised the forces and held out, thus giving much trouble to the enemy. Firishtā, however, records that the minister of Paramardi resolved to hold out and caused his master to be assassinated when he was preparing the tribute to be paid.[34] This theory of violent death of Paramardi is, however, not accepted by all. In spite of this resistance the fort could not be defended. As the reservoirs of water in the fort dried up due to a severe drought, this last resistance also broke down, and on Monday, the 20th of Rajab, the Candella army was compelled to capitulate. The Fort thus fell to the Muslims, who destroyed the temples and converted them to mosques, and in the words of Nizāmi, "the name idolatory was annihilated." The invaders, no doubt, procured a considerable booty by plundering the establishments in the fort. The government of Kāliñjar was then conferred on Hāzābaruddin Hāsān Ārnāl.

After the occupation of Kālañjar, Kutubuddin directed his army towards Mahobā and subdued it. Firishtā's reference to Mahobā as the capital of the principality of Kālpi, has been taken by Dr. Ray to indicate that Mahobā and the surrounding regions were no longer part of the Candella dominions,[35] which, however, is not true.

Thus ended the long reign of Paramardi, the last great ruler of the Candella dynasty, who had a chequered career. It was during his reign that the Candella power rose to its height. His reign was also marked by serious reverses which crippled the Candella power almost irreparably.

---

[34] *T.F.*, I., P. 197.
[35] *D.H.N.I.*, II., P. 722.

CHAPTER X

AFTER PARAMARDI : TEMPORARY RESTORATION UNDER TRAILOKYAVARMAN.

Trailokyavarman.

It has already been mentioned that the Pṛthvīrāj Rāso refers to one Samarjit as a son of Parmāl, who recovered Mahobā from Pajjun Rāi, the *Thānāpati* of Pṛthvīrāj, and held the territory between Kālañjar and Gayā, till he himself was defeated and killed by Binaeuddin, a Musalmān. Binaeuddin, according to some scholars, may be a misreading for Bāhāuddin Tughril, the governor of Bāyānā in 1196 A.D.[1], who later became the head of a state in Central India after the death of Kutubuddin. But there is no epigraphic corroboration of the facts stated in the Rāso regarding this. The Candella inscriptions, on the other hand, give the name of Trailokyavarman as the immediate successor of Paramardi. Trailokyavarman, the earliest of whose records is dated in V.S. 1261, i.e., 1205 A.D.[2], within a period of three years from the date of the last record of Paramardideva (Kālañjar Inscription of 1201 A.D.[3]), ruled for about 36 years, as understood from the Rewā Copper Plates of 1240-41 A.D.[4] Thus it appears that in spite of the crippling attacks on the Candellas during the reign of Paramardi, their power was not entirely lost, and that a fresh lease of life was given to it by Trailokyavarman. This successor of Paramardi quickly recovered Kālañjar from the Turkish occupants of the hill fortress and once again the Caṇdella ruler Trailokyavarman found himself justified in using the family's favourite title 'Kālañjarādhipati'. The recapture of the fortress from the Turks is clearly indicated in the Gārrā Plates of Trailokyavarman[5] himself as well as in the Ajaygaḍh Inscription of Vīravarman[6].

[1] *T.F.*, P. 195; *I.A.*, XXXVII., P. 145, f.n. 50.
[2] The Gārrā Plates., *E.I.*, XVI., P. 272-77.
[3] *J.A.S.B.*, XVII., Pt. I (1848), P. 313-17.
[4] *I.A.*, XVII., P. 224-36.
[5] *E.I.*, XVI., P. 272-77.
[6] *ibid.*, I., P. 327, 329., V. 7.

The object of the issue of the Gārrā Plates is to record the grant of Kaḍohā-grāma in the Pāniūlī viṣaya (modern Pānnā)[7], and Lohasihaṇi-grāma in the Vikrauṇi viṣaya (modern Bijāwār District)[8], to Rāuta Sāmanta, son of Rāuta Pāpe, of the Bhāradvāja gotra, who was killed at Kakaḍadaha in a battle with the Turuṣkas.[9] The Ajaygaḍh record describes Trailokyavarman as a vertitable Boar incarnation of Viṣṇu, whose superhuman power was shown in recovering the Candella state, submerged by the waves of the Turuṣka invasion.[10]

Available evidence therefore indicates that although the Candella power was eclipsed by the Turuṣka invaders, who captured the Kālañjara fort, lying under their occupation for sometime, Trailokyavarman was able to strengthen his position to such an extent that its recapture was made possible and actually accomplished under his leadership. But the success must have been won at the cost of valuable lives. It is to be learnt from the Gārrā Plates that in the battle at Kakaḍadaha Rāuta Pāpe laid down his life. A grant of 'Mṛtyukavṛtti'[11] was made for the maintenance of the family of the deceased warrior who had contributed to the victory of the Candellas. The improvement of the Candella position in the reign of Trailokyavarman, as depicted in the Ajaygaḍh Inscription, cannot be regarded as unreal in view of the specific details discussed above. The assumption of the title of 'Kālañjarādhipati' by Trailokyavarman after its reconquest by him seems to have been quite proper.

That the fortress passed out of the Muslim hands and remained with the Candella chief is also evident from the account of the Tabaqāt i Nāsiri, in which it is stated that in the year 631 H. (A.D. 1233) Mālik Nusratuddin Tāishi led an army from Gwāliyur towards Kāliñjar, causing discomfiture to the Rāe of Kāliñjar,[12] who had not the courage

[7] "Pāniūlī-viṣayāntahpātī Kaḍohagrāme" L. 7., *E.I.*, XVI., P. 275.
[8] "Vikrauṇi-viṣayāntahpātī-Lohasihaṇīgrāma". L. 7. *ibid.*, XVI., P. 276.
[9] "Kakaḍadaha Turuṣka-yuddhe-mṛta" L. 10-11, *ibid.*, P. 275. "Kakaḍadaha Turuṣkena saha yuddhe mṛta". L. 11, *ibid.*, P. 276.
[10] *E.I.*, I., P. 327., V. 7.
[11] *ibid.*, XVI., P. 275-76.
[12] *T.N.*, I., P. 732-33.

to face his enemy. The Muslim General plundered the city and obtained a fabulous booty. Thus it is a clear proof that the fort must have continued to be in the possession of the Hindus until 1233 A.D. The Ajaygaḍh Rock Inscription not only gives credit to Trailokyavarman for the recovery of Candella dominions but also mentions that he was 'a very creator in providing strong places' (durgga-pravidhāna-vedaḥ),[13] which probably means that a reshuffling of fortifications at Kālañjar was carried out after it had been recaptured by him. The Muslim account says that he fled without giving a fight to the Turkish attackers in 1233 A.D. But on this point one cannot however vouch for the strictest accuracy of the Muslim writer.

The victory at Kakaḍadaha, recorded in the Gārrā Plates[14] evidently gave back to the Candellas the prospect, which they were fast losing in the estimation of the contemporary political powers, and more than that, confidence in their own strength and capacity, without which further development was impossible. Trailokyavarman after this momentous victory marched along the south-eastern side to the north Bāghelkhand, and extended his power at the cost of the Kalacuris. It may be mentioned that the Mahārāṇakas of Kakareḍika (modern Kakreri) were feudatories of the Kalacuri rulers Jayasiṁha and Vijayasiṁha, as recorded in the Rewā Grants of 1175 and 1195 A.D.[15] But the Rewā Grants of 1240-41[16] show that the same family of the Mahā rāṇakas of Kakareḍika had subsequently transferred their allegiance to the Candella ruler Trailokyavarman. In referring to their new overlord the praśastikāras of the the Mahāraṇaka family used even the epithets particularly associated with their previous master, the Kalacuris, viz., "Paramabhaṭṭāraka Mahārājādhirāja Parameśvara Parama-Māheśvara Vāmadevapādānudhyāta Paramabhaṭṭāraka Mahārājādhirāja Parameśvara Parama-Māheśvara Trika-

[13] *E.I.,* I., P. 329., V. 7.
[14] *ibid.,* XVI., P. 272.
[15] *I.A.* XVII., Pp. 224-30
[16] *ibid.,* Pp. 230-36.

liṅgādhipati nijabhujopārjita aśvapati gajapati rājatrayādhipati Trailokyavarmmadeva kalyāṇa vijaya-rājye"

The exact date of this transfer of authority is however not indicated in these records, but it must have happened some time between the years 1205 and 1240 A.D. It is quite likely that the incident came about close on the heels of the victory of the Candellas over the Turks at Kakaḍadaha in about 1205 A.D., which revived the political importance of the Candellas. Some light is thrown on this matter by the damaged Tripuri Inscription of Kalacuri year 962 (1211 A.D.), as deciphered by Dr. N. P. Chakravarti, and the Dhureṭi Copper Plate of K. 963 (1212 A.D.).[17] The former refers to the Kalacuri ruler Vijayasiṁha and evidently was issued during his reign. But the latter acknowledges Candella Trailokyavarman as the ruling sovereign. If the contention of Dr. Chakravarti in reading the date of the Tripuri record is admitted then it may reasonably be presumed that the area passed under Candella occupation sometime in K. 962-63 (1211-12 A.D.).[18] What is more significant in this connection is that the record mentions one Malayasiṁha, a Mahāmahattaka and Māṇḍalika, appointed as a minister (mantrin) by Trailokyavarman. He is identified with a Sāmanta and Māṇḍalika of the same name, mentioned in the Cedi records of K. 944 and K. 962. That is, this Chief officer of the Kalacuris not only transferred his allegiance to the Candellas but served the Candella king in the capacity of his minister.

The find of the Panwār hoard of coins which included some of the coins of Madanavarman also led scholars to presume an extension of the Candella boundaries in the northern Bāghelkhand region during the reign of Madanavarman.[19] But a simple find of a coin-hoard of a particular royal family in a region adjacent to its own is not always a sure proof of the extension of administrative boundaries, as coins could be carried from one place to a neighbouring region for various

[17] *E.I.*, XXV., P. 1.
[18] *ibid.*
[19] *D.H.N.I.*, II., P. 711.

reasons. On the other hand the Rewā Grants of the Mahārāṇakas of Kakareḍika owing allegiance to the Cedi rulers,[20] as mentioned above, furnish positive evidence of the latter's hold on the region upto 1195 A.D. The presumption that the region had formerly been conquered by the Candellas from whom it was recaptured during the gloomy period of Paramardi's reign, is not also based on indisputable evidence.[20a] The find of the Panwār hoard on the basis of which a previous Candella occupation is sought to be proved cannot be regarded as a dependable piece of evidence. The Dhureṭi Copper Plate of the Śaiva teachers (1212 A.D.)[21] and the Rewā Grants of 1240-41 A.D.[22] of the Mahārāṇaka family, accepting Candella Trailokyavarman as their overlord, furnish however a positive proof of the expansion of the Candella territory to the upper courses of the Śon in the northern Bāghelkhand, and the continuance of the Candella hold on the area even at the time when the Kālañjar fortress was lost to the Muslims.

The Rock inscription from Ajaygaḍh of the time of Bhojavarman refers to the subjugation of the tribals, viz., the Bhillas, the Śabaras and the Pulindas (ājñākarān-pallinivāsinoyaṁ cakāra Bhillān-Śabarān-Pulindān)[23] by Kāyastha Ānanda, a military officer of Trailokyavarman, who appointed him as the governor of Jayadurga or Ajaygaḍh fort (durggādhikāre nṛpatiḥ pracakre). Vāse or Vāseka, the elder brother of Ānanda, was also an important military leader under Trailokyavarman. His victory against 'the irresistible Bhojuka' (Bhojukaṁ yudhi yuddhadurmmadanidhiṁ), who was 'rending the kingdom into two' (dvairājyaṁ janayantaṁ), is highly eulogised in the record.[24] The identity of Bhojuka is most uncertain. Kielhorn has suggested the identification of Bhojuka, killed by Vāseka, with Aśvavaidya Ṭhakkura Bhojuka,[25] father of Abhayadeva of

---

[20] *I.A.*, XVII., P. 224-30.
[20a] *D.H.N.I.*, II., P. 794, *C.I.I.*, IV, P. cv-cvi.
[21] *E.I.*, XXV., Pp. 1 ff.
[22] *I.A.*, XVII., Pp. 230-36.
[23] *E.I.*, I., P. 334., V. 22.
[24] *ibid.*, V. 19.
[25] *ibid.*, P. 332.

Ajaygaḍh Stone Inscription of the time of Vīravarman, dated 1268 A.D. In the absence of clearer evidence it is difficult to accept the contention. But from the nature of the expression 'rending the kingdom into two' it may be presumed that Bhojuka was an internal enemy of considerable power and influence, possibly a rebel trying to create disaffection against Trailokyavarman. For the signal service rendered by Vāseka he was decorated with the title of 'Viśiṣa' of Jayadurga by Trailokyavarman and was granted the village of Varbhavarī.[26]

Thus we find that Trailokyavarman was an able ruler who did much to save the Candella power from annihilation and also contributed to its expansion in a most difficult period of its history. He came to the throne at a very critical moment, when the fortunes of the state were enveloped by darkness. The particular merit of his service is emphasised in the passage which stated that he was 'a Viṣṇu in lifting up the earth immersed in the ocean formed by the streams of the Turuṣkas'.[27] At the time of his accession the Candellas were in a miserable plight. The citadel of Kālañjar was then under a Muslim governor[28] and the seat of government had to be shifted to Ajaygaḍh. It was due to Trailokyavarman's superb organising power that the Candella strongholds were recovered by him and Candella authority established from the Betwā in the west to the Śon in the east, and from Bāṇḍā and Hamirpur districts in the north to Pānnā in the south. Trailokya was not an insignificant chieftain of his time. The Mahā rāṇakas of Kakareḍika were among the feudatories who accepted him as their overlord.[29]

It is not unlikely that the fort of Kālañjara could not be permanently annexed by the Muslims as a result of the attack in 1233 A.D. Cunningham[30] refers to a passage in the Tabaqāt i Nāsiri[31] which may indirectly render it likely

[26] *ibid.*, P. 334., V. 17.
[27] *E.I.*, I., P. 327, 329. V. 7.
[28] *Elliot.*, II., P. 232.
[29] *I.A.*, XVII., Pp. 230-36.
[30] *A.S.R.*, I., P. 457.
[31] *T.N.*, I., P. 680-83., *Elliot.* II., P. 348.

that Trailokyavarman ruled over Kālañjar as late as 1247 A.D. The account mentions a Rāṇā named '*Dalaki wa Malaki*' as ruling in a mountainous tract not far from Kara (Allahabad District) which was plundered by Ulugh Khān in the reign of Sultān Nāsiruddin in 645 A.H. (1247 A.D.). According to Firishtā '*Dalaki wa Malaki*' (and not two Rājāhs, *Dulky* and *Mulky*, as translated by Briggs) resided at Kālañjar.[32] Cunningham holds that the correct original form was '*Tilaki wama Deo*' (Trailokyavarmmadeva), which was corrupted as *Dalaki wa Malaki* by Persian calligraphists.[33] If the contention of Cunningham is accepted, the story quoted above may be taken as applying to Trailokyavarman, who must have in that case ruled for a few more years till 1247 A.D. But the question arises as to whether he did recapture the fortress of Kālañjar once again after its fall in 1233 A.D. It may be mentioned here that Kālañjar remained in the possession of Vīravarman, the son and successor of Trailokya. It seems quite probable that Tāishi, the Muslim invader, plundered the fortress, which was not really conquered, and that the Candellas did not lose possession of it, which continued to remain in their hands in spite of repeated attacks till the 16th century.

Vīravarman.

Vīravarman succeeded Trailokyavarman to the throne, but the exact date of his accession is not known. The earliest record is dated in 1317 V.S.[34] (1259-60 A.D.). If 'Dalaki wa Malaki' of Tabaqāt-i-Nāsiri[35] is taken to be identical with Trailokyavarman, Vīravarman may be presumed to have ascended the throne sometime between 1247 and 1259 A.D. Of his reign we have the following records. (1) the Chārkhāri Plate of V.S. 1311[36], (2) the Ajaygaḍh Rock Inscription of V.S. 1317, (3) the Jhansi Inscription of V.S. 1318[37],

[32] *T.F.*, I. P. 237.
[33] *A.S.R.*, I., P. 457.
[34] *E.I.*, I., P. 325-30.
[35] *Elliot.*, II., P. 348.
[36] *E.I.*, XX., Pp. 132-34.
[37] *ibid.*, App. No. 560.

(4) the Dahi Plate of V.S. 1337[38], and (5) the Gurhā Sati Stone Inscription of V.S. 1342 (1286 A.D.)[39]. Two more inscriptions from Kālañjar were noticed, one by Cunningham, which traced the Candella genealogy from Vijayapāla to Vīravarman, and the other by Kielhorn, dated in V.S. 1340 (A.D. 1283)[40], which falls within the reign-period of Vīravarman. Another stone inscription dated V.S. 1372 (1315 A.D.)[41] of the reign of Vīravarman, was found from Ajaygaḍh. But as we have an Ajaygaḍh record of V.S. 1345[42] (A.D 1288), in which Bhojavarman is mentioned as the king, Dr. Ray doubted the proposed reading of the date, and that of the name of the king, recorded in the other inscription[43]. It is not unlikely, as suggested by Cunningham, that Vīravarman of the latter record might have been a second prince of the same name succeeding Bhojavarman sometime after 1288 A.D.

The Chārkhāri Plate (V.S. 1311) mentions the battle of Sondhi, in which one Dabhyuhaḍavarman of Candreśvarānvaya was defeated by Rāuta Abhi, a general of Vīravarman[44]. Sondhi is identical with Seondhā fort, now called Kānhārgarh on the banks of the Sindh river in the Datiā State. Rai Bahadur Hiralal, who has edited the inscription suggests that it was a battle between persons of the same family, viz. the Candellas[45]. It is difficult to believe that Dabhyuhaḍavaraman was a member of the Candella family, occupying any portion of the territory against the lineal descendant of Trailokyavarman. On the other hand the suggestion that the gift of a village to the general who achieved the victory would accrue religious merit to the predecessors of the king[46], indicates that he was either a usurper or a rebel trying to create troubles within the state.

---

[38] *ibid.*, App. No. 600.; *A.S.R.*, XXI., Pp. 74-76.
[39] *ibid.*, App. No. 608.
[40] *ibid.*, App. No. 604.
[41] *A.S.R.*, XXI., P. 54.
[42] *E.I.*, XXVIII., P. 98-107.
[43] *D.H.N.I.*, II., P. 732., f.n. 4.
[44] *E. I.*, XX., P. 133. Ll. 13-14.
[45] *ibid.*, P. 132.
[46] *ibid.*, P. 133., Ll. 12-13.

Vīravarman fortunately had not to encounter any Muslim attack during his rule, at least the Muslim chronicles do not mention any. He seems to have enjoyed a peaceful reign maintaining direct control over a large part of his ancestral territory including Khajurāho, where a unique gold dramma of Vīravarman has been recovered[47]. If the evidence of the findspots of the records of his reign is taken into consideration, it may be permitted to draw such an inference about the extent of his kingdom. His dominion, comprising the fortresses of Kālañjar and Ajaygaḍh, extended upto the Betwā on the west, near which was found the Gurhā Stone Inscription. The evidence of the Dahi Grant suggests that the western boundary extended further. This inscription seems to claim that his territory was bounded by Nalapura or Narwar and Gopagiri or Gwālior in the north-west, and Madhuvana or Mathurā in the north.[48] According to this record, Balbhadra Mallaya "an illustrious chief of distinguished bravery" is said to have conquered the lord of Narwar (Nalapurapati) Gopāla, the ruler of Mathura (Madhuvanakādhipa) and Harirāja of Gwālior (Gopagiri). Dr. D. C. Sircar reads 'Nalapurapati' as an epithet for 'Gopāla'[49], and, identifies him with Gopāla of Yajvapāla family, of whom a number of stone inscriptions were found at Narwar in the Shivapuri district of the former Gwālior state[50]. Some of these records, dated in V.S. 1338 current (or V.S. 1337 expired), Caitra sudi 7, Friday, (28th March 1281 A.D.) were found in Baṅglā, a small village near Narwar fort, inscribed on stone pillars commemorating warriors who lost their lives fighting on behalf of Gopāla against Candella Vīravarman.[51] Some of the records claim to have obtained victory repulsing the invading King Vīravarman. Thus the Dahi grant and the Baṅglā records are mutually corroborative, though, of course,

[47] *C. C. I. M.*, I., p. 224; *J. A. S. B.*, 1889, Pt. 1., p. 34.
[48] *A. S. R.*, XXI., pp. 74-76.
[49] *I. H. Q.*, XXXII., p. 405.
[50] *Annual administration report of the Archaeological Department of Gwalior State*, V. S. 1991 (1934-35); *Gwālior Rājyake Abhilekh* (Hindi) by H. N. Dvivedi.
[51] *E. I.*, XXXI; *I. H. Q.* XXXII. p. 403; The battle is stated to have been fought on the banks of the river Baruā (modern) and seems to have lasted only for a day. Vīravarman was accompanied by four other Kings, as stated in two of the Baṅglā records. Evidently they were his allies or vassals.

with the partisan's bias on either side. The nett result, therefore, as suggested by Dr. Sircar, was that "the army of Vīravarman invaded the Kingdom of Yajvapāla Gopāla and succeeded in penetrating as far as the immediate neighbourhood of the latter's capital at Nalapura (Narwar). The Candella King was most probably repulsed after having gained some initial successes."[52] It should be pointed out that there is hardly any corroborative evidence in support of the other claims advanced in the Dahi Grant. It is not clear how in the face of the growing power of the Muslims in the second half of the 13th and the first half of the 14th centuries, it was possible for the Candellas to have held sway over such an extensive kingdom without fighting a battle with the Muslims. The Muslim accounts, including Firishtā, mentions Sultān Nāsiruddin's subjugation of Bundelkhand and his apointment of a governor in about 1251 A.D. The regions subdued were Gwālior, Chanderi and Mālwā.[53] But the Muslims could not completely eliminate indigenous rule in the principalities mentioned above, where local dynasties are known to have continued, although much reduced in power.

Verses 8 and 9 of the Ajaygaḍh Record (1317 A.D.)[54] in a conventional style paint him as a great fighter. He is described as one who delighted the damsels of heaven by sending them, as lovers, the hostile heroes whom he cut down in the field of battle. He is compared with Viṣṇu riding on Garuḍa, and also with Śiva roaming about on his bull, extirpating elements of wickedness on the earth, which may mean that he ruled with firmness at a time when disorderly forces were trying to gain the upper hand.

The Ajaygaḍh record of V.S. 1317 was issued to record the benevolent and pious activities of the chief queen of Vīravarman, named Kalyāṇadevī, who built a well with perennial water, a hall for the supply of its water, and a tank at Nandipura (Jayadurga)[55]. The record also refers to the genealogy

[52] *ibid.*, One of the records mentions Vīravarman as 'Caṁdilla' (Candella) and some others refer to his association with 'Jejāhuti' and 'Jejābhukti'.

[53] *C. H. I.*, III., p. 68.

[54] *E.I.*, I., P. 327, 329.

[55] *ibid.*, Pp. 328, 330. V. 18-20.

of the queen. She hailed from the Dadhīci -vaṁsa (V. 10), and was the daughter of Maheśvara (V. 11)[56], who was revered even by the crowned heads. His mother was Vesaladevī, the daughter of king Govinda (V. 13), who according to Cunningham, may have been identical with king Govindarāja of Narwar (Nalapura).

Bhojavarman.

Vīravarman appears to have been succeeded by Bhojavarman between the years V. S. 1342 (1286 A.D.) and V.S. 1345 (1288 A.D.). As already mentioned, the last dated record belonging to the reign of Vīravarman is V.S. 1342, while the earliest known of Bhojavarman's is dated V.S. 1345. It is probable that Bhojavarman was the son and successor of Vīravarman, but there is no definite evidence on the point.

The available records assigned to the reign of Bhojavarman are all found from Ajaygaḍh. They are, —(i) a Stonc Inscription dated in V.S. 1345[57] (ii) a Sati stone record dated V.S. 1346,[58] and (iii) a Rock Inscription, which is undated.[59] Excepting the Sati Record, both the other Ajaygaḍh inscriptions were issued by ministers of Bhojavarman, the dated one by Kāyastha Nāna, and the undated one by another Kāyastha, named Subhaṭa, the *Kośādhikārādhipati*. These records, however, do not throw any light on the political condition of his time, nor do they ascribe any achievement to Bhojavarman. It is evident that the Candellas had now little scope or opportunity left for conspicuous action in the political field. But a study of documents of their ministers reveal that though the power of the Candellas must have been declining, their administrative organisation was maintained with the help of efficient councillors and officials, whose loyalty to the throne was an inherited virtue.

It is not possible to ascertain the exact limits of Bhojavarman's dominion due to paucity of data. But that the

[56] *A.S.R.*, XXI., P. 51.
[57] *E.I.*, XXVIII., P. 98-107.
[58] *ibid.*, XX., P. 135.
[59] *ibid.*, I., P. 330-38.

Ajaygaḍh fort was still under the possession of the Candellas is evident from two records mentioned above. The Kālañjar fort was also under the Candellas till V.S. 1365, when in a Sati Stone Record found in the territory held by a feudatory prince, Mahārājaputra Vāghadeva, the last known Candella ruler, 'Śrīmad-Hammīravarmadeva', their overlord, is mentioned as 'Kālañjarādhipati' (Lord of the Kālañjar fort).[60] That the Candella occupation of the fortress of Kālañjar did not cease in the intervening period is evident from the Chārkhāri record of V.S. 1346, which also refers to Hammīravarman as 'Kālañjarādhipati', though the reigning king was Bhojavarman.[61] The question whether Hammīravarman held the fort of Kālañjar as Bhojavarman's viceroy, or independently as the latter's rival, has raised controversy. Rai Bahadur Hiralal suggests that the absence of the grandiloquent titles in the case of Hammīravarman indicates that he was never recognised as the Mahārāja while his elder brother, Bhojavarmadeva was on the throne.[62] The view that the two were brothers is not based on any evidence, but is a pure assumption, which may be probable, but cannot be proved to be true. Further, the explanation offered by Hiralal regarding the assumption of the most favourite epithet of the Candella rulers, viz., Kālañjarādhipati, by the brother of the reigning prince, is also a guess. It may not be unlikely that Bhojavarman had a short reign and that after his death in V.S. 1346, Hammīravarman occupied the throne in the same year sometime before the month of 'Bhādrapada.'[63]

Hammīravarman.

The last known ruler of the Candella family was Hammīravarman, of whom we have a copper plate grant in V.S. 1346 mentioned above. In that record he has been definitely mentioned as meditating on the feet of Sri Vīravarmana-

[60] *ibid.*, XVI., P. 11., f.n. 1, 2.
[61] *ibid.*, XX., P. 134-36.
[62] *ibid.*, P. 135.
[63] The date of the record as given in *ibid*, P. 136, L. 13 is "Saṁvat 1346 samaye/ Bhādrapada Vadi 12 Ravau/ Puṣyanakṣatre//".

deva.[64] It is difficult to prove that they were brothers, as already stated. The succession appears to have, however, been peaceful.

Three records are available for his reign. Those are, (i) the Chārkhāri Plate of V.S. 1346, (ii & iii) two Sati Stone inscriptions, one from Ajaygaḍh fort[65] and the other from Bāmhni,[66] a village in the Dāmoh District in the Central Provinces. The findspots of these records suggest that Hammīravarman not only held the ancestral dominion of the Candellas including Mahobā region in the Hamirpur district and Ajaygaḍh, but also portions of Dāmoh and Jabalpur districts of the Central Provinces, on either side of the Bhānrer range of the Vindhyas. The Bāmhni Sati record furnishes the interesting information that Mahārājaputra Śrī Vāghadeva, the local ruler, described as a 'Pratihāra chief', was a feudatory of Candella Hammīravarman. Both these Sati records being dated in V.S. 1365 indicates that Hammīravarman had a fairly long reign of at least about 20 years from V.S. 1346 to V.S. 1365. Another Sati record has been found from a village named Salaiyā, 3 miles from Bāmhni in V.S. 1366 (A.D. 1309), which mentions '*Alayadina Sultāna*' (Sultan Ālāuddin) as the reigning king[67]. Thus with the occupation of Bundelkhanḍ by Ālāuddin the history of the independent Candella dynasty came to an end by 1309 A.D. Vestiges of the Candella power may have lingered after this date in some small fortified areas, but the glories of the Candellas became a part of ancient legend, which could not be revived under the imperial sway of the Muslim rulers.

---

[64] *ibid.*, p. 135., L. 6.
[65] *ibid.*, XX., p. 134, f. n. 2.
[66] *ibid.*, XVI., p. 10., f. n. 2; *ibid.*, XIV., p. 30.
[67] *ibid.*, XVI.m p. 11., f. n. 2.

CHAPTER XI

ADMINISTRATION

Inscriptions of the reigns of the Candella rulers do not furnish a systematic and consistent account of their administrative organisation. It is clear however that their government, as in other contemporary states, was wholly of the prevailing monarchical type. The Candella King was the pivot of the administrative structure, without whom the state had no existence. He must have enjoyed an authority, which presumably was not subject to any constitutional check exercised by a popular assembly or any other such institution, to which no reference has been made in their extant records. Theoretically the constituents of the state, were the 'Sapta Prakṛtis', as conceived by the political thinkers of ancient India. The Māu Inscription alludes to '*aṅgāni sapta*'[1], the seven constituent parts of the state structure, leaving the expression undefined. By this must have been meant, the king (svāmī), the ministers (amātya), the realm (janapada), the capital (durga), the treasury (kośa), the army (bala), and the ally (mitra)[2]. Thus the other 'limbs', besides the king, were functioning in the Candella state. As known from the inscriptional sources there were ministers in the Candella kingdom, representing the 'limb' known as 'amātya'. Military power (bala), without which the Candellas could not have expanded their territory, must have also functioned as an effective limb. That the treasury, i.e., the kośa, constituted another essential element of the state, is shown in the use of the expression 'kośādhikārādhipati'.[3]

The King

The Candella kings generally assumed the usual imperial

---

[1] *E. I.,* I., p. 198., V. 8.
[2] *Mbh., S. P.,* 69, 65. *Manu,* IX., 294. *K. A.* (*Shamasastry*)., VI., 1., p. 287.
[3] *E. I.,* I., p. 335., V. 29.

titles in their official documents, viz., Parameśvara, Paramabhaṭṭāraka, Mahārājādhirāja, &c. But it is of interest to note that the early rulers of the family upto Yaśovarman are mentioned in the records simply as, rājan,[4] nṛpa,[5] mahīpati,[6] kṣitipa,[7] nṛpakulatilakah,[8] kṣitidharatilakah[9], &c. The usual imperial designations were used by their successors from the time of Dhaṅga, who succeeded Yaśovarman. Yaśovarman, it may be mentioned, was the real architect of the greatness of the Candellas, but, as he retained at least a show of allegiance to the Imperial Pratihāras, he did not assume any mark of formal independence. The conquest of Kālañjar by Yaśovarman was an important incident in the history of the Candellas, and this was signified by the assumption of the epithet of 'Kālañjarādhipati' by his successors. Another title, Parama-Māheśvara, frequently adopted by the Candellas in some of their records symbolises their devotion to the Śaiva cult.

The influence of the Kalacuris, whom the Candella rulers defeated, is noticed in the adoption of the *Gaja-Lakṣmī* emblem on the latter's seals and coins. To the same influence was due the assumption of the well-known Kalacuri titles by some of Candella rulers, viz., "Parama-Māheśvara Śrīmad Vāmadevapādānudhyāta", and "Trikaliṅgādhipati nijabhujopārjit-āśvapati-gajapati-narapati rājatrayādhipati", pre fixed to the name of Candella Trailokyavarman in the Rewā copper plate of Kumārapāla.[10] The Dhureṭi copper plate[11] issued shortly after the conquest of Rewā area by Trailokyavarman also reveals that, besides the Kalacuri titles, some titles of the Gāhaḍavāla rulers viz., 'Paramabhaṭṭāraketyādi-samasta rājāvalīvirājamāna' ('The king endowed with all the royal titles, commencing with Paramabhaṭṭāraka'), 'vividha-vidyā-vicāravācaspati' (expert like a Vācas-

4 *ibid.*, p. 327., V. 5.
5 *ibid.*, p. 334., V. 15 uses 'nṛpati' *ibid.*, p. 142, V. 21.
6 *ibid.*, p. 141., V. 14.
7 *ibid.*, p. 327., V. 7. Uses of 'kṣitipāla', 'kṣitidhara' and 'kṣitibhuja' are also found in other records.
8 *ibid.*, p. 126, 132., V. 23.
9 *ibid.*, p. 129., V. 43.
10 *I. A.*, VII. pp. 230-36.
11 *E. I.*, XXV., p. 2.

pati or Bṛhaspati in the pursuit of different sciences) and 'Kānyakubjādhipati' (lord of Kānyakubja), were used with the name of the Candella king. Some of the titles are specially significant. The description of the king as "vividhavidyā-vicāra-vācaspati" proves that he must have been acquainted with the sciences studied in his time which led to the sharpening of his intellect and development of his power of judgment. A Satī record of the time of Hammīravarman (A. D. 1308)[12] and the Chārkhāri Copper Plate of Hammīravarman (1346 V.S.)[13] also use the title 'rājāvalītrayopeta' for the ruler, evidently implying 'aśvapati', 'gajapati', and 'narapati'. In L. 12 of the Dhureṭi Copper Plate Trailokyavarman is given the epithet, 'Triśatīrājyādhipati' (the lord of the kingdom consisting of three hundred), which is not met with elsewhere.[14]

None of these records excepting the Chārkhāri Plate of V.S. 1346 is an official document of the Candella rulers. Hence it may be doubted if all the titles mentioned above were officially assumed by them. It may be noted that those titles occur particularly in the records connected with these areas which had been under the Kalacuri or the Gāhaḍavāla rule. Another interesting title used by Candella Hammīravarman himself and also attached to the names of his predecessors in the Chārkhāri plate of V.S. 1346 is 'Sāhi',[15] probably indicative of the growing Muslim influence in the courts of northern and central India.

Succession.

The Candella monarchy was normally hereditary, the son succeeding the father on the throne. Even if the son was a minor, it was customary to instal him on the throne. The legendary Parmāl Rāso gives instance while referring to the case of Paramardi, who was only a boy of five when called upon to succeed his father.[16] Early accession to the throne by

[12] *ibid.*, XVI., p. 10., f.n. 4.
[13] *ibid.*, XX., p. 134-35.
[14] *ibid.*, XXV., p. 5.
[15] *ibid.*, XX., p. 134-35.
[16] *P. R.*, II., V. 108., p. 28.

Paramardi is proved by epigraphic testimony, where he is described as "bālopi netā."[17] It was necessary to make some sort of arrangement for the actual administration of the territory if such a situation arose, but we have no information about that.

The Candella records do not contain any hint of rivalry for the throne in the royal family. If the reigning king died without leaving any male issue, the throne passed without any trouble to the younger brother of the deceased ruler. The history of the Candellas furnishes two cases of peaceful succession by collateral members. Jayaśakti, one of the early rulers, having no direct heir, was succeeded by his younger brother, Vijayaśakti. It is noteworthy that both the names are mentioned in the records of the latter's successors. Kīrtivarman also came to the throne after the death of Devavarman, his elder brother. Another interesting case is that of Pṛthvīvarman, who ascended the throne after the death of his nephew, Jayavarman.[18] There is no evidence to show that these were cases of disputed succession. Rai Bahadur Hiralal suggests that Hammīravarman was a younger brother of Bhojavarman on the evidence of non-assumption of the royal title, 'Mahārājādhirāja', by the former in the Chārkhāri Plate of 1346 V.S., Bhojavarman being the ruling sovereign then, as known from the Ajaygaḍh Rock Inscription of the same year.[19] In that case this was also a case of undisputed succession by a younger brother, though the relationship is difficult to be proved.

Khajurāho record of V. S. 1059[20] and a Kālañjar record[21] refer to voluntary abdication of the throne by Dhaṅga and Jayavarman respectively. Dhaṅga, who had lived upto one hundred years, may have abdicated on the ground of infirmity due to old age. Jayavarman retired because, as he himself declared, he felt wearied of government.

[17] *E. I.*, I., p. 327., V. 6.
[18] *ibid.*, pp. 198, 203., V. 12.
[19] *ibid.*, XX., p. 135.
[20] *ibid.*, I., pp. 137-47., V. 55.
[21] *J. A. S. B.*, 1848., Pt. I., pp. 318-19.

The eldest son of the reigning king was regarded as his heir-apparent, while the younger sons were often appointed to responsible posts. The Dudāhi stone inscription[22] refers to Devalabdhi, and his father, Kṛṣṇapa, a son of Yaśovarman, which suggests that his family had a special position in this region. Dudāhi viṣaya was an outlying district of the Candella kingdom, and it acquired a political importance due to its common frontier with the Paramāras. Pratāpa, the younger brother (bhrātā kanīyān) of king Madanavarman is described in a Kālañjar inscription[23] as a very influential person in the court, and he undertook diverse works of public interest, including erection of temples, construction of tanks and gardens and providing care for the sick and indigent subjects.

There is reference to the ritual of coronation ceremony (mūrddhābhiṣikta)[24] which a new king had to pass through on his accession to the throne. Details are not indicated in any of the records. But the signs of royalty, as referred to in different inscriptions are, siṁhāsana[25] (throne), pādapīṭha[26] (foot stool), ātapatra[27] (royal umbrella), mauli[28] (head garland or the crowṇ), &c. These indicate that the usual splendour and majesty were associated with the royal office of the Candellas. There are references also to the royal retinue and the royal palace.

Personal qualities.

An idea about the requisite qualities of a king can be formed from the eulogistic references to the Candella monarchs in their inscriptions. As described in these records, they were of handsome appearance, (kandarpakalpākṛteh,[29] saurūpāṅgah,)[30] of impressive personality (pauruṣa),[31] learning

[22] *I. A.*, XVIII., p. 237.
[23] *J. A. S. B.* (1848), Pt. I., p. 318, L. 15.
[24] *E. I.*, I., p. 327., V. 11.
[25] *ibid.*, I., p. 122, L. 9.
[26] *ibid.*, p. 209., V. 10.
[27] *ibid.*, p. 201., V. 42.
[28] *ibid.*, p. 197., V. 5.
[29] *ibid.*, p. 125., V. 11.
[30] *ibid.*, p. 126., V. 21.
[31] *ibid.*, p. 128., V. 33.

(vidyāvadātahṛdaya[32]), proficiency in arts and poetic talents (kāvyālaṁkārachando-lakṣaṇaguṇagaṇādhiṣṭhāna),[33] virtuous and of pleasing conduct ('subhacarita-pavitrah',[34] 'sadvṛttasya ca sadma'),[34a] devoted to Dharma ("Dharmavatsalah" "Dharmādhārah" "Dhārmmikah" "Dharmmamekohi-sakhā"),[35] &c. Their ability to protect the state against internal and external enemies in the same way as a 'kulavadhū' is protected, and their ability to eradicate social evils (kaṇṭakaśodhana) as well as their tolerant attitude and policy to different forms of religion are also referred to. Their munificence is often highly spoken of and they are described as the veritable 'kalpataru', the tree that fulfills all desires.[36]

Not only in the Candella inscriptions but everywhere when a king is praised, either in epigrahic or literary records, these qualities are attributed to him. It may however be pointed out that the Candella praśastikāras considered such qualities to be essenial for a king. In view of the duties which the kings had to perform, these qualities were required for efficient administration and pursuit of a successful policy at home and abroad. They were well in accord with the practical requirements of satesmanship and administration.

Divine comparisons.

Kings of the Candella family, as was customary in those days, have been compared to some of the deities of the Brahmanical pantheon or legendary heroes. The family claims to have originated from the Moon-God, and mythological sages, like Marīci, Atri, &c., of the Candravaṁśa. Moreover later rulers like Kīrtivarman and Trailokyavarman are often compared to Viṣṇu. In the Deogaḍh Rock

---

[32] *E.I.*, P. 141, V. 17

[33] *ibid.*, XX., p. 127., L. 8. Some of the Candella rulers were eminent poets and scholars. Parmardi claims to have composed an eulogy to Purāri (Kālañjar Insc.). Bidā (Vidyādhara) is stated to have offered a poetical composition to Māhmud (Firishtā).

[34] *ibid.*, I., p. 198., V. 6.

[34a] *ibid.*, V. 9.

[35] *I. A.*, XVI., p. 203; L. 11.; *E. I.*, I., p. 143, V. 31; *I. A.*, XVI., p. 205; L. 5; *E. I.*, XX., p. 127, L. 11.

[36] *E. I.*, I., p. 198., V. 9.; *ibid.*, p. 125., V. 4.; *I. A.*, XVI p. 202., L. 1., *E. I.* XXXI (Bhārat kalā Bhavan Plates of Madanavarman, V. S. 1192).

inscription Kīrtivarman is likened to Viṣṇu without his usual weapon, 'gadā' (agadam nūtanaṁ Viṣṇum..).[37] and in the Mahobā inscription to Puruṣottama (Viṣṇu).[38] Trailokyavarman is described as 'Turuṣkakulyambudhimagna-dhātri-samuddhṛtiṁ Viṣṇuriva pratanvan'[39] (Just as Viṣṇu, who lifted up the earth in his Varāha incarantion, so Trailokyavarman revived the Candella power, submerged in the ocean formed by the streams of the Turuṣka invaders). It is also claimed for Kīrtivarman in the Deogaḍh record that 'surely Yudhiṣṭhira, Sadāśiva and Rāmacandra—all entered his body'.[40] Brahmā, Dharma, Indra, Kāla, Kubera are some of the other deities with whom the Candella kings are often placed on equal footing. They are also compared to Yudhiṣṭhira, Bhīma, Arjuṇa, Karṇa and Rāma as well as to Bṛhaspati and Śakra. Thus though absolute divinity is not directly claimed, equation with divinities and legendary characters of great celebrity served the purpose of glorifying the sanctity of the hereditary monarchy of the Candellas. The praśastikāras, it may be noted, took up the ideas contained in the Mānava Dharmaśāstra[41] and other such texts regarding the divinity of the king.

Duties and functions.

The supreme position in the state belonged to the king. Final authority in regard to the military and administrative functions of the state rested with him. Epigraphic evidences bear ample testimony to the military campaigns directed personally by the different Candella rulers.[42] It is well known that the Candella power was founded on territorial conquests. Quite naturally therefore, the Candella records give the utmost importance to the part played by the kings personally in military matters. Some of the Candella kings are definitely mentioned to have led their armies in person.

---

[37] *I. A.*, XVIII., p. 238., V. 3.
[38] *E. I.*, I., p. 219., V. 26.
[39] *ibid.*, p. 327., V. 7.
[40] *I. A.*, XVIII., p. 238.
[41] *Manu.* VII., 3-8.
[42] *E. I.*, I., p. 197-98., V. 3-4, 8-10; *ibid.*, p. 217-22., V. 17, 22, 23, 26; *I. A.*, XVI., p. p. 201., V. 3; etc.

Kings themselves are responsible for the formulation of their policies of peace and war. Ministers and military leaders, of course, helped the king in such matters, but, as the Parmāl Rāso shows, Paramardi once disregarded the expert opinion of high military officials and launched a battle with Pṛthvīrāj Cauhān.[43]

Kings' concern in affording protection to the people against internal and external dangers is best evident from the description of the state as '*kulavadhū*'. (kulavadhūmiva vasundharāṁ nirākulāṁ paripālayannavikala viveka nirmalikṛtamati..). This conception is evidently based on the idea that a state is, like a wife, depending entirely on the husband for the protection of her person and honour. As it is the sacred duty of the husband to protect her, so also is the duty of the king to protect his subjects, who are helpless like a wife and should be defended by the king.

Epithets like 'parā-rakṣā bhūteṣvapi' (carefully protecting all beings—Māu Insc., V. 13), 'trasta-trāṇa-praguṇa-manasāṁ' (Khajurāho Insc., II. V. 9), 'trasta-trātari' (Khajurāho Insc., V. 25, protecting the distressed), 'apāsya prajānāṁ bhayaṁ' (removing the fear of the subjects,-Māu Insc., V. 39), 'hṛdi prajānāmātaṅkaśaṅkuṁ' (weapon to destroy fear from the hearts of the subjects, Khajurāho Insc., IV., V. 17), &c., indicate that the Candella rulers were particularly careful in the matter of maintenance of the security of their kingdom. The period was full of troubles and dangers. There were not only external dangers, evil forces were also at work within the Candella territory. The people were afraid of dire calamities threatening them from all sides. A striking emphasis is therefore placed on the king's power to remove terror from their minds.

There are numerous references in the Candella records to the 'weeding out of thorns' ('kṛtya kaṇṭaka śodhanaṁ janapade'—Māu Record., V. 39, 'ucchinnah kaṇṭakaugha' Māu Record., V. 8, 'dūrādhah kṛta kaṇṭakasya'—Baṭeśvar

---

[43] *P. R.*, pp. 42-43.

Insc., V. 24, 'sphītaṁ rājyaṁ akaṇṭakaṁ'—Rock Insc. of Bhojavarman, V. 20, 'kṣapita nikhila duṣṭah'—Māu Record., V. 6, and 'duṣṭaprahantā'—Rock Insc. of Vīravarman, V. 9), i.e., extermination of the wicked and subversive elements from the kingdom. These references show that the Candella rulers were alert and watchful, and they took stern steps to exterminate all elements of disorder. The king was regarded not only as the supreme administrative head but also he claimed to be the guardian of the traditional social order. The Māu stone inscription describes Sallakṣaṇa as one encouraging and even forcing people of various castes to remain true to their traditional duties.[44] Like all others the king also was subject to Dharma. He was afraid of the consequences resulting from the violation of the sacred law (bhīrurdharmmāparādhe)[45] on his own part. Dharma, which must mean the laws and injunctions embodied in the Śāstras, was the only guide of the king (Dharmmam-ekohi-sakhā)[46] in the performance of his duties in his personal as well as in his public life.

The religious activities of the Candella kings were attested by their erection of temples and installation of Saivite and Vaiṣṇavite as well as Jain images. Their interest was apparently not confined to Hindu religion, they were broad-minded enough to extend their patronage to Jainism and Buddhism also.[47]

Kings are described as 'janānandasundarah'[48] 'sajjanānandajananah'[49] i.e., one who pleases the people. The use of these epithets indicate the value which the Candella rulers attached to obtaining popularity amongst their subjects.

Writers of legal texts[50] prescribed royal tours of inspection

---

[44] *E. I.*, I., p. 198, 203., V. 13.
[45] *ibid.*, p. 126., V. 20.
[46] *ibid.*, XX., p. 127., L. 11.
[47] There are a number of inscriptions issued by Jain worshippers, some of whom were '*kulāmātyas*' of Candella rulers (*I. H. Q.*, XXX., p. 183). Mahārājaguru Vāsavacandra claims to have been held in honour by Candella Dhaṅga (*E. I.*, I., p. 135-36). The Chārkhāri Plate (V. S. 1236) while granting a village to some Brahmins excluded 5 *halas* of land previously endowed to a Buddhist monastery (*E. I.*, XX., p. 130. L. 14).
[48] *E. I.*, I., p. 141., V. 15.
[49] *I. A.*, XVI., p. 205., Ll. 5-6.
[50] *Śukranīti* I., V. 374.

as a measure to check administrative corruptions and guard against the oppressive officials. The duty, as enjoined by them, was sought to be carried out by the Candella rulers. Their charters were issued when they were on tours in the different parts of their dominions. Dhaṅgadeva, when at Kāśikā (Benares), gave the village Yullī situated in Usaravāha to Bhaṭṭa Yaśodhara in V.S. 1055 (998 A.D.).[51] Devavarman, when at Suhavāsa-samāvāsa encampment, gave the village Kaṭhahau in the Rājapura-avasthā to Brahmin Abhimanyu.[52] Madanavarman, when in residence near Bhaillasvāmin (modern Bhilsā), gave ten ploughs of land of the village of Bamharaḍā in the Sūḍali-viṣaya to Brahmin Rāhulaśarman,[53] and from his camp at Pareyīgrāma he gave 2¼ *padas* of land in Valahauḍā grāma in Mahisineha Viṣaya to Paṇḍitā Somaśarman.[53a] Paramardi, when in the camp of Sonasāra confirmed a long list of land grants made by his grand-father, Madanavarman during the latter's encampment at Vāridurga.[54] A number of records were issued by Paramardi from Vilāsapura, which is identified with Pachār. The Bhārat Kalā Bhavan Plate of Paramardin (V. S. 1239) was issued from Sallaksaṇa-Vilāsapura.[54a]

The Candella records are completely silent about the judicial functions of the king. It is quite probable that the usual functions of the Indian king in the period were also performed by the Candella kings.

An important function of the king was the selection and appointment of his ministers and the important officials after due 'tests' ("parīkṣya samyak") which reminds us of the '*upadhās*' prescribed in the Arthaśāstra of Kauṭilya.[54b]

Personal life.

Inscriptional sources give little information about the

---

[51] *I. A.*, XVI., p. 201.
[52] *ibid.*, p. 202.
[53] *ibid.*, p. 207.
[53a] Bhārat Kalā Bhavan Plates of Madanavarman, V. S. 1192 *E. I.* XXXI. p. 309-13
[54] *E. I.*, IV., p. 153.
[54a] *ibid.*, XXXI., Dr. D. C. Sircar thinks that this is identical with Vilāsapura.
[54b] *K. A.*, I., Chap. X.

personal life of the king. These sources occasionally refer to Krīḍāgiri (pleasure mount) and Kelisarasi (swimming pools)[55]. Details about the royal sports are not available, but evidently they were on such occasions gaily attired and accompanied by an equally gay retinue, which included particularly youthful damsels. The pleasure mount of Vākpati on the Vindhya mountain was resounded with the sweet notes of his 'excelle-encies' sung by the Kirāta women, seated on spotless lotuses, and on which groups of peacocks were made to dance by the bubbling noise of water-falls rushing down from its tops (Khajurāho Insc., II., V. 13). Amorous dalliances of the king within the harem are also mentioned in the Nānyaura Plate of Dhaṅga (V.S. 1055).

The Candella king attended dramatic performances. The drama Prabodhacandrodaya was staged in the presence of Kīrtivarman, who evinced great interest in it.[56] Hunting, which must have been a popular royal sport, has been portrayed in some of the sculptured panels of the Khajurāho temples. Duels between elephants or between a lion and an elephant were also arranged as a thrilling sports item.

Ministers.

The Candella kings had their ministers to advise them on matters of policy and also to help them in executing their projects. Some of their ministers claim to have served the royal family on an hereditary basis. The Māu stone inscription refers to a family of ministers serving the Candellas from the time of Dhaṅga to that of Madanavarman.[57] Similarly the Baṭeśvar inscription refers to Lāhaḍa, who was the Chief minister of Madanavarman, while his son, Sallakṣaṇa, and grandson, Puruṣottama, held the same position under Paramardideva.[58] Birth was not always the sole criterion in the selection of ministers. Learning, experience, power of judgment and capacity for leadership were some of the qualities which a minister had to possess (Maulaḥ sadvaṁśajanma

[55] *E. I.*, I., p. 125.
[56] *P. C.*, p. 13.
[57] *E. I.*, I., pp. 195-207.
[58] *ibid.*, I., pp. 210-11., V. 20, 22, 28.

suciramalamatiḥ śastravid-dṛṣṭakarmma vāgmī dakṣah pragalbhaḥ kạrīturaga-rathārohābhijñaḥ kṛtastraḥ Mantre gūḍho'nurāga prabhṛtiguṇayutaśca......mantrimukhyasya cakre//.—Māu Record, V. 41). Different 'tests' were applied to ascertain the qualities of candidates before their appointment as ministers ('parīkṣya cakre' ibid., V. 21). The Chief minister was designated '*Mantrimukhya*'. The essential qualifications for this high post are mentioned in inscription. They were to be 'Sarvvopadhāśuddha' (Māu Record, V. 21), i.e., successful in all the requisite tests to which they were put. (Reference may in this connection be made to Kauṭilya's theory of 'upadhās' or allurements to test the character of ministers).[58a] The ministers should be (nayaprayoge gahaṇe sudakṣah) highly expert in the abstruse conduct of politics, endowed with understanding, uprightness (Yuktaścet sacivo guṇairabhijña prajña—Māu Record, V. 31), and similar other qualities, as well as experienced in the working of the different administrative departments. Ananta, who, it is said, 'counselled the very heart of the king' (Mantrī mantrādhikāre sumahati hṛdayam gūḍha viśrambha kṛtye nityaṁ Kīrtivarmmeśvarasya/ibid., V. 30), and therefore, occupied a position like that of a Privy Councillor, had earlier worked as 'the captain of horses and elephants' (hastyaśvanetā), and of 'the forces of the town' (purabalādhyakṣa) and 'protector of properties' (ekasvagoptā). His son, Gadādhara, having success fully combed the state of the seditious and subversive elements (kṛtvā kaṇṭaka-śodhanaṁ—ibid., V. 39), and having efficiently managed the departments of Kośa (Finance) and Daṇḍa (Law and Order) of the realm, was appointed a *Pratihāra* by king Jayavarman (ibid., V. 40); and later, for his knowledge and practical experience he was made the 'mantrimukhya' by Pṛthvīvarman (ibid, V. 41), in which capacity he continued during the reign of his successor Madanavarman.

There is a vagueness in the use of the terms, *mantri*, *saciva* and *amātya*. It is consequently difficult to say whether these terms

[58a] K. A., I., Chap. X.

indicated functional or other differences. Along with these terms are also mentioned the expressions, mantrimukhya (Māu Record V. 41), sacivesu-mukhya (Baṭeśvar Record, V. 28) and amātya-mantrīndra (Deogaḍh Record, V. 5). The mantrimukhya was the chief of mantrins or ministers. Similarly the sacivas had a principal, and the amātyas, who were either identical with or different from the mantrins, had a chief of their own. It is not unlikely that all these expressions applied to the chief of ministers. There must have been therefore a Council of Ministers, headed by the Mantrimukhya. Evidently he was the most important official in the state, almost next to the king, and for his experience and knowledge he must have exercised considerable influence over the king. The available Candella records provide names of some Chief ministers in different periods, viz., Prabhāsa, during the reigns of Dhaṅga and Gaṇḍa (Māu Record, V. 20-21), Vatsarāja of the time of Kīrtivarman (Deogaḍh Record, V. 5), Gadādhara of Pṛthvīvarman and Madanavarman (Māu—V. 41-42), Lāhaḍa also of Madanavarman (Baṭeśvar—V. 19-20), Sallakṣaṇa and Puruṣottama of Paramardi (ibid., V. 22-24, 27-28).

Some of the ministers counselled the king in secret and confidential matters. Ananta, to whom we have already referred, is described in V. 30 of the Māu Record as the foremost adviser of the king, and enjoyed his complete confidence in all secret matters of policy. Thus it appears that the policy of the king must have been largely formulated with the help of this minister, who was in all probability the highest authority of the Political Department (mantrādhikāra).

In some epigraphic passages, e.g., in the Māu and the Baṭeśvar records, the importance of the chief minister's portfolio is so vividly painted that it may not be wrong to suppose that sometimes he was the power behind the throne, the king almost looking like a puppet in his hands. The policy of Prabhāsa, the Chief minister of Dhaṅga and Gaṇḍa, was so effective that it became 'trivarga-phalaprada' (Māu—V. 22) i.e., Dharmma, Artha and Kāma. His grandson, Śivanāga, by his efforts claims to have rendered all rulers tributaries to his master, Vidyādhara (ibid., V. 24). Verse 31 of the Māu Stone inscription, referring to Ananta, Kīrtivarmana's Privy Councillor, records that it is no wonder for the king to surpass even the son of Dharma by his fame, good acts and prosperity, when the king has for his guide a minister of the calibre of Ananta. Gadādhara, his son, was also highly eulogised for elevating the status of the Candella kings, Pṛthvīvarman and Madanavarman by the proper application of the six diplomatic expedients (ibid., V. 42), which are also enunciated by Kauṭilya, viz., *Ṣāḍguṇyam.*[59] Paramardi, it is said in the Baṭeśvar inscription, placed the whole burden of government on the arms of his Chief minister, Sallakṣaṇa.

If the glories of the ministerial families, as claimed in their own records, are taken to be real, the claims of the Candella kings will fade into insignificance. It will not be safe to regard the accounts given in the records of the ministers as free from exaggerations, nor will it be prudent to deny the vital role which some of the able ministers played, relying on the fulsome praises bestowed upon the kings in their own documents.

Ministers are not known to have been representatives of the people, but they were selected by the king on the basis of merit and other considerations. Therefore, constitutionally, they held their offices at the pleasure of the king. There is, however, no case of removal of a minister on record.

There must have been a regular secretariat or ministerial establishment, '*mantrādhikāra*', under the Chief minister, other ministers, acting under his guidance, were entrusted with different duties. Of the multifarious activities of the ministers, counselling the king on matters of policy, i.e., foreign affairs, was among the principal duties performed by the chief minister. For example, Gadādhara, already referred to, claims to have reduced all princes to dependency by

[59] *K. A.*, VII., Chap. I., (Shamasastry) pp. 293-96.

applying the six expedients, viz., peace, war, marching, sitting encamped, dividing his forces, and alliances with more powerful kings, and so forth, according as the exigencies demanded—(Māu Record, V. 42).

Only on one occasion the post of '*saṁdhānavigraha-mahāsaciva*' (Minister of Peace and War)[60] has been mentioned. This office was held by Gadādhara during the reign of Paramardi. Thus the portfolios of war and peace were under his charge. It may not be unlikely that Gadādhara of this Record and Gadādhara of the Māu Record, who had been found functioning as the Chief minister during the reigns of Pṛthvīvarman and Madanavarman, were identical. Śivanāga, of the time of Vidyādhara, though not explicitly mentioned as a Minister of peace and war, performed the functions appropriate to this office, as he is said to have rendered other rulers tributaries to his master (Māu—V. 24). Vatsarāja, the 'amātyamantrīndra' of Vidyādhara, is also stated in V. 6 of the Deogaḍh Inscription to have indeed become famous, a very Vācaspati in his unique office of the counsellor, having quickly subdued enemies on all sides by his counsel and excellent valour. A casual mention of '*Sāṁdhivigrahika*' is found in the Dhureṭi Copper Plate.[61]

Suppression of internal enemies and maintenance of law and order within the state were among the functions assigned to the Chief minister and his department. Thus Sallakṣaṇa, the Chief minister, is described in V. 24 of the Baṭeśvar record to have succeeded in bringing the 'seditious people' to book (durādhah kṛta kaṇṭakasya). This particular work may not have always been carried out personally by the chief minister, but was delegated to a minister enjoying his confidence or to a trusted official. Thus the Māu Record refers to Gadādhara, a son of Ananta, performing the duties relating to '*kaṇṭakaśodhana*' (weeding out of thorns) during the reign of Sallakṣaṇavarman, when his father held the office of the Chief minister in the kingdom (V. 39). Ajaygaḍh Rock Insc., of the time of Bhojavarman mentions one Ālhu

[60] *E. I.*, I., p. 211., V. 30.
[61] *ibid.*, XXV., pp. 1. ff.

of the Vāstavya Kāyastha family, who was engaged in the administration of the city gates and thoroughfare (pratoli-adhikāra) particularly in keeping down wickedness(V. 13).

The *Pratihāra* seems to have enjoyed the rank and designation of a *saciva.* The Pratihāra was not a mere doorkeeper to usher in those who come to meet the king. He was the chief of the royal body-guards and master of ceremonies. His official duties required him to keep close to the king's person. As the king's security was much dependent on his services, the king was careful about the choice of his Pratihāra. This is evident from V. 40 of the Māu record, which states,-'King Jayavarman eagerly appointed him, i.e., Gadādhara, the chastiser of enemies and famous for his greatness, near his own person, in the office of Pratihāra'. It is quite probable that before his appointment as Pratihāra, Gadādhara must have shown his ability in his work relating to 'kaṇṭakaśodhana'. The King seems to have flourished with the loyal support of this influential family, as is evident from the fact that Gadādhara's father, Ananta, was the Chief minister, while he served as a 'saciva' and 'pratihāra'. Verse 10 of the Ajaygaḍh Rock Inscription of Bhojavarman shows that Gaṅgādhara,[62] a favourite councillor (sacivobhirāma) of the Vāstavya kāyastha family was appointed 'kañcukī' (chamberlain) by Paramardi after due consideration. His younger brother, Jaunādhara, who was a valiant warrior himself, assisted Gaṅgādhara in his work (sahakarmacārī—V. 11).

The Treasurer was another saciva. Subhaṭa, a saciva, was in charge of Treasury establishments (*kośādhikārādhipati*).[63] Gadādhara, another saciva, whom we have already mentioned as a Pratihāra, for some time held the portfolios of kośa and daṇḍa (kośasya daṇḍasya ca—Māu Record, V. 39). The function of the saciva in charge of kośa may have been wide enough to include duties relating to supervision over collection of revenue, as well as its expenditure.

[62] In rendering the verse to English, Kielhorn gives the name as Gadādhara, though in the text it was mentioned as Gaṅgādhara. The facsimile of the record in Pl. XV., *A. S. R.*, XXI, L. 5, also shows it as 'Gaṅgādhara.'

[63] *E. I.,* I., p. 335., V. 26.

'Bhāṇḍāgārapati', the superintendent of royal stores, is mentioned only in one occasion.[64]

Two other ministers are mentioned in epigraphic records with no indication of the functions assigned to them. One of them was Gaṇapati, a minister of Vīravarman (Ajaygaḍh Rock inscription of 1281 A.D.),[65] and the other was Nāna under Bhojavarman (Ajaygaḍh Stone inscription of 1288 A.D.).[66]

We may now consider the organisation of the Judicial Department in the Candella kingdom. The Khajurāho record of V.S. 1059 refers to Bhaṭṭa Yaśodhara, a royal priest, placed in charge of the Judiciary, *Dharmmādhikāra* (the department of Dharma), by Candella Dhaṅga. Next to the king, who must have usually represented the highest tribunal, this royal chaplain, in charge of Dharma, must have been the highest authority in judicial matters including the interpretation of law as embodied in the Smṛtis and their Commentaries.

In this connection we may refer to another term, '*Dharmmalekhi*', mentioned in the Semrā and Nānyaura 'C' Plates, and the Bhārat Kalā Bhavan Plate of Paramardin (V. S. 1239).[67] This has been taken to mean a 'writer of legal documents.' Evidently Pṛthvīdhara of the Vāstavya race, who composed the long and complex document, revalidating some former grants of lands, was a technical expert in drafting legal documents (Dharmalekhī). The composer of the Chārkhāri Plate (V. S. 1236), Śubhānanda has also been described as a Dharmalekhī (E. I., XX., P. 131). The expression '*Arthalekhi*' has been used in the Dhureṭi Copper Plate (ibid., XXV), evidently to denote the same function. The work done by them was probably similar to that usually performed by a pleader or a solicitor in modern times.

Lastly we may refer to the high officials of the Secretariat (mānyān adhikṛtān). They are mentioned in different Candella records variously as *Kāyasthas*, *Karaṇikas*, *Adhi-*

[64] *ibid.*, V. 30.
[65] *A. S. R.*, XXI., p. 52.
[66] *E. I.*, XXVIII., p. 103, 106., V. 24.
[67] *E. I.*, IV., p. 170; *I. A.*, XVI., p. 208., *E. I.*, XXXI.

kṛtān and *Lekhakas*. Although different designations are mentioned in different records, it is likely that their functions were identical. The Kāyasthas thus held a prominent place, as is shown from their frequent mention in the land grants of the Candellas. We have already referred to the Vāstavya Kāyastha family to which Gaṅgādhara and Subhaṭa belonged. Kāyasthas are also mentioned in connection with the drafting of legal documents,[68] and they figure as a class to whom grants are communicated. *Akṣapaṭalika* (keeper of accounts) is mentioned in the Chārkhāri Plate, though in connection with the drafting of the record.[69]

Ajaygaḍh rock inscriptions of the times of Kīrtivarman and of Bhojavarman mention a family of Vāstavya Kāyasthas, who hereditarily held high and responsible offices under successive Candella rulers.[70] Ṭhakkura Jājuka of this family, who was appointed by king Gaṇḍa to superintend all the affairs of the state (Sarvvādhikārakaraṇesu sadā-niyuktah), received the gift of a village, named Dugauḍa, from the king.[70a] To another member of this family, Vidana, the king is stated to have entrusted the responsibility of the realm (vinyasta-rājyaṁ—V. 15).[70b] Two other members of this family received the unique decoration of '*Viśiṣa*', accompanied by grants of lands. Maheśvara, the son of Jājuka, was made the Viśiṣa of Kālañjara, and was awarded the village, named Pipalāhika, by king Kīrtivarman (V. 9).[70c] Vāse or Vāseka was also appointed the Viśiṣa of Jayadurga or Ajaygaḍh (durge Jayākhye viśiṣādhikāre) along with the grant of the village of Varbhavarī by king Trailokyavarman (V. 16). Viśiṣa is rather an unusual designation, not met with in any other record. In all probability it refers to an administrative post associated with a fort. Alternatively, the term Viśiṣa may have been used as a title conferred on officials in recognition of their

---

[68] Khajurāho Insc. of V. S. 1011-Karaṇika Jaddha Gauḍa; Khajurāho Insc. of V. S. 1059—Kāyastha Jayapāla of Gauḍa; Semrā, Icchāwār and Mahobā Plates—Pṛthvīdhara of Vāstavya family; Pachār Plate—Subhānanda (Vāstavya).

[69] *E. I.*, XX., p. 128.

[70] *ibid.*, XXX., pp. 87-90, & I., pp. 330-36.

[70a] *ibid.*, V. 6 & V. 7. respectively.

[70b] *ibid.*

[70c] *ibid.*, The grant of the village, Pipalāhika to Maheśvara is also mentioned in the record of Kīrttivarman.

meritorious services, which seems to have been accompanied by a gift of land.

The inscription also refers to the traditional theory relating to the sanctity of '36 towns', famous for the settlement of the Kāyasthas'[71] Thus it appears that the Kāyasthas enjoyed an honourable status in the Candella Court.

The royal court was adorned by one or more official poets. The *Kavi* was generally a Brāhmaṇa, who was honoured for his knowledge and literary gifts. Most of the inscriptions were composed by these kavis.[72]

Vaidya (the official Physician), Āṭavika (forest officer) and Dūta (messenger, who communicated royal orders and grants) also enjoyed a place of prominence among the officers of the Candella state.

Military Department.

That the Army under the Candellas was administered efficiently cannot be denied, for the growth of the Candella kingdom itself was an unmistakable proof of the strength of the army and superiority of its organisation. The supreme leader of the army was the king himself. He often led the army personally in military campaigns. The minister in charge of war and peace (Saṁdhānavigraha-mahāsaciva or Sāṁdhivigrahika) was evidently the political adviser to the king in military matters relating to the declaration of war and the settlement of terms of peace.

The Army had its Commander in chief designated as *Senāpati,*[73] who must have led the forces in the battle-field. Besides, there were special officers in charge of elephants and cavalry, *hastyaśvanetā.*[74] The defensive organisation was also looked after by specially appointed officers. The *Purabalādhyakṣa* was the Superintendent of the forces defending the capital city. *Koṭṭapāla,* referred to in the Dhureṭi Copper Plate, may be regarded as the Officer in charge of defence of

[71] 'Ṣaṭ-triṁśati karaṇa karma nivāsapūta āsanpurah' *E. I.*, I., p. 333., V. 2.
[72] Khajurāho Insc. (V. S. 1011) Kavi Mādhava; Khajurāho Insc. (V. S. 1059) Kavi Rāma; Rock Insc of Vīra, Poet Ratnapāla; Baṭeśvara Record, Devadhara.
[73] Senāpati Madanapālaśarman—Icchāwār Plate., *I. A.*, XXV., p. 205.
[74] *E. I.*, I., p. 20., V. 30.

small towns. The office of the *Ekasvagoptā* also appears to have been a military one. His duty was to protect properties, i.e. buildings etc., under the control of the army. It may be noted that the functions of the Purabalādhyakṣa and the Ekasvagoptā are found to have been combined and entrusted to the same officer. The forts must have had a governor (durgādhipa). Paṁsuha, son of Śrī Ayo, is mentioned to have been appointed as a governor of Jayadurga along with its approach roads (pratolikānvita Jayapura-durgādhipa).[75] The office of the governor of the fort was clled *durgādhikāra*. Ānanda, the younger brother of Vāseka, the Viśiṣa of Jayapura, is stated to have been made the governor of the fort by the king.[76] The *Aśvavaidya* or the Veterinary Surgeon, mentioned in the Candella record,[77] must have been attached to the army.

Even Kāyasthas and Brāhmaṇas were entrusted with responsible military functions. Jaunādhara and Mālādhara, younger brothers of Gaṅgādhara, belonged to the Vāstavya Kāyastha family, which, as already mentioned, produced illustrious administrators. Both the brothers have been described as distinguished warriors (vīramukhya). The Pachār Plate refers to Senāpati Madanapālaśarman, evidently a Brāhmaṇa. In recognition of meritorious military services grants of land were used to be made in their favour. Madanapālaśarman received the grant of a village, as recorded in the Pachār Plate of the time of Paramardi. The Dahi Grant refers to one Mallaya as a distinguished soldier being similarly rewarded.[78] The Chārkhāri Plate of Vīravarman records the grant of a village to one Rāuta Abhi for a deed of valour in the battle of Sondhi (Sondhisaṁgrāma.... kṛta-vīryātiśayo prasāde).[79] There was also the system of granting pension, '*Mṛtyukavṛtti*', to heirs of persons killed in battle. The Gārrā Plates of V.S. 1261 (1205-1206 A.D.) record

[75] *ibid.*, XXVIII., p. 104., L. 20. Ajaygaḍh R. I. of Kīrtivarman records the conferment of the authority over the gates ofthe Kālañjara fort (Kālañjaradvāravarādhikāram) upon Maheśvara, *ibid.*, XXX. p. 88.

[76] *E. I.*, I., p. 335., V. 22.

[77] *A. S. R.*, XXI., p. 51.

[78] *ibid.*, pp. 74-76.

[79] *E. I.*, XX., p. 133.

grants of lands to Rāuta Sāmanta, son of Rāuta Pāpe, who was killed at Kakaḍaḍaha in a battle with the Turuṣkas (Kakaḍaḍahe Turuṣka-yuddhe mṛta Rā. Pāpe putrasya Sāmanta nāmne prasādena mṛtyukavṛttau śāsanaṁ kṛtvā pradattāiti//).[80]

Administrative Divisions.

The Candella kingdom, generally known as Jejābhukti or Jejākabhukti, was for administrative reasons divided into a number of districts, subdivisions and village-groups. The village must have been the unit of administration. Some villages were organised into unions—thus there were village-groups, comprising of 5, 12 or 18, villages, viz., Pīlikhini-pañcela and Iṭāva-pañcela in Dudāhi, and Isarahāra-pañcela in Vaḍavāri ; Khaṭau-dvādaśaka, Rālhasaṭkaṭa-Ṭaṇṭa-dvādaśaka and Hāṭ-āsṭadaśaka in Vikaura Viṣaya (Semrā Plates).

Rewā Copper plate grants of the Mahārāṇakas of Kakareḍikā mention an expression, '*Pattalā*', denoting a territorial unit larger than a village, as the villages, Rehi and Agaseyi are stated to have been included in the Vaddharāpattalā and the village Ahaḍapāda in the Khandagaha-pattalā. Dhureṭi Copper Plates refer to Dhovahaṭṭa pattana situated in Dhanavāhipattalā.[80a] Pattalā might have denoted a type of village-group. Bhārat Kalā Bhavan Plates of Madanavarman (V.S. 1192) refer to Astavāla-grāma in Eracchapattalā, Pipalahā in Tintiri-pattalā,[80b] Vasauhā and Mahuāli in Kolavā-pattalā, Goulā in Vāndiuri-pattalā,[80c] Dādari in Navaraṭha-pattalā, Denavaḍa and Valahauḍa in Mahisinehapattalā and Dāvaha (or Dāveha) in Nandāvana-(or, Nandāvena)-pattalā. Navaraṭha-pattalā seems to be the same as the Navarāṣṭramaṇḍala-viṣaya of the Chārkhāri Plates.

---

[80] *ibid.*, XVI., p. 272.

[80a] Dhovahaṭṭa has been identified by Dr. N. P. Chakravarti with Dhureṭi. Mm. Mirashi thinks that 'it is more likely to be Dhobaṭ, near Makundapur, about 10 miles south by west of Rewā.' Dhanavāhi-pattalā, according to him, 'may be identical with Dhanavāhi, 22 miles to the south west of Dhobaṭ'. (*C. I. I.*, IV. p. 371.

[80b] Tintiri-pattalā may be identified with Teonthār tehsil of Rewā, and the village Pipalahā with Pipal-(oau) mentioned in the Ālhā Ghāt Stone Inscription. (*I. A.*, XVIII. pp. 213-14).

[80c] Vāndiuri seems to be identifiable with the modern Banda district.

Similarly Eraccha and Nandāvena pattalās of this record may be taken as identical with the viṣayas of the same names in other Candella records. It may be suggested that either pattalā and viṣaya were used in an identical sense or that the pattalā bearing viṣaya name might have been used for the sadar subdivision of the district. Names of the following villages are met with in the available Candella records.- Yullī, Durvvāharā, Bamharaḍā, Ranasuā, Raṇamaua, Kamanauda, Vijaulīgrāma, Śeṣayīgrāmā, Uladāna, Dudāhi, Navasahahatthidahā, Patha, Vaḍavāri, Nandinī, Dhanaurā, Kaḍoha, Lohasīhani, Kakaraḍaha, Rehi, Agaseyi, Deddu, Lauvā, Dugauḍa, Pipalāhika, Varbhavarī, Bhūtapallikā Kumbhaṭibhaṭagrāma, Ṭumṭumāgrāma, Kokaḍa-(or, Kīkaḍa)grāma, Sugauḍa, Ahaḍapāda, Pareyi-grāma, Astavāla, Pipalahā, Vasauhā, Goulā, Dādari, Denavaḍa, Valahauḍa, Dāvaha, Mahuāli, Vavauḍā and Iṭalā. Most of them are however unidentifiable.

We do not find sufficient details about the system of village administration under the Candellas. Royal grants were communicated among others to Brāhmaṇas, Kuṭumbins (house-holders) and Mahattaras (village-headmen or dignitaries). They were possibly associated with the vilage administration. It is not however clear whether these Mahattaras were royal dignitaries entrusted with local administration. The Mahattama is mentioned in the Nānyaura Plate 'B' of V.S. 1107. He had a larger jurisdiction than the Mahattara, as he is mentioned in the record to be associated with the 'janapada' ("Mahattama-janapādan"). The Dhureṭi Plates of Trailokyamalla describe Malayasiṁha as the 'Mahāmahattaka-mantri-māṇḍalika'. (L. 5).

The next larger unit was '*avasthā*' or subdivision, e.g., 'Rājapura-avasthāyām Raṇamaua-saṁvaddham Kaṭhahaugrāme', (Kaṭhahau village, attached to Raṇamaua, included in the Rājapura-avasthā.-Nānyaura Plate 'B'.). Another expression which seems to be almost synonymous is '*Pratibaddhaṁ*' as it also stands for a subdivision, e.g., 'Usaravāha pratibaddham Yullīnamadheyagrāmam.' (Nānyaura Plate 'A').

The term *Viṣaya* signified a definitely larger administrative area. A number of viṣayas are mentioned in the Candella inscriptions, viz., Suḍāli viṣaya (near Bhilsā), Vikaura viṣaya (Madanpur), Dudāhi viṣaya (Lalitpur), Vaḍavāri viṣaya (Berwārā, Lalitpur), Nandāvana viṣaya (Banda district), Eracha viṣaya (Hamirpur), Pāniuli viṣaya (Pānnā), Vikrauni viṣaya (Vikaura in Saugor district) Karigāva viṣaya (Jhansi), Kirayiḍa viṣaya (near Mahobā), Dahi viṣaya, Vedesaitha viṣaya, Antarvedi viṣaya (Ganges-Jumna Doab) and Pītaśaila viṣaya[81] (unidentified).

Bhārat Kalā Bhavan Plates of Madanavarman mention Mahisineha viṣaya, and the Pāśuni viṣaya has been mentioned in a copper plate grant of Paramardin. Both these viṣayas are unidentifiable. But it may be suggested that the Pāśuni Viṣaya was most probably the valley of the Paisuni river which flows through the eastern part of the Banda district before it meets the Yamunā. Maṇḍala and Viṣaya often denoted the same sense, as we find in the Chārkhāri Plate of V.S. 1108, that the village named Bhūtapallikā is situated in the Navarāṣṭramaṇḍala which is described as a viṣaya.

The term '*Bhukti*' is not known to have been used by the Candellas in the sense of an administrative division larger than a viṣaya. Their kingdom itself was known as 'Jejākabhukti.' *Bhaṭṭāgraharā* villages or those which had been granted rent-free to Brāhmaṇas often find mention in the Candella records, e.g., Ḍhakāri, Naṁgava, Phaṇḍiva, Mutāusa and Mutautha. Some of the cities and towns, and places important for *royal encampments*, as known from the Candella records may be mentioned here, though all of them are not identifiable. Viz., Tarkkārikā, Suhavāsa-samāvāsa, Bhaillasvāmi-samīpāvāsa (mod. Bhilsā), Kharjuravāhaka (Khajurāho), Ramaṇipura, Madanapura, Sonasāra-samāvāsa, Vāridurga (probably Barigār), Gahilu, Vilāsapura (probably Pachār), Vaḍavāda, Jayapura or Nandipura (Ajaygaḍh), Kāśikā (Kāśī,) Kakareḍikā (Kakreri), Padmāvatī

[81] *Vide ante.* Chap I. P. 15. An explanation of the term has been suggested. For S. L. Katare's Suggestion vide E.I., XXX. p. 89

(Narwar), Dhovahaṭṭapattana (Dhureṭi or Dhovaṭ, Rewā), Kīrttigiridurga (Deogaḍh), Gopagiri (Gwālior), Kakaḍadaha (mod. Kukurooa), Kālañjara and Sondhi (Seondhā fort, now Kānhārgarh).

Revenue Administration.

Sufficient importance was attached to the administration of *kośa* (treasury). It is evident from the fact that it was placed under the charge of a minister, if not the Chief Minister, as seems to be likely from the evidence already mentioned. The kośa was believed to be one of the integral constituents of the state.

Land must have been one of the chief sources of the revenue collected by the Candellas. The rate of the land tax is not explicitly mentioned in their records, but it was customary in many places to raise this tax at the rate of 1/6th of the produce of the soil. Increased rates were also current; variations of rates sometimes were due to the quality of the cultivated land and abnormal financial or political situation. The list of revenue terms found in the records comprise, Bhāga, Bhoga, Kara, Paśu, Hiraṇya, Daṇḍādāya, Cāṭādipraveśa and Śulka.

The expression 'Bhāgabhogādikaṁ'[82] probably means the king's customary grain-share, assessed on the produce of the fields, and realised in kind, as distinguished from 'hiraṇya', realised in cash on certain special kinds of crops. Bhāgabhogādikaṁ may be identical to an almost similar expression 'Bhāgabhogakara.' But Bhāga, bhoga and kara may be considered separately also. Bhāga was the traditional 1/6th share of the crop due to the king, the quantity of which may be altered, as stated in the legal texts. Bhoga, as Dr. Ghosal holds,[83] stands for the periodical supplies of fruits, firewood, flowers and the like, which the villagers had to furnish to the king. It may indicate the state's share of the profits (bhoga) derived from the possession of the particular land, which are stated to be eight in number e.g., Nidhi (treasure-trove),

[82] *E. I.*, IV., p. 153., L. 117-19; *ibid.*, XX., p. 133., L. 15; *ibid.*, p. 136., L. 15-16.
[83] *Hindu Revenue System.*, p. 290.

Nikṣepa (underground deposits), Pāṣāṇa (stones), Siddha (land already under cultivation), Sādhya (cultivable waste land), Jala (water), Akṣiṇī (present profits) and Āgāmi (future profits). Of these Nidhi, Nikṣepa and Pāṣāṇa are specifically mentioned in the Chārkhāri Plate, V. S. 1346.[84] Kara has been differently interpreted by different scholars. According to their views, it was—(i) a periodical tax over and above the king's grain share, (ii) an emergency tax in addition to the grain share, and/or (iii) a tax upon merchant's profits. (*Hindu Revenue System. P. 293*).

Hiraṇya was probably a cash levy on some special kinds of crops, the customary grain share being levied on ordinary crops. It may also mean certain cash impost over and above the normal bhāga. Paśu is a revenue term, denoting a tax on cattle, but is often used in epigraphic documents along with the term hiraṇya in a rather conventional way.

Daṇḍādāya was receipts from court fines and punishments. Śulka must have denoted taxes and duties on merchandise, realised from traders. The expression 'cāṭādipraveśa' (entry by irregular soldiers and others), mentioned in some of the Candella land grants, may indicate the expenses paid by villagers for the maintenance of irregular troops, if and when, they were posted in the localities, either for the maintenance of internal peace or to meet any other emergency.

It appears from the evidence discussed above that the source of revenue exploited in the Candella kingdom were identical with those known in many other parts of contemporary India. No new revenue term is to be met with in the Candella records.

Different types of land may be discovered in the words,- sāra, uṣara, nimna, unnata, sthāvara, jaṅgama, jala, sthala, gartta and pāṣāṇa, used in the Candella land grants. It is probable that such classification was necessary for an accurate assessment of royal dues. These terms are also found in contemporary records of other dynasties. It is evident therefore

[84] *E. I.*, XX., p. 136., L. 12.

that the Candellas did not introduce any novel feature in the fiscal arrangement of land.

Detailed *boundaries of land*, as furnished in the available grants, testify to the importance assigned to accurate measurements. The Mahobā Plate of Paramardideva describe a piece of land granted in the village of Dhanaurā as 'bounded on the east by the nālā belonging to the barber, on the south by a nālā, on the west by the embankment of Bhaṭahada tank, on the north by a brahmin's land and tank-embankment.'[85] Similarly the Augāsi Plates mention 'an ant-hill by a madhuka tree' as the western boundary of a gift land. The village boundaries were well known, "prakhyāta catuh-sīma paryantam." Boundary pillars or 'grāmadaṇḍakas' are mentioned in the Augāsi Grant.[86] The Chārkhāri Plate (V. S. 1108) refers to 'sīmatṛṇakāṣṭhaka' of the village Bhūtapallikā.[87]

Land was measured on the basis of its sowing or ploughing capacity. The Augāsi Grant records the grant of '*ten ploughs of land*' (hala-daśa aṅkopi hala 10) of the village Vamharaḍā in the Suḍāli viṣaya to the brahmin Rāhulaśarman. Similarly the Chārkhāri grant mentions a gift of five ploughs of land (pañcahalāni).[88] The Semrā Plates while recording a long list of land gifts exclude a plot of land measuring four ploughs (halacatuṣṭayāvacchinnāh). The sowing capacity as a possible unit of measurment is mentioned in the Pachār Plate, where it is said that a '*prastha*' of seeds was to be sown in each '*vādha*' of land. But the total land donated was mentioned in terms of *hala*, i.e., daśahalāvacchinnābhūmih, ten ploughs of land to be sown wth 7½ droṇas of seed.[89] The term Vādha is also mentioned in the Mahobā Plate, the land donated being 60 square vādhas (dairghye vādha 10 vistare vādha 6 jātavādha ṣaṣṭhyānvita), equivalent to five halas.[90] The evidences mentioned above

---

[85] *E. I.*, XVI., p. 12., L. 8.
[86] *I. A.*, XVI., p. 208.
[87] *E. I.*, XX., p. 127.
[88] *ibid.*, p. 130., L. 14.
[89] *ibid.*, X., P. 48., L. 8.
[90] *ibid.*, XVI., p. 12. 12., L. 11-12.

point out the importance of hala or the ploughing capacity as the popular unit of measurement of cultivable plots of land in the Candella state. Land for the dwelling place is found to be measured in terms of '*hasta*' (cubits). A plot of land measuring 52 square cubits for dwelling purposes is recorded to have been given to a brahmin in the Mahobā plate. The Semrā Plates refer to the *Pada* measurement, plots measuring padadvayaṁ, padamekaṁ, padārddhaṁ, padacaturthāṁśa, padaṣaṭ-aṅkatopi pada 6, padacatvāriṁśad-aṅkatopi pada 43, were donated to brahmins. Two of the Bhārat Kalā Bhavan plates also mention 'Pada' measurements, but in another we find reference to '*lāva*' or '*lava*' measurement. Inscriptions concerned do not however furnish specific details about these measures, which must have been current in the Candella territory.

Exemptions from payments of land-revenue and other taxes were sometimes granted to Brahmin teachers and scholars. *Brahmadeya* villages or lands with immunity from taxes, given to such brahmins probably constituted the *Bhaṭṭāgrahāras*. The Deed of gift in such a case not only fully states the terms of immunity but also gives in the conventional style the condition of perpetual enjoyment conferred on the grantee (candrārka samakālaṁ putrapautrādanvayānugāminyah) with complete proprietary rights (karṣataṁ karṣayataṁ dānādhāna vikrayaṁ vā kurvvataṁ na kenacid kācid vādhā karttavyā—Semrā Plates). That these were not merely conventional statements is evident from the fact recorded in the Dhureṭi Copper Plates[91] that a village had been mortgaged (*vittabandha*) by a Saivite religious instituion. The mortgagee was given all the rights of collecting taxes. As suggested by Dr. N. P. Chakravarti, the village was to be held by the mortgagee as pledge as long as he wishes, probably meaning thereby, till all the dues were cleared. The deed of mortgage was registered in the court of the "Pañcakula."[92] Bhaṭṭāgrahāra villages are those rent-free villages granted to brahmins.

---

[91] *ibid.*, XXV., p. 1. ff.
[92] *C. I. I.*, IV p. 373, f.n. 6. The village-Pañcāyet is likely to be a modern equivalent of '*Pañcakula*.'..

Besides Brahmadeya, Candella grants refer to lands given in lieu of salary for official duties, or as a reward for any meritorious service rendered either in the civil or military capacity. The most interesting type of land grants mentioned in two of the Candella records, known as the Gārrā plates, is '*Mṛtyukavṛtti*'. This term is found applied to a grant made to the heir of a valiant soldier, who laid down his life in a battle against the Turuṣkas.

CHAPTER XII.

SOCIAL AND ECONOMIC CONDITIONS

The Candella records do not contain sufficient information about social life or organisation. The picture that can be drawn on the basis of the data furnished is more or less a conventional one and does not present any distinctive feature worth mentioning.

Names of the four *varṇas*, the Brāhmaṇa, Kṣatriya, Vaiśya and Śūdra occur in the Candella records. The position of the Brāhmaṇa in society was the highest, and life was to be in accord with the 'Dharma,' or the sacred laws of the Hindus.

The Candella Rājputs\must have regarded themselves as true representatives of the Kṣatriya caste, but their origin was obscure. They claim to be descended from the Moon God (Candra Vaṁśa), and call themselves 'Candrātreyas' in their own records. The Parmāl Rāso refers to them as the 'Kṣatriya of a high order' (छोनी छत्रिय).[1] They depended on the Brāhmaṇas for the recognition of their social status, and tried to win their support and confidence by expressing their loyalty to 'Dharma', and anxiety not to violate it in any way (bhīrur-dharmmāparādhe).[2] As required by Śāstric injunctions they also took up the responsibility for upholding the social structure based on caste. In the matter of administration too, the Candella rulers were very often guided by Brahmin ministers and counsellors, who appear to have exercised their personal influence on the royal actions and measures, which contributed not only to the expansion and consolidation of political authority but also to the strengthening of the Brahmanic hold on society.

In the legendary Parmāl Rāso certain duties are expressly stated as constituting the code of honour applicable to the

[1] *P. R.*, I. V. 121, P. 12.
[2] *E. I.*, I. p. 126, V. 20.

Kṣatriyas. '*Svāmihita*' or 'welfare of the master' is pointed out as the supreme objective of a Kṣatriya. The warrior should, if required, freely lay down his life.[3] It was commonly believed that if one died fighting for the king, he would have a place in the heavenly world, and on the other hand, if one betrayed the cause of the master his place would be in the hell.[4]

To kill or strike soldiers already wounded, or those who had taken shelter, was considered unworthy. This is condemned in the Rāso.[5] To march against an enemy without exhausting the armoury of peace was also not considered advisable or proper. A messenger was to be sent to him, as the Rāso says, with an ultimatum asking for a peaceful surrender.[6] If the enemy did not agree, then only a military attack was to be launched. If he wanted time to prepare himself to meet the attack, truce was granted. When Pṛthvīrāja reached the outskirts of Mahobā with his strong army, Parmāl wanted a two month's time to recall his military leaders, Ālhā and Udal, which was readily agreed upon by the former.[7]

The extreme fidelity of kṣatriya wives is shown by the Parmāl Rāso referring to instances of their self-immolation on the funeral pyres of husbands dying in the battle field.[8]

Position of the Brāhmaṇas.

The Brāhmaṇas generally kept themselves engaged in the performances of six-fold duties ('ṣaṭ-karmmābhiratah', 'ṣaṭ-sukarmmasuratarṁ bahuśrutarṁ')[9], as enjoined in the sacred text,—yajana, yājana, adhyayana, adhyāpana, dāna and parigraha. Rai Bahadur Hiralal takes the prominent mention of the expression 'ṣaṭ-karmmābhirata' to stand for six yogic practices, which are more awe-inspiring than the ordinary six duties of a brahmin.[10]

[3] 'Svāmihita tana diyava' (*P. R.*, p. 96); 'Pahile svāmihite śis diya phiri pucchava mama vatta' *ibid.*, p. 79.
[4] *ibid.*, p. 72, V. 59.
[5] *ibid.*, pp. 42-47, V. 67-68.
[6] *ibid.*, pp. 71-72, 98.
[7] *ibid.*, pp. 97-102.
[8] *ibid.*, p. 86.
[9] *E. I.*, I., p. 146, V. 53; XX, p. 128.
[10] *ibid*, XX, p. 126.

Grants of lands and dwellings were made to Brāhmaṇas of renowned 'gotras' and 'pravaras', well versed in the Vedic rituals. The Candella rulers offered sacrifices (hutabhuji hutvā) before ceremonially making grants and endowments on auspicious occasions like the solar eclipse ('rāhugraste divākare'-Semrā Plate), the lunar eclipse ('somagrahe'-Icchāwār plate and Chārkhāri Plate, V.S. 1108), ('rāhugraste niśākare'-Nānyaura Plate 'A'), the full-moon day ('Māghe-māsi pūrṇimāyāṁ'-Augasi Plate); ('Kārttika-paurṇamāsyām'-Nānyaura Plate 'A'), the Saṁkrānti ('Makaragate savitari'-Mahobā Plate), Viṣuva-Saṁkrānti (Bhārat Kalā Bhavan Plates of Madanavarman), the death anniversary of parents ('ātmīya-mātuh sāmvatsarike' -Nānyaura Plate 'B'), 'Puṣyānakṣatre' (Chārkhāri Plate of Hammīravarman), eighth day of the dark fortnight of the month of Kārttika (Pachār Plate) and the seventh day of the bright fortnight of the month of Caitra (Chārkhāri Plate of Paramardideva). Paramardin made a gift of some lands to a Brahmin "when he was at the Maṇikarṇikā-ghaṭṭa at Śrī Vārānasī, apparently in the course of a pilgrimage" (Bhārat Kalā Bhavan Plate of V.S. 1247).[10a] It thus appears that injunctions of the sacred Brahmanical literature about the efficacy of 'dānas' (gifts), made on holy occasions, were duly observed by the Candella rulers.

Gifts to Brāhmaṇas included land and dwellings as well as gold, money, grain and cows.[11] In case of land grants official documents inscribed on copper plates (tāmrakaṁ, tāmrapaṭṭaṁ and Śāsanaṁ) were generally issued. *Tulāpuruṣa dāna* is referred to in verse 52 of the Khajurāho Record of V.S. 1059.[12] It is one of the Mahādānas prescribed in the Smṛtis, when gold and valuables weighed against the person of the donor were donated to brahmins. The Parmāl Rāso refers to '*Bhāṇḍayajña*', the ritualistic forms of which are not mentioned. But it appears from the Rāso that on the occasion, temples were to be erected and donations made to brahmins.

[10a] *ibid*, XXXI.
[11] *ibid.*, XX., p. 127, L. 16-17. 'Kanaka-go-dharā-dāna.'
[12] *ibid.*, I. p. 146.

The Candella kings were very active in erecting temples of Śaiva and Vaiṣṇava worship, for which learned brahmins were appointed as priests. They also took particular interest in settling brahmins of the Vājasaneya, Chāndogya and Bābhṛccya Schools. It may be concluded that the vedic study was zealously encouraged and patronage was extended by the state to teachers engaged in keeping the lamp of vedic learning burning in the country.

Obedience of the pupils to their teachers was referred to indirectly in the fragmentary Mahobā inscription (Gurumupāsta..śiṣyavad).[13] Pupils, in the traditional brahminical manner, resided with their teachers, and the latter's dwelling places are stated in a Candella record to have resounded with the chants of the vedic hymns by crowds of students. ('Dvijāśrayasya', 'Tasyām śruternninada-saṁghaninādītayam').[14] These perhaps refer to educational institutions which grew up in the dwelling places of brahmin teachers.

Subjects comprising the course of study included Sanskrit language and literature (Saṁskṛta bhāṣā and sāhitya) in all its aspects, viz., Kāvya, alaṁkāra, chanda and lakṣaṇa (Chārkhāri Plate, V.S. 1109, L. 8), Grammar (Śabdānuśāsana) and Śruti, particularly the Vājasaneya and the Chāndogya śākhās. The Bābhṛccya śākhā has also been mentioned in the Chārkhāri Plate of V. S. 1108 (L. 16). Familiarity with the science of polity and economics (Arthaśāstra) and law (Dharmaśāstra) with their later commentaries, is clearly indicated by the frequent references to be found in the inscriptions to technical terms and doctrines connected with those branches of learning. Sometimes the sciences to be studied are mentioned, as being fourteen in number, '*Vidyāścaturdaśakalā*'. These must have been the four Vedas, six Vedāṅgas, Mīmāṁsā, Nyāya, Dharmaśāstra and Purāṇa. The brahmin teachers were 'ever ready to expound fully the different subjects, viz., the Vedas, Vedāṅgas, Itihāsa and Purāṇa' (Veda-Vedāṅgetihāsa-purāṇa mīmāṁsā vyākhyā-tatpara—Chārkhāri Plate of Devavarman—L. 17).

---

[13] *ibid.*, I. p. 222,. L. 13.

[14] Rock Insc. of Bhojavarman. V. 4.

'*Astravidyā*'[15] or the science relating to military weapons and their use, was a subject which must have been cultivated particularly by the warrior class. But even the Kāyasthas who were not warriors professionally are known to have been well versed in the use of weapon, as the Ajaygaḍh record of the time of Bhojavarman shows.

Brahmins with diverse designations, such as, Dvivedī, Trivedī, Caturvedī, Śrotriya, Agnihotri, Paṇḍita, Dīkṣita, Rāuta and Ṭhakkura, figure in the Candella records. The terms 'Śrotriya' and 'Agnihotri' might be applied to all brahmins, who performed the duties of their caste, and possessed requisite qualifications. But the brahmins were engaged not only as teachers and priests, they were also employed in high administrative offices. Some brahmin families were hereditarily engaged in administrative duties, such as, those of the Chief Minister, the Minister of War and Peace, the Privy Councillor, &c., The office of the Court Poet (Kavi) was also generally held by the Brahmins. Poet Rāma of the Śabara vaṁśa was the composer of the Khajurāho Inscription of V.S. 1059 (V. 58). The services of the brahmins particularly in the administration of justice were valued. Their intimate acquaintance with the sacred laws must have been considered as a special qualification for the performance of judicial duties. The Khajurāho Inscription refers to the appointment of a royal priest, Bhaṭṭa Yaśodhara, as the Dharmmādhikāra. Even the army was not closed to the brahmins, if they were qualified. There is an instance of a brahmin, Madanapālaśarman, being appointed as a Senāpati (Icchāwār Plate). In local administration too, brahmins held an influential position, as orders regarding royal grants were to be communicated to them like other public officials.

The Kāyasthas.

It is difficult to say if the Kāyasthas had already been formed into a caste. But the functions attributed to some

[15] *ibid.*, V. 25.

Kāyastha dignitaries in the Candella inscriptions were certainly of great influence and responsibility. Special importance attaches to a Kāyastha, descended from Vāstu, and hence called the *Vāstavya Kāyasthas*, dwelling near Kālañjar. The Ajaygaḍh record of Nāna, a minister of the Candella King Bhojavarman, refers to the origin of the Kāyasthas from the sage Kaśyapa (v. 14).[16] '*Gauḍa Kāyastha vaṁśa*' is referred to in the Khajurāho Inscription of V.S. 1011 (Karaṇika Jaddha, son of Jayanāga of Gauḍa), and of V.S. 1059 (Kāyastha Jayapāla of Gauḍa country). Another Candella Inscription from Ajaygaḍh of the time of Bhojavarman refers to the theory of sanctity of 36 towns, which was due to the Kāyasthas (ṣaṭtrimśatih-karaṇakarmma-nivāsapūta-āsanpurah) residing in those places.[17] One of the towns as mentioned in the record is Tarkārikā which, however, is not identifiable.

The Kāyasthas, according to the Smṛtis, were royal officials engaged in the act of scribes, writing state documents, or maintaining public accounts. Karaṇas also denote a group of officials like the Kāyasthas, discharging almost identical duties and responsibilities. It may not be unreasonable therefore to presume that the two expressions were used to denote the same group of people. In addition to the usual functions of the Kāyasthas, i.e., those of the scribe, the writer of documents and the keeper of accounts, of which there are ample evidences in the Candella records, they were often entrusted with highly responsible duties, connected with the offices of the Saciva, the Pratihāra, the Kośādhikārādhipati, &c., as indicated in the Ajaygaḍh Rock Inscription of Bhojavarman. Distinguished members of the community were decorated with the title of 'Viśiṣa' of the Kālañjara or of the Jayapura forts. Two such cases are mentioned in the Ajaygaḍh Record. Māheśvara or Maheśvara, the son of Jājuka, was made the Viśiṣa of Kālañjara by King Kīrtivarman (v. 8), and later Vāse or Vāseka was appointed as the Viśiṣa of Jayadurga (Ajaygaḍh) by Trailokyavarman (v. 17). The Ajaygaḍh

[16] Ajaygaḍh R. I. of Kīrtivarman also makes an identical reference. *E. I.*, XXX. p. 90., V. 3.

[17] *ibid.*, I., p. 337, V. 2.

Inscription pays eloquent tribute to their military achievements thus, Jaunādhara, the brother of Gadādhara, the royal chamberlain, fought at Kālañjara with conspicuous distinction (v. 11), and his younger brother, Mālādhara, was also a well known warrior of his time (v. 12).

Inferior castes seem to be referred to in a general way by the comprehensive term, '*Saṁkīrṇavarṇa*', used in the Khajurāho records of V.S. 1059 (v. 59). Presumably there were other social groups in the Candella territory, but they are not enumerated. The Meḍas and the Caṇḍālas were known, and however low their social status may have been, they were not ignored, as they were given a place in the conventional list of officials and communities, occuring in connection with grants. The Chārkhāri Plate of V.S. 1346 includes Nāpita (barber), Mahara and Dhīvara (fisherman) in the list.[18]

Marriage and position of women.

Marriage within one's own caste (varṇa) seems to have already become the general rule. Candella Harṣa married a suitable lady of equal caste (savarṇṇā), named Kañchukā, from the Cāhamāna family.[19] Yaśovarman had for his wife, Puppā, hailing from a noble family (mahāvaṁśe samutpannā).[20] Madanavarman had three queens, "Maharājñī Vālhaṇadevī, Rājñī Lakhamādevi and Rājñī Cāndala (Candela)-devi", as known from the recently discovered Bhārat Kalā Bhavan copper plates of Madanavarman, dated in V.S. 1192 (1136 A.D.). The chief Queen of Candella Vīravarman was Kalyāṇadevi, the grand daughter of Śri Cādala of the Dadhīci-vaṁśa,an object of reverence for the Kṣatriyas (bhujajanmavandyah-Ajaygaḍh Rock Inscription of of V.S. 1317).[21] The brahmin ministers of the Candella ruler were also careful in selecting brides from equally illustrious families (mahāvaṁśa. V. 33, sat-kula. v. 34—Māu Candella Inscription).[22]

[18] *ibid.*, XX., p. 136, L. 10.
[19] *ibid.*, I., p. 126, V. 21.
[20] *ibid.*, I., p. 144, V. 40.
[21] *ibid.*, I., p. 327, V. 10.
[22] *ibid.*, I., p. 200.

Polygamy in the princely society is indicated by the expression, 'Sapatnī' (co-wife) in the Khajurāho Rock Insc. V.S. 1059., v. 59, and by the names of three queens of Madanavarman furnished by the Bhārat Kalā Bhavan Plates. The Ajaygaḍh Record refers to Kalyāṇadevī's recognition as the Chief Queen,[23] which implies the existence of other queens of lesser rank. The Chief Queen (Mahiṣī) enjoyed a distinctive position even in the royal court. Reference may in this connection be made to the part played by Malhandevi, the queen of Paramardideva, during Candella-Cauhān conflict.[24] Brahmins also could take more than one wife. Ananta, the most favourite minister of Kīrtivarman, had two wives, as stated in the Māu Record.[25]

The use of 'Sindura' (vermillion) on the forehead by married women must have been very popular, as it is repeatedly mentioned in the Candella records and shown in the sculptures of Khajurāho. The married women are described as 'Sīmantinī'.[26] On the death of the husband it was the custom, as it is now among Hindu women, to remove the sindura mark (nihsindurita,[27] sindurabhūṣaṇavivarjitāmāsyapadmaṁ),[28] along with the jewellery, such as, necklaces of pearls, &c., (utsṛṣṭahāra-valayaṁ-kucamaṇḍalaṁ).[29] External signs by which widowhood is indicated in Hindu society seem to have been widely in use in the Candella country, and with these signs must have been also associated the usual austerities which a Hindu widow is required to perform.

The puranic idea of womanly chastity and devotion to the husband was upheld. If an ideal marriage in the royal family was to be depicted, the Candella court-poet would find ready illustrations in the divine couples, Girijā and Śiva ("Sthāānohśarīrārdhakaṁ......Girijām")[30] and, Śrī and the

---

[23] *ibid.*, I., p. 328, V. 14.
[24] *P. R.*, p. 97.
[25] *E. I.*, I., p. 200, V. 34.
[26] Khajurāho Insc. V. S. 1059., V. 13.
[27] *E. I.*, I., p. 141, V. 13.
[28] *ibid.*, p. 129, V. 41.
[29] *ibid.*
[30] Ajyagaḍh Record., V. S. 1317, V. 1 & 16.

enemy of Kaiṭabha, i.e., Viṣṇu (Śrīriva-Kaiṭabhāre).[31] Reference may in this connection be made to the marriage of a Candella princess, Naṭṭā or Naṭṭākhyadevī, as described in the Benares Grant of Kalacuri Karṇa.[32] Devotion of Arundhatī and Anusūyā to their husbands, Vaśiṣṭha and Atri, the great Puranic sages respectively, are also cited as ideals in the Candella records.[33]

To protect a married woman from all kinds of danger and harm was apparently regarded as a sacred duty. In the Candella records the kingdom is compared to a 'Kulavadhū', to be defended by all means. The kulavadhū's life and security were so much valued because she and her husband were partners, bound up with ties of common duties, and because by bearing children she was an instrument of perpetuating his line, and for the repayment of the debt which he owed to his ancestors. The birth of a son raised the status of the wife, and was an occasion for jubilation. Kañchukī, the queen of the Candella king Harṣa, by giving birth to the prince, Yaśovarman, came to deserve the esteem and honour enjoyed by Kṛṣṇa's mother, Devakī, and she walked with her head erect (putror-janmonnataṁ-śirah).[34]

Women generally had to stay indoors in their own apartments (antahpurikā), not accessible to the outsiders, where they kept themselves occupied with their household duties. Some of the Candella queens however seem to have taken part in public affairs, or took interest in enterprises beneficial to the people. The Parmāl Rāso eloquently refers to the influence of the queen of Parmāl Candel (Paramarddideva) in court life as well as in the administration of the state. Kalyāṇadevī, the queen of Vīravarman, undertook some works of public utilty, such as the construction of a well and a maṇḍapa or rest-house for the pilgrims. The enlightened outlook of Queen Kalyāṇadevi, as depicted in

[31] *ibid.*

[32] *E. I.*, II., p. 306, V. 8.

[33] 'Vaśiṣthadayitā'—Ajaygaḍh Record. V. S. 1317, V. 16; 'Anusūyātri-muneriva'—Māu Record, V. 33).

[34] *E. I.,* I., p. 128.

Verse 17 of the Ajaygaḍh Record (V.S. 1317),[35] indicates that the queens, particularly the Mahiṣī or the Chief Queen, had to be well-educated.

When women of royal family were captured by the enemy after a military victory, resulting in the death of their husbands, poets sympathise with the agony of their widowhood, which sometimes was accentuated by the humiliation suffered through imprisonment.[36] What is suggested is that they were so devoted to their husbands that they would rather die than surrender themselves to their captors. It is to be observed however, that the authors of the inscriptions of the Candella rulers were careful in avoiding suggestions which might reflect on the moral character of their victorious patrons, when they described the sufferings of these women The object was to give an impressive account of their valour and might.

The picture that is furnished by the Candella records is that of women in high society. It is not therefore possible to form any definite idea about the life of women in general, who must have in all likelihood been contented with their domestic duties.

'Offering of water to the deceased parents' on the occasion of their death anniversary and on occasions of the performance of meritorious acts, like grants of lands to brahmins and scholars, find repeated mention in the Candella records. Besides 'Sāmvatsarika' of the mother of Devavarman referred to in the Nānyaura Grant of V. S. 1107, we find the use of the expressions, 'Saṁtarpya' and 'pitṛtarpaṇaṁ kṛtvā' (offering of water to parents) before the recording of grants of lands to brahmins.

Among popular festivals and recreations mention may be made of hunting expeditions and elephant fights as well as dance and musical performances, which have been amply demonstrated in numerous sculptured panels of the Khajurāho temples. The Khajūrāho inscription of V.S. 1011 also mentions that when the splendid temple of Viṣṇu was erected by

[35] *ibid.*, p. 328.
[36] *ibid.*, p. 145, V. 46.

Yaśovarman at Khajurāho, there were great festivals in which gods also participated.[37]

Special amusements and sports, probably amorous in character (surata-krīḍā),[38] were provided by pleasure-mounts and lakes, respectively called, krīḍāgiri and kelisarasi.[39] They were entertained by Kirāta women singing to the accompaniment of peacock's dances. Some kind of popular folk-songs was probably sung on these occasions, to which royal patronage was extended.

The cultured people enjoyed performances of Sanskrit dramas. A highly philosophical drama written by Śrī Kṛṣṇa Miśra, named Prabodhacandrodaya (Riśe of the Moon of perfect intelligence), was staged in the presence of King Kīrtivarman and his courtiers at the instance of Śrī Gopāla, a 'sahaja-suhṛt' of the king.

Economic Condition.

Agriculture must have been one of the principal occupations of Bundelkhaṇḍ during the Candella period, as in other parts of India. The 'hala' or plough is prominently mentioned as an instrument of cultivation. Land was measured according to the number of ploughs used in cultivating it. The system of measuring land on the basis of its 'seed capacity' was also in vogue. The equation between the 'hala' measure and the measure based on 'seed capacity' was also known. Thus 7½ 'droṇas' of land was identical with 10 halas (Sārddha-droṇa-sapta parikalita prastha pratyeka vādha vyavasthayā daśa-halāvacchinnā-bhūmih-Pachār Plate).[40] The 'droṇa', of course, was a kind of a dry measure of weighment of agricultural products and each droṇa contained 16 'prasthas'. The instance cited shows that it was usual that one 'prastha' of seed was to be sown broadcast (vāpagatya) on each 'vādha' of land. Vādha, evidently, was the unit of the measurement of land surface. Hence 7½ droṇas of seed

[37] *E. I.*, I. p. 129., V. 42.
[38] *I. A.*, XVI, p. 201, L. 5. This is also evident from innumerable 'mithuna' sculptures on the walls of the Khajurāho temples
[39] *E. I.*, I. p. 125, V. 13.
[40] *ibid.*, X. p. 48, L. 8.

mean 120 prasthas, cultivable by 10 halas, i.e., 12 prasthas or $\frac{1}{8}$th of a droṇa of seed for each hala of land. This is more clearly explained in the Mahobā Plate of Paramardideva, which refers to "pādona-droṇa catuṣṭayā parikalita prastha pratyeka vādha vyavasthayā dairghye vādha 10 vistare vādha 6 jātavādha ṣaṣṭhyānvita"[41] i.e., 60 prasthas of seed ('pādona' being less by a quarter or 4 prasthas i.e., 64-4= 60 prasthas) to be sown in 5 halas of land at the rate of one prastha of seed per square vādha of land.

Attention was paid to irrigation work for the facility of cultivation. The Khajurāho Inscription of V.S. 1011, for example, refers to the construction of embankments to divert the course of a river (v. 26), evidently for the benefit of the peasantry concerned. Expressions like '-nālā' (canals), 'puskariṇī' (tanks) and 'bhiṭi' (embankments) are met with in different Candella records. These were usually located near the cultivable plots of land, apparently to supply water to the fields.

Arts and Crafts.

There were men engaged in occupations other than agriculture also. Various crafts and professions are mentioned in the Candella records, and these may have been generally followed on a hereditary basis gradually developing caste-like features in their respective organisations. The inscriptions refer to Rūpakāra (sculptor), Rītikāra, Pitalakāra and Pitalahāra (brazier), Sūtradhāra (architect), Vaidya (physician), Aśvavaidya (veterinary surgeon), Nāpita (barber), and Dhīvara (fisherman).

The epithet '*Śilpin*' was not probably applied to a craftsman until he became an expert in his line. The title '*Vijñānin*' was apparently superior to the title 'śilpin'. This was reserved for those senior śilpins only who attained further skill and efficiency in their respective crafts. Pālhaṇa, the engraver of the Semrā Plates of V.S. 1223, is described as merely a metal-carver, Pitalakāra. But the Icchāwār Plates

[41] *ibid.*, XVI, p. 12. L. 11-12,

of V.S. 1228, issued about five years later, mention him as a 'śilpin', and further experience for about two more years made him a 'vijñānin', as claimed in the Mahobā Plate of V.S. 1230. In the Pachār Plates of V.S. 1233 and the Chārkhāri Plates of V.S. 1236, the same craftsman has been mentioned as a '*vaidagdhi-viśvakarmmanā*', a master of the art and craft. Probably by then he had reached a stage in his career when his knowledge was not confined to the bare technicalities of the craft, but embraced a wider field, including the aesthetic aspect of the craft, which was recognised by the aristocratic patrons of art and culture. Rai Bahadur Hiralal observes that no improvement in the skill of this particular individual is discernible in the workmanship of the plates mentioned above.[42]

It is also noticed that Rāma, the builder of the well and the maṇḍapa at the Ajaygaḍh fort during the reign of Candella Vīravarman, is described as '*Vaidagdhi*' in the inscription on a stone in the same fort (V.S. 1317).[43] Sūtradhāra Chiccha, who built the Khajurāho Temple, was '*Vijñāna-Viśvakarttā*', as mentioned in the Khajurāho stone inscription of V.S. 1059.[44]

Trade.

Prominent traders or bankers, who were known as Śreṣṭhis, occupy a very influential position due to their wealth and organisational leadership. Sometimes they came forward with gifts and donations for the maintenance of religious establishments or to set up images of deities for public worship. Most of the gifts recorded were made by the Śreṣṭhis of the Grahapati family, who were worshippers of Jīnanātha. It seems that the trade was mostly in the hands of the Jains, who formed a wealthy community in the Candella territory. That they exercised some influence even in the Candella court is evident from epigraphic records. The Khajurāho Jain Temple Inscription of V. S. 1011 describes one Pāhila of the

[42] *ibid,*. XX., p. 128.
[43] *ibid.,* I. p. 228, V. 22.
[44] *ibid.,* p. 146, V. 60.

Grahapati family as held in high honour by king Dhaṅga (Dhāṅgarājena mānya),[45] and the Darbāt Śāntinātha image inscription of V.S. 1132 refers to Śreṣṭhis Pāhila and Jīju as hereditary ministers (kulāmātyavṛnda) of King Kīrtivarman.[46]

There were markets (āpaṇa) in the towns, in which there were streets of shops where wares were kept for sale (vaṇijānāṁ vīthipathe).

Exchange & Currency.

The coins of the Candella rulers are available from the middle of the 11th century A.D. Early Candella rulers have not left any coinage of their own. It has been supposed, however, that the Gādhiyā coins may have been used by them as serving the purposes of a metallic currency until they introduced their own coinage.[47] The terms '*pala*'[48] and '*hāṭaka*',[49] mentioned in some of their inscriptions, have been taken by some to denote 'gold pieces'. But there is no independent evidence in support of the presumed use of 'pala' and 'hāṭaka' as coin denominations in any period. 'Pala' is known to be a unit of gold measure, while the dictionary meaning of 'Hāṭaka' is 'gold'.

Kīrtivarman is found to have been the first Candella king to strike coins in his own name. His gold coins, both dramma (app. 63 grains) and half-dramma (app. 31 grains), are very similar in design to the coins of the Kalacuri ruler, Gāṅgeyadeva. The reverse of these coins shows a rudely executed figure of a goddess generally seated cross-legged, identified with Lakṣmī or Pārvatī.[50] On the obverse is inscribed the name of the Candella ruler in bold characters. Probably the original Kalacuri types, to which these Candella coins bear kinship, were in circulation in the Candella dominion when it came under the temporary occupation of

---

[45] *ibid.*, p. 136.
[46] *I. H. Q.*, XXX, pp. 183-85.
[47] *I. A.*, XXXVII., pp. 147-48.
[48] *E. I.*, I. p. 143, V. 33.
[49] *ibid.*, p. 146, V. 52.
[50] *I. A.*, XXXVII, p. 147.

Lakṣmīkarṇa. They were later imitated by the Candellas after they had recovered their dominion from the clutches of the Cedis.

The dramma coins of Kīrtivarman (Gk. Dramma standard) are not very rare, according to Smith,[51] but there are only three specimens of his half-dramma coins (one in the Indian Museum, one in the British Museum and one in Hoey's Cabinet). The next ruler, Sallakṣaṇa, continued the same series of gold coins. His drammas are very rare, but five of his quarter-drammas are noticed by Smith. Sallakṣaṇavarman spells his name as 'Hallakṣaṇa' in the coin legend. His copper coins present a unique feature : viz., 'Hanumān (the monkey-god) under a canopy' is found in place of the Lakṣmī figure on the obverse. For the next ruler, Jayavarman, we have as many as eleven Hanumān-type copper drammas (60 grains). Dr. A. S. Altekar refers to an unique 'Arddha-dramma' coin (30 grains), belonging to this ruler.[52] It has the figure of the 'Hanumān in flying pose' on the reverse. It is a die-struck coin. Cunningham noticed a silver coin of Jayavarman in the collection of the British Museum, but it can not be traced now. Copper coins of the usual Hanumān type are also available for the reign of Pṛthvīvarman. One such coin, weighing 16.2 grains, probably one quarter dramma piece, had been acquired by the British Museum.

The largest number of available Candella coins belong to Madanavarman. These may be classified according to their denomination :—(i) Gold drammas, (60 grains), (ii) Gold quarter drammas, (15 grains), and (iii) Copper quarter drammas, (15 grains). Cunningham noticed two gold drammas, six gold quarter drammas and two copper quarter drammas, during his tours in Bundelkhand. V. A. Smith notices one gold dramma and two gold quarter drammas.[53] Later 48 more gold coins (8 large, weighing between 13.16 to 16.07 grains) were found in a hoard in a village named

---

[51] *ibid.*, p. 148.
[52] *J.N.S.I.* V. p. 33.
[53] *C. C. I. M.*, p. 253.

Panwar in the Teonthār tehsil, of the Rewāh state.[54] So far no silver coin of this king has been noticed, excepting a single doubtful one, viz., a quarter dramma in the collection of Mr. Hoey. But this may have been made actually of heavily alloyed base gold, like many of the Candella coins.

For the long reign of Paramardi we have however, a solitary specimen of a base gold dramma (61.4 grains) from Khajurāho, of the usual Lakṣmī type.

Later, Candella rulers, who revived the political power of the dynasty after it had suffered serious reverses at the hands of the Cauhāns, continued to issue coins of their own. We have specimens of gold and copper drammas of Trailokyavarman. Though the findspots of the gold coins are not known, a copper one was discovered in the Bāndā district, which may be presumed to have been included in Candella dominion in the early part of the 13th century A.D.

The last Candella king, for whom we have independent coinage, is Vīravarman. A unique gold dramma of this prince was discovered at Khajurāho, and now preserved in the Indian Museum cabinet.[55] Very recently another gold coin of Vīravarman has been noticed by Mm. Mirashi.[56] It was found from the ancient site at Tripuri, the capital of the Kalacuri rulers, near Jabalpur. The coin weighs 46 grains, and is 7″ in diameter. The legend inscribed on the coin, as read by Mm. Mirashi is "Śrīmad-Virava(r)ma-dha(rā) devo". The epithet 'dharādeva' (a divinity on earth) in the coin-legend has been explained by Mm. Mirashi as being regarded as a god.

---

[54] *J.A.S.B.* (*Num. Sup*). XXII. p. 131.
[55] *C. C. I. M.*, p. 254.
[56] *J. N. S. I.*, XVI., pp. 236-38.

CHAPTER XIII

RELIGION

Traditions current in Mahobā regard Manīyā Deo (Devī), a tribal deity of the aboriginal people of the area, as the tutelary deity of the Candellas[1] throughout their history. A shrine dedicated to the goddess exists at Mahobā, where a rude figure is carved on a projecting boulder. There is another small temple of Maniyā Devī on the hill of Maniyāgarh (Rājgarh), the site of a large ruined fort on the left bank of the Ken river, from the remains of which has been found an image of a female with sword in hand. This has been identified as the figure of Maniyā Devī, from whom the 'garh' derives its name. According to Beglar,[2] it does not appear improbable that she was a sort of compromise between the Brahmanical Pārvatī and the naked female worshipped to this day by some tribes of Gonds. In the bardic account of Cānd also reference is made to Maniyādevī as the goddess of the Candellas to whom they appealed in times of danger.

The extant epigraphic records as well as the numerous temples of the Candella rulers testify to the wide prevalence of the Brahmanical religion amongst them. The Candella kings were generally worshippers of Śiva, but the records reveal that they were tolerant to worshippers of other faiths. Some of the Candella kings appear to have been staunch Vaiṣṇavites. The non-Brahmanical religions, Jainism and Buddhism, also received occasional patronage from the Candellas.

To ascertain the condition of religious worship in Jejākabhukti under the Candella rule, we may discuss different sectarian religions separately.

---

[1] *I. A.,* XXXVII. p. 137.

[2] *A. S. R.,* VII. p. 43.

Brahmanical Religion.

A study of the Candella inscriptions reveal that Brahmanical theism in its different aspects beginning from the '*trayīdharmma*' (the three Vedas) to the Purānic conception of cult divinites was prevalent among the rulers and their subjects. The records are mostly concerned with Brahmanical sects. Invocations are offered to different gods at the beginning and at the end of these records.

In the Khajurāho inscription of V. S. 1011 the king is invoked to protect the laws of the 'three Vedas'. The prosperity of the Brahmins in particular was an object aimed at.[3]

But undoubtedly the utmost predominance was enjoyed by the Puranic religion with its idea of Trinity (Brahmā, Viṣṇu & Śiva) as well as its innumerable myths and legends connected with different gods and goddesses.

The importance of '*tapas*' (religious austerities) is acclaimed in some records as means of achieving great power and influence (nirantara tapas tīvra prabhavaṁ).[4]

Religious *sacrifices* also find mention in a Candella record, though indirectly, by way of comparison with battles waged by Yaśovarman. V. 17 of the Khajurāho record of V. S. 1011 states, '(Yaśovarman) never tired at the sacrifice, where terribly weilded sword was the ladle, where the oblation of clarified butter was made with streaming blood, where the twanging of bow-strings was the exclamation of 'vaṣaṭ' and at which exasperated warriors marching in order, were the priests, successful with his counsel (as with sacred hymns), sacrificed like beasts, the adversaries in the fire of enmity, made to blaze up high by the wind of his unappeased anger.'[5]

The above description gives us an idea of the procedure of sacrifices, which included oblation of clarified butter by means of ladles on the sacred fire with the exclamation of 'vaṣaṭ' and the utterance of sacred hymns and accompanied by the sacrifice of beasts. Sacrifice to the sacred fire is also

[3] *E. I.*, I. pp. 129, 135.
[4] *ibid.*, pp. 125, 130. V. 7.
[5] *ibid.*, pp. 126, 131.

mentioned in connection with grants of lands &c., to brahmins in the Semrā, Mahobā and Chārkhāri copper plates.[6]

That the Candella rulers conceded an important place to the Brahmanical religion and philosophy will also be evident from a number of inscriptions recording grant of lands and other gifts to immigrant scholarly brahmins, who were encouraged to settle in the Candella dominion. Mention of the distinguishing gotras, pravaras, as also of the particular Śākhā or caraṇa of the vedic study, to which they belonged, in the land-grants of the Candellas, indicate that popularisation of the different aspects of vedic studies was one of the objects of the Candella rulers.

Grants of lands were also considered as acts of piety leading to the increase of religious merit (puṇya) of the donor and his deceased parents (mātāpitror-athātmanah). The records sometime mention the particular occasion when donations were made.[7] A number of Khajurāho records indicate that lands and dwellings as well as valuable gifts in connection with erection of temples were given not to a single priest but to a number of brahmins.[8] It may be reasonably presumed therefore that there was a regular hierarchy of priests who looked after the diverse affairs of the temple and conducted the daily worship. Some of them were called royal priests or priests of the royal household, who in addition to their priestly functions were occasionally charged with some administrative duties (e.g., Bhaṭṭa Yaśodhara, the royal priest, was made an aministrator of justice, Dharmmādhikāra).[9] Besides the priests mention is made of the temple dancers. The Kālañjara Pillar inscription in the temple of Nīlakaṇṭha[10] refers to one Mahānācanī Padmāvatī, the chief of the dancing girls attached to the shrine. She was of the type of temple dancers (Devadāsis), dedicated to the service of the God for life, found in other parts of India. Temple

---

[6] *ibid.*, IV. p. 158. L. 14; *ibid.* XVI. p. 13. L. 19; *ibid.* XX. p. 130. L. 10.

[7] For Inscriptional references to such occasions for gifts *vide ante.* chap. XIII.

[8] *E. I.*, I. p. 146. V. 53; "dhanadhānyadhenu-vasudhādānena sammānitah/ saudhesu sphaṭikādri-kūṭa vikaṭeśvāropita brāhmaṇāh//"

[9] *ibid.*, p. 146. V. 56.

[10] *A. S. R.* XXI. p. 34.

dancers are also seen depicted on the sculptured panels of the Khajurāho temples. The same record also mentions one Mahāpratihāra (Chief door-keeper) Saṁgrāmasiṁha, attached to the temple. Evidently he was a temple official, either appointed by the king or by the priests.

Vaiṣṇavism.

Some of the early rulers of the Candella family including Yaśovarman, were devout worshippers of Viṣṇu. The earliest definite reference to the worship of Viṣṇu occurs in the Khajurāho Inscription dated V.S. 1011 (953-54 A.D.).[11] The record begins and ends with invocation to God Vāsudeva,—'Oṁ namo Bhagavate Vāsudevāya'. The king Yaśovarman is described here as 'one anxious to worship the feet of Viṣṇu, the enemy of Madhu' (Madhuripu-caraṇārādhane yah satṛṣṇah). It records the erection of a magnificent temple dedicated to Viṣṇu, the golden pinnacles of which illuminated the sky, and became, it is said, the object of attraction even for the denizens of heaven. The image, that was installed in the temple, was also a highly valuable one (Vv. 42-43).

This temple has been identified by Cunningham with the Vaiṣṇava temple, known as the Caturbhuja temple at Khajurāho. It is 98′ ft. in length and 45′ 3″ in breadth. The four subordinate shrines are placed as usual at the four corners of the terrace, and the fifth one dedicated to Garuḍa, the vehicle of Viṣṇu, has however disappeared. Inside the sanctum of the temple is a rare Viṣṇu image having three heads and four arms (4′ 1″ high) standing in an elaborately carved toraṇa frame. The middle head of the image is human, but the side ones are those of Narasiṁha (Man-lion) and Varāha (the Great Boar) incarnations of Viṣṇu. Other incarnations of the God are also portrayed in bas relief on the door-jamb within the temple. The 'avatāras' of Viṣṇu, it seems, were highly popular with the Candellas. The Khajurāho inscription of V.S. 1011 in its opening verse

[11] *E. I.*, I. pp. 123-35.

eulogises the different incarnations of Viṣṇu, viz., Varāha Vāmana and Narasiṁha, in which forms He relieved the world from the oppression of the demons (Daityas). He is also referred to in the same verse as Śakra and Daityārāti.

The popularity of the *avatāra* cult will be further evident from the Dudāhi ruins, which consist of temples dedicated to the Varāha incarnation of Viṣṇu.[12] In the principal group of the ruins may be noticed a Varāha temple with a figure of a boar under a four-pillared canopy. Besides there are two other boar statues, one of which is called the 'Bācchā' (the little pig) in the same group. In the second group of the ruins also there is a statue of the Varāha incarnation. To its left is the image of the Earth goddess (pṛthivī) and beneath it is a Nāga with a twisted body. These ruins, on the evidence of the inscription found there,[13] may be assigned to Devalabdhi, the grandson of Yaśovarman. This proves that this grandson of Yaśovarman imbibed his grandfather's faith in Vaiṣṇavism.

There are other inscriptional evidences also which speak of the Candella rulers' leanings to the Vaiṣṇavite faith. In the Deogaḍh Rock inscription we find that Kīrtivarman (A.D. 1098) is likened to Viṣṇu.[14] Kīrtivarman is again compared to Puruṣottama (Viṣṇu) in the Mahobā inscription.[15] Jayavarman (A.D. 1117), the grandson of Kīrtivarman, according to a Kālañjar fragmentary inscription (No. 2), was also devoted to Viṣṇu.[16] Again the Rock inscription of Vīravarman compares the Candella ruler Trailokyavarman to Viṣṇu. It is said that Trailokyavarman (1st half of 13th cent. A.D.) revived the Candella power, which had been submerged in the ocean formed by the streams of the Turuṣkas, just as Viṣṇu, who lifted up the earth in his Varāha incarnation.[17]

Besides at Khajurāho we come to notice two temples dedicated to Varāha and Vāmana incarnations of Viṣṇu.

---

[12] *A. S. R.*, X. p. 90.
[13] *I. A.*, VIII. p. 237.
[14] *ibid.*, p. 238. V. 3.
[15] *E. I.*, I. 219. V. 26.
[16] *JASB.*, (184), p. 321; *A. S. R.* XXI. pp. 34-35.
[17] *E. I.*, I., pp. 329., V. 7.

The Varāha temple (20′ 4″ × 16′) has a colossal monolithic statue of the boar (8′ in length and 5′ high), carved all over with multiple figures of gods and goddesses. The Vāmana temple also, besides containing the image of Vāmana (the dwarf), 4′ 8″ high, has the figures of Varāha, Vāmana and Nṛsiṁha carved in the niches within.

Another sculpture of interest is an 11-headed image of Viṣṇu, enshrined in the central niche of the Citragupta or Bharatji's temple at Khajurāho. The central head is that of Viṣṇu, while the remaining ten represent his ten incarnations.

As for the erection of temples dedicated to Viṣṇu, we have already referred to the activities of Yaśovarman. Similar measures were also undertaken during the reign-periods of some of the later rulers of the family. The Māu stone inscription of the time of Madanavarman records the erection of a temple to Viṣṇu by the family of his ministers.[18] The record opens with usual invocation to Viṣṇu. Baṭeśvar inscription of the time of Paramardi also uses similar invocatory language at the beginning—'Oṁ Oṁ namo Bhagavate Vāsudevāya'.[19] It appears that Paramardi extended similar patronage to Vaiṣṇavism, as, one of his ministers, Sallakṣaṇa erected two beautiful temples, one to Viṣṇu and another to Śiva. As for the Viṣṇu temple, V. 25 of the inscription records:

> "Prāsādo Vaiṣṇavastena nirmmitontarvahan-Hariṁ
> Mūrddhnā spṛśati yo nityaṁ padamasyaiva
> madhyamaṁ//".[20]

During the reign of Bhojavarman, Nāna, one of his ministers (saciva), claims to have caused an image of Hari to be placed on the celebrated fort of Jayapura (Ajaygaḍh) (V.S. 1345-A.D. 1288).[21]

The numerous temples at Khajurāho including those which are in ruins are attributed to the Candellas. A number of them were dedicated to Viṣṇu. But the names of the Candella rulers who built these temples are not generally preserved in extant records.

---

[18] *ibid.*, I., pp. 202, 206., V. 46.
[19] *ibid.*, p. 208.
[20] *ibid.*, p. 211.
[21] *ibid.*, XXVIII., pp. 104, 107., V. 33.

In the western group of temples is the shrine now known as the Devi Jagadambi (Jagadambā) or Kalī temple. It contains an image of the river-goddess Gaṅgā, standing in her vehicle, Makara, which appears to have been substituted for the original Viṣṇu image. It is however not known when this substitution took place. That the temple was originally vaiṣṇava is shown by the image of Viṣṇu carved over the entrance to the sanctum. Another temple in the same group, now known as the Pārvvati temple, was also vaiṣṇava originally, as the lintel of the sanctum bears on its centre a figure of Viṣṇu, which led scholars to identify it as a vaiṣṇavite shrine. But the Viṣṇu image appears to have been replaced at a later date by that of Pārvvati or Gaurī, on the pedestal of which is carved the figure of a godhā or godhikā (lizard).

In the eastern group there are several mounds marking the sites of ancient temples. Some of these must have been vaiṣṇava temples. The ruined temple, now known as Kākra Maṛh, is identified as vaiṣṇavite by the finds of the door-frame to the sanctum and its four pillars. A four-armed image of Viṣṇu is enshrined in the Javāri temple, lying close to the Khajurāho village.

The southern group includes a temple near the Jaṭkāri village, in which there is a large-sized Viṣṇu (9′ ft. high).

Sectarian attempts to depict Viṣṇu as superior to Śiva and Brahmā, the two other members of the Trinity, are to be noticed in both Candella inscription and sculpture. In V. 1 of the Khajurāho record it is claimed that 'Hari is higher than Hara, as the latter holds on his head Gaṅgā, an offering to the feet of Viṣṇu'. On the lintel over the entrance to the sanctum of the Lakṣmaṇa temple at Khajurāho is a figure of Lakṣmī with Brahmā and Śiva to her left and right, as if supplicating the consort of Viṣṇu.

In inscriptions the deity is generally invoked under the names, Viṣṇu, Hari and Bhagavāna Vāsudeva; in some records other names also occur, such as, Murāri, Mādhava,

[32] *ibid.*, I. P. 124.

Puruṣottama, Nārāyaṇa, Upendra, Śauri, Śakra, Daityārāti, &c., as well as the names of the different forms of his incarnations such as, Varāha, Vāmana, Nṛsiṁha and Rāma.

His consort is mentioned as Lakṣmī, Śrī, Kamalā, &c. Sarasvatī or Puṣṭi, a consort of Viṣṇu is found depicted on the body of the great Varāha image of Khajurāho. The Jaṭkāri Caturbhuja temple possesses a peculiar sculpture on its outer wall, a lion-headed female. Possibly this is the female counterpart of the Narasiṁha incarnation of Viṣṇu.

Some *Coins* and *Seals* (attached to the copper plates of some of the later Śaiva rulers of the Candella dynasty) bear a representation of Lakṣmī. The device may have been borrowed from the Kalacuris whom the Candella rulers defeated. The seals bear in relief the figure of a four-armed goddess sitting in 'Lalitāsana' on a double-petalled lotus (viśva padma) or on a four-legged stool with an elephant standing on an expanded water lily on either side and holding an upturned pitcher over the head of the goddess. The central image is of *Gaja-Lakṣmī*, Mahā Lakṣmī or Kamalā, the consort of Viṣṇu. Lakṣmī, when in the company of her consort, is portrayed with two hands, but while depicted singly, she is endowed with four hands with elephants anointing her from both sides. Mahā Lakṣmī, according to the Mārkaṇḍeya Purāṇa, is one of the forms of the Great Mother, the consort of Śiva. It is to be noted that the rulers using such seals called themselves 'Parama-Māheśvara' (devout worshippers of Śiva). Hence the use of the Gaja-Lakṣmī symbol did not conflict with their Śaiva faith. Moreover it may be mentioned that Gaja-Lakṣmī figures are noticed in some early seals, coins and relief carvings of the pre-Christian period, even before the rise of the worship of the cult divinities. She was originally a folk-goddess, the presiding deity of beauty, wealth and fortune, and as such, became an object of adoration for all sects and religions in later periods. The adoption of this emblem by the Candella rulers was therefore not due to any sectarian bias but for the continued prosperity of their kingdom.

The mount of Viṣṇu was Garuḍa, but in the Rāma incarnation *Hanumān* (the monkey) becomes his chief devotee. Some Candella coins bear the figure of Hanumān on one side. At Khajurāho is found a large statue of the monkey-god with a short dedicatory inscription, dated 922 A.D., on its pedestal. Another colossal image of Hanumān, head having broken off, has been found from the 'Baniyā kā barāt' ruins of Dudāhi.[23] Hanumān was also originally a folk-god for strength and vigour, later absorbed in the Hindu pantheon and worshipped to this day as such. It is not surprising therefore that the Candella rulers adopted the monkey-symbol on their coins, and some bulky images, signifying strength and vigour, are found in the Candella country.

It is thus evident that Viṣṇu worship continued in the Candella country throughout the period of Candella rule, though the predominant religion during this time was Śaivism.

Śaivism.

Śaivism was already a popular religion in the north and central India long before the advent of the Candellas. Kālañjar, which became one of the major strongholds of the Candellas, was popularly known for many centuries as an abode of Nīlakaṇṭha Śiva. It is of interest to note that Yaśovarman who, by occupying the fortress of Kālañjar initiated an era of greatness in the history of the Candellas, was himself a vaiṣṇavite. But from the time of his son and successor, Dhaṅga, the Candella rulers became devout worshippers of Śiva, and Śaivism since then became practically the royal religion in the Candella dominion.

For Dhaṅga we have the evidence of the Khajurāho inscription of V.S. 1059 (A.D. 1002-03)[24]. It opens with the usual invocation to Śiva (Oṁ Oṁ namah Śivāya), and also some verses in praise of the different forms and aspects of that god. viz., Rudra, Digambara, Śūladhara, Maheśvara and Paśupati. This inscription records that Dhaṅga erected

[23] *A. S. R.*, X., p. 90.
[24] *E. I.*, I. pp. 137-47.

a magnificent temple of Śambhu, where he installed two liṅgas, one of which was made of emerald (marakatamayaṁ tuṅgaṁ liṅgaṁ), and the other of stone. It is stated that the glories achieved by Dhaṅga were due to the grace of the god, Śiva, whom he worshipped ardently. According to the Śaiva Purāṇas, a 'Ratnoja' liṅga is installed by votaries on the fulfilment of some cherished object. Dhaṅga may have set up the emerald liṅga to mark his attainment of a superior political status.

The temple, referred to in the Khajurāho record as having been built by Dhaṅga, has been identified with the Viśvanātha temple at Khajurāho (89′ 1″ in length and 45′ 10″ in breadth), where the said inscription was found. There is an image of Śiva Viśvanātha, to whom the temple is dedicated, at the centre of the lintel of the sanctum. The emerald liṅga has however disappeared and been replaced by one of common stone. The temple has in front of it a smaller temple (31′ 3″×30′ 9″) dedicated to Nandī, the bull-mount of Śiva. It contains a highly polished colossal statue of Nandī (6′ ft. high and 7′ 3″ long).

The Khajurāho record also refers to the distribution of great quantities of gold, grain, cows and monies, as well as lands and dwellings to pious brahmins,[25] evidently for the maintenance of the temple and for making regular arrangements for the worship of the deity, installed in it.

There was another temple, dedicated to Śiva Vaidyanātha, near the Viśvanātha temple, from the ruins of which was unearthed an inscription, which is now placed on the wall of the Viśvanātha temple. It is dated in V.S. 1058 (1001-02 A.D.), and records the erection of the temple in honour of Śiva Vaidyanātha, by one Kokkalla of the Grahapati family.[26] A number of buildings were given to pious brahmins when the temple was erected, as on the other occasion mentioned above.

Besides, there are numerous Śaivite temples in different parts of the Candella dominions stylistically attributable

[25] *ibid.*, I. p. 146, V. 53.
[26] *ibid.*, pp. 147-52.

to the Candella period. Inscriptional material regarding these temples is however wanting. One belonging to the early group is a small temple dedicated to Śiva, built partly of granite and partly of sandstone on the embankment of the lake called Lālguān Sāgar at Khajurāho. Another temple, the largest extant at Khajurāho, is known as the Kandarya Mahādeva temple. In length it measures 102′ 3″, in width 66′10″ and in height 101′9″. It had four subsidiary shrines at the four corners, which now no longer exist. Inside the sanctum stands a marble linga. Close to the shrine of Kandarya Mahādeva is another ruined temple of Mahādeva, in which the image of the deity is carved on the middle of the lintel of the sanctum.

The holiest of the Khajurāho temples, which is still in religious use, is the Mātaṅgeśvara temple. The entire floor of the inner sanctum is occupied by a large 'Gaurīpaṭṭa' (20′ 4″ in diameter and 4′ 5″ in height), on which is set a highly polished colossal liṅga, 3′ 8″ in diameter and 8′ 4″ in height.

One of the finest temples at Khajurāho is the Dulādeo (the heavenly bride) temple, originally dedicated to Śiva, whose figure, as usual, appears carved on the lintel over the entrance to the sanctum. But the original image installed in the sanctum was substituted by the liṅga, now existing.

There is epigraphic evidence of the erection of a temple to Śiva at Baṭeśvara, near Agra, during the reign period of Paramardideva by his Chief Minister, Sallakṣaṇa.[27] Though the temple has not been identified, yet Baṭeśvara is traditionally famous as a holy place for the worshippers of Śiva.[28] The present temple of Baṭeśvara Mahādeva, of course, does not appear to be very old, but the liṅga, enshrined in the sanctum of the temple, is of a colossal size, not unlike other liṅgas of the Candella temples.

The Nīlakaṇṭha temple at Kālañjar is also a small one, but its importance to the Śaivites can hardly be exaggerated.

---

[27] *ibid.,* I. pp. 205-14. Cunningham locates the findspot of the inscription at Singhanpur-Baghāri, near Mahobā.

[28] *P. R.,* p. 61.

The temple might have been in existence from the Gupta period, but pillars of the maṇḍapa, which belong to the Candella school, indicate that sufficient additions to the temple were made by the Candella rulers. Just outside the maṇḍapa of the temple there is a rock-cut reservoir (Kuṇḍ) and a large-sized figure of Kāla Bhairava (24′ ft. high), an attendant of the god Śiva. According to scholars, the Bhairava image is one of the '*līlā mūrttis*' (incarnatory images) of Śiva.

At Mahobā, the capital of the Candellas, almost all the Hindu temples were utterly destroyed, but Cunningham noticed among the ruins, the remains of a Śiva temple, fragments of the '*argha*' of a liṅgaṁ and a black-stone bull (the vehicle of Śiva)".[29] Another Śiva temple, entirely of granite, was also noticed by him at the village of Rāhilya, 2 miles from Mahobā. The village is traditionally associated with Rāhil Barm or Rāhilavarman (c. 900 A.D.), the great-grand father of Dhaṅga.

It is quite common to come across invocation to Śiva in the epigraphic records of the period of the later Candella rulers. The Deogaḍh Rock inscription, Mahobā inscription, Kālañjar fragmentary inscription (No. 2) and another Kālañjar record of Paramardi invoke Śiva thus,—"Oṁ Oṁ namah Śivāya"[30] The Ajaygaḍh Rock inscription refers to Kedāra (Śiva) as—"Oṁ Oṁ namah Kedārāya"[31]

Dhaṅga's devotion to Śiva is pronouncedly proclaimed in V. 55 of the Khajurāho record, which states that after living for one hundred years, Dhaṅga ended his life at the holy confluence of the Prayāga, while meditating on Rudra (Śiva).[32] Besides we find direct evidences of Śiva worship by Vidyādhara, Madanavarman and Paramardi. Vidyādhara is described as a votary of Śiva in the Madanpur stone inscription.[33] Madanavarman and his grandson, Paramardi, both are stated to have worshipped the divine husband of Bhavānī before making grants of lands to Brāhmaṇas, as

[29] *A. S. R.*, II., p. 441.
[30] *I. A.* XVIII. p. 238; *E. I.*, I. p. 231.; *J.A.S.B.*, 1949, Pt. 1., p. 313, 317.
[31] *E. I.*, I. p. 333.
[32] *ibid.*, p. 146.
[33] *A. S. R.*, X., p. 100.

recorded in the Semrā, the Icchāwār and the Mahobā Plates. Pratāpa, Madana's younger brother, who was a very influential person in the court, undertook diverse works of public interest including erection of temples and installation of images of Śiva, Kamalā and Kālī.[34]

The long Sanskrit inscription found on a large black stone slab leaning against a pillar opposite the entrance of the cave temple of Nīlakaṇṭha at Kālañjar is claimed to have been composed by the king Paramardi out of his innate faith on Purāri (Śiva).[35]

Ajaygaḍh Rock inscription of the time of Bhojavarman refers to the erection of a temple (Devālaya) to Śiva Kedāra by one Subhaṭa of the Vāstavvya Kāyastha family, who was appointed as a saciva (minister) and Kośādhikārādhipati (Superintendent of Treasury) by the Candella king.[36]

The devotion of the Candella rulers to Śaivism is definitely indicated by the assumption of the title of 'Parama-Māheśvara' in their official documents, viz., the Nānyaura Plate 'B' (Devavarman), Nānyaura Plate 'C' and Kālañjar inscription no. 4 (Madanavarman), Semrā Plates, Icchāwār plate, Mahobā plate, Pachār plate and Chārkhāri plate 'B' (Paramardi), Garrā Grant (Trailokyavarman), Chārkhāri plate 'C' (Vīravarman) and Chārkhāri plate 'D' (Hammīravarman).

Śiva has been worshipped in the *liṅga* form all over India from a very early period. The Candellas also were adherents to the worship of Śiva in the liṅga form. This is shown by the installation of liṅgams made of black-stone, sand stone, marble and even of emerald, to which we have already referred. The colossal form of the liṅgams set up by the Candellas constitutes a remarkable feature, which cannot but attract our attention. *Mukhaliṅgams* or liṅgams with human faces carved on them are not usually met with in the Candella territory excepting one four-faced image (Caturmukha liṅgam) enshrined on the pedestal in the sanctum

[34] *J.A.S.B.* 1848., p. 317. L. 27.
[35] *ibid.*, p. 313.
[36] *E. I.*, I. p. 335.

of the so-called Brahmā temple on the bank of the Khajur Sāgar. The four-faced image was earlier mistaken for an image of Brahmā.[37] The great liṅgam of Nīlakaṇṭha Mahādeva at Kālañjar has two silver eyes fixed on it.[38]

But the worship of the human form of Śiva was also not unknown to the Candellas, and in some of the temples human figures of Śiva were installed, e.g., in the Dulādeo temple at Khajurāho, where the figures of Śiva is carved on the centre of the lintel over the entrance to the sanctum. The liṅga now enshrined in the sanctum is a substitute for the original image, which cannot be traced. In some other temples also carving of the image of Śiva on the lintel is noticed viz., the ruined temple of Mahādeva situated between the Kandârya and the Devi Jagadambā temples, and Śiva-Viśvanātha temple in the western group of the Khajurāho temples. Another noteworthy image of the deity is found in the Devi-Jagadambā temple—a three-headed eight-handed Śiva carved in relief in the lower niche of the western facade. The figure of Śiva is also seen carved on the body of the monolothic image of Boar. At the Varāha temple is carved the image of the marriage of Śiva and Pārvvatī (Kalyāṇa-sundara-mūrtti). Another image, a four-armed one, of Śiva may be seen on the outer wall of the Jaṭkāri-Caturbhuja temple.

Śiva is mentioned in the Candella documents in diverse forms depicting the various aspects of the deity. The Khajurāho records give us the following names,—Rudra, Śambhū, Digambara, Śūladhara, Maheśvara, Paśupati, Marakateśvara, Vaidyanātha and Chandramauli; The Semrā and Mahobā Plates—Viśveśvara, Bhavanīpati and Somanātha; Kālañjar Inscriptions—Nīlakaṇṭha, Purāri and Girijābhartuh; Ajaygaḍh Rock Inscription—Kedāra; Madanpur Inscription—Candraśekhara, Tryambaka and Tripurāntaka; Deogaḍh Rock inscription—Sadāśiva; Rewā copper plate—Vāmadeva; the Māu stone inscription—Indumauli, and Baṭeśvar record—Pañcānana.

---

[37] *A. S. R.*, II., p. 430.
[38] *ibid.*, XXI., p. 33.

The consort of Śiva, i.e., *Śakti* or Devī, is also often eulogised in the Candella records. She is mentioned in her different names as Maheśvarī, Bhavānī, Girijā, Kālī, Nagendrakanyā, Mahiṣāsuramarddinī, Bhāratī and Pārvvatī. The earliest evidence of Śakti worship in the Candella kingdom is found at Khajurāho in the Chaonṣaṭ Yoginī temple, in which there were 65 cells (of which 35 have survived). Excluding the lager cell, the other 64 correspond to the number of Yoginis or female attendants of the goddess Kālī. Cunningham was of opinion that there was a temple in the centre of the courtyard, consecrated to Kālī or Śiva, of which no remains have been discovered.[39] Stylistically the temple, built entirely of granite, is assigned to c. 900 A.D. Inscriptional evidence regarding the dedication of a separate temple of Kālī may be gathered from the Kālañjar fragmentary record, referring to the installation of an image of Kālī in a temple.[40] Some peculiar images of the goddess Cāmuṇḍī, a skeleton figure, may also be seen at Kālañjar, one beside the statue of Kāla Bhairava, and another near the Nīlakaṇṭha temple.[41] Cāmuṇḍī or Cāmuṇḍā, is one of the Sapta-Mātṛkās (others being Brahmeśvarī, Kaumārī, Vaiṣṇavī, Vārāhī & Indrānī). According to Varāha purāṇa however there is another Mātṛkā, called Yogeśvarī, bringing the total number to eight—'Aṣṭa-Śakti'. On the Ajaygaḍh fort there are figures of eight Śaktis, carved in a row on a rock near the Tarhāoni gate.[42] One of these Aṣṭa Śakti images again is Cāmuṇḍī, as noticed from the inscribed pedestal.

There are some specimens of composite sculpture also,—viz., Umā-Maheśvara or the āliṅgana-mūrtti, Śiva's marriage or Kalyāṇa-sundara mūrtti and Arddhanārīśvara mūrtti. The last one is particularly interesting, as in this image Śiva and Śakti are merged in one body in a sitting posture, as engraved on the outer wall of the Jaṭkāri-Caturbhuja temple. A number of standing as well as sitting Arddhanārīśvara

---

39 *ibid.*, II., p. 417.
40 *J.A.S.B.* 1848, p. 317, L. 27.
41 *A. S. R.*, XXI., p. 33.
42 *ibid.*, XXI. p. 47.

images are however seen on the walls and niches of Khajurāho temples.

The image of *Nandin* (a bull), the Vāhana or vehicle of Śiva, is almost an indispensable adjunct to a Śaivite shrine. Invariably the figure of the bull is there, either in the maṇḍapa of the temple or in the outer courtyard, with its face turned towards the deity. In some temples however Nandin is more comfortably accomodated in the separate maṇḍapa outside the main temple, but just in front of the main entrance to the sanctum. The sculptural representations of Nandin are seen at Khajurāho both singly and in the company of its master.

Minor Cults.

The survey of Brahmanical worship of the region would remain imcomplete without a reference to other Purānic and pseudo-Purānic gods and goddesses, who are mentioned in different records, or whose sculptural representations are found.

Let us begin with *Gaṅeśa.* There is no evidence to prove the existence of the Gāṇapatyas in the region particularly during the period of the Candella rule. Gaṅeśa is mentioned in the Khajurāho record[43] as a member of the family of Śiva, a parivāra-devatā. Mūṣaka, (the mouse), the popular mount of Gaṇeśa, is represented in the Khajurāho sculptures. At Ajaygaḍh we come across a statue of Gaṇeśa (Vināyaka), claimed to have been set up by Gaṇapati, the minister of Candella Vīravarman, in the Ajaygaḍh Rock Inscription of V. S. 1337, (A.D. 1281).[44] The Dhureṭi Plates of Trailokyamalla open with invocations to Gaṇapati and to Śiva.[44a]

Subrahmaṇya or Kārtikeya, another god of Śiva's family is conspicuously absent. But in the row of pillars carved over the fourth cave near the Nīlakaṇṭha temple at Kālañjar are two armed figures called 'Mahādeo ke pute', (Sons of Mahādeva).[45] One of them with bow and arrow in hand is popularly

[43] *E. I.*, I., p. 140.
[44] *A. S. B.*, XXI., p. 52.
[44a] *C. I. I.*,, IV. p. 371 (Oṁ namah Śivāya / Gaṇapataye namah).
[45] *J.A.S.B.*, 1848., p. 321.

known as 'Bīr Badh'. It seems probable that the people by regarding him as a son of Śiva, identify the image with that of Kārtikeya .

Brahmā, an important member of the Purāṇic Trinity, lost his status in the later age. and there is no sect or class owing special and exclusive allegiance to this divinity. In other words, there is no Brahmā cult like the Vaiṣṇavas and the Śaivas. But Brahmā continued to receive offerings from both the Vaiṣṇavites and the Śaivities, and inscriptional references may be noticed in some of the Candella records. Sculptural representation of the god may also be seen in the temples of both the cults. In the Candella dominon also we find figures of Brahmā depicted on the walls of some of the temples. In the Caturbhuja or Lakṣmaṇji temple at Khajurāho Brahmā along with Śiva is portrayed as standing on either side of Lakṣmī,[46] evidently to demonstrate the superiorty of Vaiṣṇavism over the other two cults. Brahmā is also seen carved on the body of the Great Boar statue of the Varāha temple of Khajurāho. But in the Vāmana temple is found the image of Brahmā along with his consort, Brahmāṇī. The Dhureṭi Plates of Trailokyamalla in an invocatory verse refers to 'Sarvva-suklā Sarasvatī as the consort of Brahmā'.[46a] At Dudāhi we come across what may be called a rare specimen of a shrine dedicated to Brahmā.[47] On the lintel of the sanctum is carved 'a three-headed bearded figure of Brahmā with his mount, the goose, supported by 'nava grahas' or nine planets'. The temple contains inscriptional evidence too. In one of the pilgrims' record, the writer pays his homage to 'Caturmukha' i.e., the four-faced god Brahmā, and his consort 'Sāvitrī' and uses the expression.—'Brahmāsāda praṇamati' at the end.

The worship of *Sūrya* or the Sun-god also appears to be quite popular among the Candellas. There is a temple known as the Citragupta temple or Bharatji's temple at Khajurāho, specially dedicated to Sūrya. An image of the deity, 5′ ft.

[46] *A. S. R.*, II., p. 427.
[46a] *C. I. I.*, IV, p. 371.
[47] *A. S. R.*, X., pp. 93-94.

high, is installed in the sanctum. It is seen wearing high boots and driving a chariot of seven horses. There is also an image of Sūrya in relief on the lintel above the doorway.[48] Similar Sūrya images on lintels are found in other temples at Khajurāho. On the outer wall of the Jaṭkāri-Caturbhuja temple is also carved a figure of Sūrya seated in his chariot, his seven horses being shown on the pedestal. There is a small tank at Ajaygaḍh, popularly believed to be sacred to Sūrya.[49]

Inscriptions also refer to the worship of the Sun along with Bhavānīpati by the Candella kings Madanavarman and Paramardi, while making grants of lands to brahmins. The Khajurāho record of V.S. 1011 closes with invocation to Savitṛ (the Sun god)—"Namo Savitre",[50] after invoking Vāsudeva. Evidence however is not quite clear to show that the Saura cult prevailed independently on a large scale in Bundelkhaṇḍ. But as Sūrya of the Brahmanical pantheon is a form of Nārāyāṇa ('Savitṛ-maṇḍala-madhyavarttī Nārāyaṇa'), his worship was not unusual.

Revanta and *Navagrahas* are intimately associated with the solar cult. Several reliefs of Nava-grahas are found in the Candella temples, both Brahmanical and Jaina, viz., Lakṣmaṇji temple, Varāha temple and the Ghaṇṭāi temple. Presumably there was no sectarianism in the propitiation of the planetary deities, movements of whom, it is believed, controlled human fate. There is an image of Revanta, the son of the Sun-god, depicted in bas relief on the basement of the Khajurāho temple (Lakṣmaṇji). Besides, there are reliefs of 'Aṣṭa-Dikpālas' (Guardian deities of eight directions) in some of the temples, viz., Kandarya-Mahādeva, Varāha, and Pārśvanātha (Jaina) temples, evidently to guard against the evil spirits. In some temples we find individual figures of Agni (in the Kandarya temple), and of Yama (in the Devī Jagadambā temple), who also are members of Aṣṭa-dikpālas.

Some icons of *Gaṅgā*, standing on her vehicle Makara,

---

48 *H. T.*, Vol II Kramrisch. Pl. V.
49 *A. S. R.*, VII., p. 49.
50 *E. I.*, I., pp. 129, 135.

are noticed in the Candella temples. An image of Gaṅgā is also carved on the body of the Great Boar of the Varāha temple. At the Kandarya Mahādeva temple there are representations of both Gaṅgā on Makara and *Yamunā* on Kūrma.

The account given above shows that the Candella rulers were ardent worshippers of the Brahmanical gods and goddesses, and that their reigns were characterised by noteworthy efforts to propagate their religon with a liberal and tolerant outlook. The Dhureṭi Plates of Troilokyamalla begin with invocatory verses to the three gods of the Trinity, Viṣṇu, Śiva and Brahmā, as well as to Gaṇapati[51]

Non-Brāhmaṇical Cults,—Buddhism

Of the non-Brahmanical cults, there is little trace of Buddhism during the Candella period. The only archaeological evidence of Buddhism earlier than the rise of the Candellas is furnished by a large image of Buddha, seated in 'bhūsparśamudrā' (touching the earth) on a double petalled lotus (Viśva-padma) seat, found in the Ghaṇṭāi temple site at Khajurāho. On the lotus-petals of its pedestal was inscribed the oft-quoted couplet, 'Ye dhammā hetu prabhava teṣāṁ hetuṁ Tathāgata', in characters assignable to 9th cent. A.D. Cunningham took the Ghaṇṭāi temple as a Buddhist shrine because of this find, but later the discovery of a large number of naked Jaina statues from the ruins of the temple led to its identification as a Jaina temple.[52]

Some Buddhist images have been unearthed near the Kirātsāgar lake at Mahobā, which definitely indicate the tolerance of the Candella rulers to the Buddhists. The find included some very fine sculptures of Bodhisatvas, Buddha and Tārā. They are not dated, but on a study of the characters of the short epigraphs on the pedestals of two of the images, Mr. K. N. Dixit assigns them to 11th-12th cent A. D.[53].

[51] *C. I. I.*, IV., p. 371. (Ll. 1-4.).
[52] *A. S. R.*, II., p. 431; *ibid*, XXI, p. 60.
[53] *M. A. S. I.*, No. 8.

Both the Bodhisatva Avalokiteśvara images are excellently carved and are regarded as the finest specimens of Indian sculpture. Iconographically one of them appears to be Siṁhanāda Bodhisatva (2′8″ high), and the other Padmapāṇi (2′2″). The former is seated in 'rāja-lilā' pose on a conventionally carved lion, whose face is turned towards the Master. The Bodhisatva holds an akṣamālā in his left hand and a trident entwined by a serpent is placed beside his right hand. The halo behind his head is carved in a lotus design. The body of the image is curvilinear and in high relief. His hair is coiled up, but some of the long curls fall on either shoulder. The short inscription at the pedestal refers to Chitnaka, the son of Sātana, the master painter, who was "well versed in science of all arts (Sakalavidyā kuśala)." The Padmapāṇi is also seated in rājalilā pose, but on a lotus throne, and the lotus stalks rise on either side of the image. Profuse ornaments decorate the different limbs of the deity unlike the Siṁhanāda image, which has only a simple garland in the form of a Yajñopavīta. The third image in the group is the Buddhist goddess Tārā (1′ 9″ high), with beautiful ornaments all over her body. The Goddess is seated in Vajrāsana posture with legs crossed. The left hand, holding a Nīlotpala, is in Vitarkamudrā and the right one in Varada with a miniature 'vajra' placed on the palm. The rim of the back slab has five small images of Dhyānī Buddhas. This image also has a short epigraph at its pedestal bearing the name of the donor, Citrakara, a relation of Sātana, the painter. An image of Buddha has also been found there. He is seated in Padmāsana (legs crossed) in Bhūmisparśa-mudrā. No ornament of any kind is on the body of the image, but hair has been carved in conventional curls tapering upwards, which has given it a cap like shape. The soft and rounded treatment of the limbs and fine chiselling of the facial features give the images a life like appearance. The find of these images at Mahobā point to the prevalence of the Mahāyāna Buddhism among some sections of the people of the Candella kingdom.

Another indirect reference to the existence of Buddhist

worship in the region is noticed in the Chārkhāri Plates of Paramardideva. While granting an entire village to certain brāhmaṇas, particular care was taken to exclude 5 'halas' of land belonging to a Buddhist Shrine.[54]

It is not known, when the endowment in favour of the temple was created, or by whom; but that it was respected by the Candella King is an indication of the existence of the religion during this period in however slender form it may be.

The Prabodhacandrodaya (of the time of King Kīrtivarman man) refers to the existence of the Saugata sect of Buddhists[55] evidently in the Candella country. It is claimed in the drama that the Buddhist sect lost its hold on the people at the rise of Viveka (conscience).

Jainism.

Jainism had some hold on the people, particularly the trading community (Śreṣṭhins). The Khajurāho Inscription no. 3 of V.S. 1011, carved on the left door-jamb of the temple of Pārśvanātha, records a number of gifts and endowments of gardens, named Pāhilavāṭikā, Candravāṭikā Laghucandravāṭikā, Śaṅkaravāṭikā Pañcaitalavāṭikā, Āmravāṭikā and Dhaṅgavāḍi by one Pāhila, a devotee of Jīnanātha, who claims to have been 'held in esteem by King Dhaṅga.'[56] The devotion of the 'Grahapati' family, to which Pāhila belonged, is also evidenced by the Darbāt-Śāntinātha image inscription of V.S. 1132,[57] in which it is found that during the reign of the illustrious Kīrtivarman, son of Vijayapāla, the image of Śāntinātha was installed by a group of his 'hereditary ministers' (kulāmātyavṛnda), viz., Pāhilla and Jīju. They were disciples of the Jain teacher Vāsavendu or Vāsavacandra. Of these two ministers, Pāhilla may be identified with Pāhila of the Khajurāho record, which also refers, as in the other inscription, to Mahārājaguru Vāsavacandra. In the Khajurāho inscription, however, he is not mentioned as a minister, but that he was an influential person in the court

[54] *E. I.*, XX., p. 130. L. 14.
[55] *P. C.* Act., V., pp. 176-77.
[56] *E. I.*, I., pp. 135-36.
[57] *I. H. Q.*, XXX., pp. 183-85.

of Dhaṅga, probably already a minister, is indicated by the statement that he was 'esteemed by the king'. The same family, out of their devotion to the Jaina faith, sets up an image of Sambhavanātha, as recorded in the Jain image inscription No. 8, dated V.S. 1215, during the reign of Madanavarman.[58] It further mentions the name of the father of Pāhilla, Śreṣṭhi Dedu, his son, Sādhu Sālhe, and his grandsons, Mahāgana, Mahīchandra, Śiricandra, Jīnacandra, Udayacandra and others. Another Grahapati family, devoted to Jainism, is also mentioned in inscriptions engraved on pedestals of some Jaina images, at Khajurāho. One of them refers to Śreṣṭhi Śrī Pāṇidhara, "Oṁ Grahapatyānvaye Śreṣṭhi Śrī Pāṇidhara" and another dated in Saṁvat 1205 refers to Śreṣṭhi Śrī Pāṇidhara and his sons, Śreṣṭhi Ti (tri)-vikrama Ālhana, and Lakṣmīdhara.[59] This was a family of Śreṣṭhins or bankers and merchants.

The Jaina temples of Khajurāho definitely show that Jainism flourished side by side with Brahmanical cults in the Candella territory. It is quite likely that the Jainas here enjoyed royal patronage though it is not known who built these temples. But in architectural style, elegance and details of execution the Jaina temples were at par with other Brahmanical shrines there.

Jain temples are situated to the south-east of the Khajurāho village. From the ruins of the Ghaṇṭāi temple, named after the 'bell and chain ornaments' on its pillars, were discovered several Digaṁbara Jaina images. Above the entrance to the temple is an image of an eight-armed Jaina goddess riding on Garuḍa, evidently the 'Śāsana-devatā Nirvāṇī' of the Tīrthaṁkara Śāntinātha, whose 'upāsaka' was Garuḍa. Besides, at each end of the lintel is the figure of a Tīrthaṁkara. The frieze above the lintel depicts sixteen symbolic representations, referable to the 'sixteen dreams' of the mother of Mahāvīra, the last Tīrthaṁkara.

To the south-east of the Ghaṇṭāi temple is situated a group of Jaina temples, enclosed within a modern compound

---

[58] *E. I.*, I., pp. 153.
[59] *ibid.*

wall. The Pārśvanatha temple is the largest and finest of the Jaina temples now surviving at Khajurāho (68′ 2″ long and 34′ 11″ broad). Here also is met with an image of a Jaina goddess (ten-armed), riding on a Garuḍa, carved on the entrance door of the temple, while on the lintel of the sanctum are seen seated and standing Jaina figures. There is a figure of a bull, carved in front of an ornamental throne in the sanctum, which indicates that it was originally dedicated to Tīrthaṁkara-Ṛṣavanātha or Ādinātha, the first Tīrthaṁkara. The modern image of Pārśvanātha was installed as late as 1860 A.D. The outer wall of the temple consists of statues of the Tīrthaṁkaras, arranged in tiers, and other figures of the Brahmanical pantheon as well. In the Ādinātha temple too, the original image is substituted by a modern image of the same divinity. The pillared niches of this temple represent the principal Jaina goddesses holding their respective symbols and riding on their distinctive vehicles.

The Śāntinātha temple, to the south of the Pārśvanātha temple, is however a later structure, but it was built on the ruins of the old temple and some ancient Jaina sculptures are built into its walls. The sculptures include a standing image of Ṛṣabhadeva (14′ ft. high) with his vehicle, the Bull carved on the pedestal. Cunningham noticed a short dedicatory inscription dated 1027-28 A.D. on the pedestal, which however is now hidden under plaster.[60]

Among other places in the Candella dominion mention may be made of the Dudāhi ruins where in the principal group there are remains of two Jaina temples, one of which contains a stark naked figure (12′ ft. high), and the other a squatted one with a naked figure standing on each side. In the second group at Dudāhi is noticed another Jain temple with a large square pillar 10′ ft. high, decorated with naked Jaina figures.[61] At Madanpur (24m. S.E. of Dudāhi) is a Jain temple with an inscription dated Samvat 1206 (A.D. 1149) containing the name of Madanapura.[62] In the fort of

[60] *A. S. R.,* II., p. 434.
[61] *ibid.,* X., pp. 92, 96.
[62] *ibid.,* XXI., p. 172.

Ajaygaḍh also several rows of small Jaina figures are noticed.[63] At Mahobā we come across a number of broken Jaina statues with their respective symbols. Some of them bear names inscribed on their pedestals—viz., Nemināthа, Sumathanātha and Ajitanātha.[64] Date and name of the reigning monarch at the time when the statues were set up are also inscribed in some cases. The earliest of such records noticed by Cunningham is Saṁvat 1169 (A.D. 1112). The name of Madanavarman is inscribed on the pedestal of Neminātha marked with 'shell-symbol' (śaṅkha), dated in Saṁvat 1211, and of Paramardideva on the pedestal of an unidentified Jaina image dated Saṁvat 1224.

At Buri Canderi (on the Betwā river), which was an old city founded by the Candellas, to the south of the palace-site Cunningham found 21 Jaina figures, placed against the walls, of which 19 were standing and 2 seated, identified as Supārśvanātha and Candraprabha from their symbols, 'svastika' and 'candra' (crescent) respectively.[65]

A literary evidence about the existence of the Digambara sect of Jainism is furnished by the drama, Prabodha-candrodaya.[66]

---

[63] *ibid.*, p. 46.
[64] *ibid.*, pp. 73-74.
[65] *ibid.*, II., p. 404.
[66] *P. C.*, Act.. V. pp. 176-77.

CHAPTER XIV

ART AND ARCHITECTURE

The contributions of the Candella rulers in the field of art and architecture are highly significant. The art-products to be attributed to their reigns are characterised by a maturity in style and technique, displaying many features which were specially evolved in their dominions during an age which witnessed an artistic resurgence. The Candella kings are traditionally reputed as great builders and enthusiastic patrons of art and architecture. This tradition is well confirmed by the magnificent group of temples, particularly those at Khajurāho, which was one of the most important centres of their kingdom. The Parmāl Rāso assigns to the Candella kings the construction of as many as 85 temples at Khajurāho[1], where no less than 30 are still in existence. Some of them are quite well preserved and provide us with ample scope for a detailed study and assessment of their style and composition.

ARCHITECTURE

The earliest remains.

Central India is generally regarded as the home of the early Śikhara temples, and specimens of early designs are scattered in different parts of it. But as Khajurāho did not come into prominence before the advent of the Candellas, architectural objects of the pre-Candella period are not generally found in the region. The only temple which belongs to an earlier period is that of the *Chaonṣaṭ Yoginis* situated on a low rocky ridge to the south-west of the Śibsāgar Lake. This temple originally had 64 units surrounding a rectangular courtyard (103′ ft. by 60′ ft.). This is an exceptional design, as such temples are normally circular in plan.[2] Of the 64 shrines 34

[1] *P. R.*, Book II., V. 28 & 54.
[2] *S. E.*, P. 575., *H. I.I.A.*, P. 110.

are still standing. According to Cunningham, the main temple was in the centre of the quadrangle, which is, however, now non-existent.[3] Each of the cells or small shrines is roofed with a short conical tower of early Nāgara design. This stylistic evidence along with the characters of short epigraphs on the pedestals of images leads to the conclusion that it belonged to a period prior to the rise of the Candellas, *i.e.*, about 9th cent. A.D. Its antiquity is further confirmed by the fact that it is the only temple at Khajurāho built entirely of granite,[4] whereas buff colour sandstone is used in building the typical Khajurāho temples.

Two temples are noticed at Khajurāho, which are built partly with sandstone and partly with granite,[5] and it may not be wrong to presume that they also belong to the early group, though later than the Chaonṣaṭ Yogini temple. They are,—(*i*) the Lālguān Mahādeva temple, a little to the west of the Chaonṣaṭ Yogini temple, on the bank of a lake, and (*ii*) the so-called Brahmā temple, on the eastern bank of the Khajur Sāgar. Both the temples are small in size, but it is difficult to describe their exact form, as all the component elements are not sufficiently preserved. The Brahmā temple has a pyramidal superstructure. The ground plan of it is square inside and cruciform outside, with an opening on the east, and windows on three sides fitted with thick stone lattices of simple but different patterns.

Another temple of this design is the Mātaṅgeśvara temple, just to the south of the Lakṣmaṇji or Caturbhuja temple. It is 24′ ft. square internally and 35′ ft. square externally, with an opening in the centre of each projection. There is a long flight of stairs in front of the main entrance on the eastern side. The roof again is pyramidal like the maṇḍapa halls and not curvilinear, as seen in the śikharas of the Candella Age. The simplicity of the plan and design and lack of ornamentation of these temples point to their earlier construction.

[3] *A.S.R.*, II., P. 417.
[4] *Khajurāho*, B. L. Dhama, & S. C. Chandra, P. 13.
[5] *ibid.*, Pp. 15, 26.

Candella Period: Epigraphy in temples.

Epigraphic evidences testify to a prolific architectural activity in and around Khajurāho under the auspices of the Candella kings from the middle of the 10th to the beginning of the 11th cent. A.D.[6] The earliest dated record that has been found at Khajurāho is the one inscribed on the pedestal of a colossal image of Hanumān, placed in a plain, small, modern temple, half way between the main temple sites and the Khajurāho village. It is dated in 316 of the Harṣa Era or A.D. 922.[7]

Another important inscription, dated in V.S. 1011 (953-54 A.D.) is found fixed on the wall of the portico of the Caturbhuja or Lakṣmaṇji temple.[8] This was set up to record the construction of the temple by Yaśovarman, though it was issued during the reign of his son, Dhaṅga. Of the latter we have a stone record dated V.S. 1059 or 1002-03 A.D., in the maṇḍapa of the Viśvanātha temple,[9] recording the construction of this magnificent abode of Śiva. In the same place is found another inscription dated in 1001-02 A.D., referring to the erection of a temple of Vaidyanātha by one Kokkala.[10] Pāhila, another private donor records gifts of some gardens in the reign of Dhaṅga in an inscription on the left door jamb of the Jain Pārśvanātha temple.[11] Cunningham refers to a short inscription dated in 1027-28 A.D., on the pedestal of the image of Ṛṣabhadeva in the temple of Śāntinātha.[12] The inscription is now however hidden in plaster. The temples, which bear these records amply prove that the Candella kings of the 10th cent. A.D., liberally patronised sculptors and architects whose works are illustrated in numerous temples, Vaiṣṇava, Śaiva and Jaina.[13]

[6] The Candella temples at Khajurāho are generally assigned to the period 950-1050 A.D. *H.I.I.A.*, P. 109, *Ind. Arch.*, P. 133, *H.I.E.A.*, Vol. II., P. 111.

[7] *Khajurāho*, B.L. Dhama & S.C. Chandra, P. 25.

[8] *E.I.*, I. Pp. 123-25.

[9] *ibid.*, Pp. 137-47.

[10] *ibid.*, Pp. 147-52.

[11] *ibid.*, Pp. 135-36.

[12] *A.S.R.*, II., P. 434.

[13] On stylistic and structural considerations Prof. Saraswati observes that none of the Candella temple at Khajurāho can be dated prior to the second half of the 11th cent. A.D. As suggested by Prof. Saraswati, it is not unlikely that the temples at Khajurāho, to which the inscriptions testify, suffered irreparable damage during the invasions of Sultān Māhmud, and that the extant temples very probably belonged to the period of revival of the Candella glory under King Kīrtivarman in the second half of the 11th cent. A.D. (*S.E.*, Pp. 664-66).

Temple architecture: Special features.

A temple in the Candella dominion presents the following components: the *garbhagṛha*, the *antarāla*, the *maṇḍapa*, the *ardha-maṇḍapa* and the projected portico, all on the same axis on a raised terrace (*adhiṣṭhāna*). Besides, the Khajurāho temples developed certain special features which gave them a distinctive stamp. They are,—(*i*) absence of any enclosure surrounding the temple, even if it is a *pañcāyatana* one; they are simply built on a common raised platform; (*ii*) in the plan and composition of the temples in the full-fledged Central Indian type inner ambulatory passages are provided for by extending the transepts of the projected balconies with *kakṣāsanas* round the main cella of the sanctum; the projected balconies are also repeated in the ambulatories; (*iii*) the Candella temples are found to be *saptaratha* in plan and *saptāṅga* in elevation, thus affording an integration horizontally and vertically; the three tiers of the '*jāṅgha*' (the perpendicular wall portion) are utilised in depicting sculptures of exquisite workmanship and alluring beauty: and (*iv*) the upward movement of the *śikhara* is given an added momentum by repetitions of miniature towers (*aṅgaśikharas*) surrounding the main tower.[14]

As all the temples at Khajurāho are mainly of a cognate style it is not very easy to determine accurately any chronological sequence among them. Prof. S. K. Saraswati has, however, classified the temples on stylistic considerations as those with aṅgaśikharas and those without, and the *Sāndhāra* and the *Nirandhāra* (with or without internal ambulatory passage). "As a general rule", he observes, "the temples without transepts around the sanctum cella and without aṅgaśikharas precede those that possess these significant characteristics with which the typical Central Indian temple reaches its complete form".[15]

The Vāmana temple, to the north-east of the Brahmā temple, and the Ādinātha temple, in the Jain group of

[14] This style is symbolic of the "universal sovereignty of the deity worshipped", according to Havell (*A Handbook of Indian Art*, P. 68).

[15] *S.E.*, P. 566.

temples, are without aṅgaśikharas but ornamented with interlacings of Caitya-window motifs. As such, these temples may be placed prior to the rise of the full-fledged Candella form. The temples whose towers are superimposed with aṅgaśikharas form the majority of the temples at Khajurāho, and include the Bharatji or Citragupta, the Devi Jagadambā, the Kunwār Maṭh, the Rāmacandra or Caturbhuja, the Pārśvanātha, the Viśvanātha, the Javāri and the Kandarya Mahādeva shrines. Of these again the Devi Jagadambā temple, to the south of the Citragupta temple, and the Kunwār Maṭh, being *nirandhāra* or without inner ambulatory passages, may be taken stylistically to belong to a period earlier than the *sāndhāra* ones. The Kandarya Mahādeva temple is no doubt the most exuberant form of the Candella style of architecture in which all the specialities evolved by the Central Indian architects are represented in their richest expressions.[16]

The Kandarya Mahādeva Temple: a description.

As an illustration of the Candella architecture in its perfectly developed form a description of the Kandarya Mahādeva temple may be attempted here. As is customary with the Khajurāho temples, it is of the *pañcāyatana* composition with the main shrine in the centre and four smaller subsidiary shrines at four corners,[17] now non-existent; the whole group is situated on a high plinth or *adhiṣṭhāna*. As is usual again in Central India, no enclosure wall surrounds the composition.

The main temple complex consists of all the usual component parts built on the same axis, and coordinated in such a way as to present the structure as an integrated whole, measuring 102′3″ in length and 66′ 10″ in width. The superstructures of the different adjuncts are graded in height from the front to the spire of the main sanctum, which rises to a height of 101′ 9″, as if alluding to an upward movement till it reaches its finality.[18] The roof of the different *maṇḍapas*

[16] *ibid.*, P. 572., *H.T.*, II., P. 372., *H.I.I.A.*, P. 109.
[17] The Caturbhuja and the Viśvānātha temples at Khajurāho are also pañcāyatana.
[18] *H.T.*, II., P. 367. The design of the Kandarya temple very nearly conforms to the 'Meru' type of temple of the Bṛhat Saṁhitā. *A.C.*, P. 18.

in front of the main tower may be described as pyramidal with supplementary superstructures placed all around. They are followed by the gabled roof of the *antarāla*, which connects the main *śikhara* with the maṇḍapa roof. Externally the main sanctum is *saptaratha* in plan, each *rathaka* (facet) being continued as '*pagas*' (according to the canonical texts of Orissa), all of them rising beyond the *gaṇḍi* of the śikhara, and almost touching the crowning *āmalakas*. The main tower is embellished by tiers of aṅgaśikharas, which are miniature replicas of the tower, and produce the effect of grandeur and upward movement at the same time. The *śikhara* is curvilinear at the 'gaṇḍi' portion (*i.e.* the outer wall of the Śikhara), but the curvature is not extended upto the top, at the shoulder the line goes horizontally to be joined with the neck. The spire is capped with two ribbed 'āmalakas' one above the other, the upper one being smaller, and is surmounted by the usual 'kalasa' finial without any bell shaped member in between. The maṇḍapa towers also have their own kalasas giving an admirable symmetrical look.

The body of the temple may be studied in three segments, the plinth, the wall section and the tower. The plinth or the '*pāda-bhāga*' (*pā-bhāga* according to Orissan texts), which is sufficiently high (13′ ft.), is marked by a succession of bold mouldings, thus providing ample scope for light and shade. The wall section or the cube of the *bāḍa* is again variegated with two belts or '*bāndhanās*', in between which are set up three tiers of elegant sculptures of inexhaustible interest. The upper section of the temple, the *śikhara* rises above another series of carvings which, according to the architectural texts, is called the '*baraṇḍa*', linking up the 'bāḍa' with the 'gaṇḍi' of the tower. Thus vertically the 'bāḍa' of the temple is divided seven-fold, and is called *Saptāṅga*. The heavy weight of the huge mass of masonry is further relieved by the balconied openings all through on the two side walls of the maṇḍapas and including the back wall of the sanctum. This not only eases the monotony of solidity, but also, comparatively speaking, lessens the unusual load of this massive construction. The Jain Pārśvanātha temple does not however possess balconied openings, whose place is taken by the latticed windows in the centre of the projections.

Internally too the temple bears the distinctive stamp of maturity of mediaeval artists. To enter the portals of the *mukhamaṇḍapa* one has to climb up a few steep steps of plain stone stairs and to stand beneath an exquisitely carved doorway.[19] From below the lintel project three struts of foliated form with fine *makara* motifs on either end, one of which is broken. A repetition of it may be seen inside at the doorway of the maṇḍapa. The interior of the *ardhamaṇḍapa* is rectangular and that of the maṇḍapa hall square. The transepts on either side of the maṇḍapa are stretched and extended round the sanctum cella to provide for the inner ambulatory passage. The most notable feature within is the series of open balconies on three sides of the temple scheme, supported by pairs of circular pillars with richly foliated capitals. On the outside the windows were partly shaded by stone eaves projected from the 'baraṇḍa.' The lower sections of the openings serve as 'kakṣāsanas', their parapets slanting outside. The ornate ceilings of the several maṇḍapas constitute another important architectural feature of this type of temples.[20] The designs are mainly geometrical in pattern, and each of the ceilings are formed with a series of overlapping octagonal and concentric courses of various depths, resting on a central complement of four pillars. From the apex of the ceiling comes down a stone pendant of floral design. Flying images of Gandharvas, Gaṇas and Apsarās are seen projecting from the abacus of the pillars as brackets for the support of the architraves. These, together with numerous other images set up in the niches, lintels and door frames and on the 'jāngha' outside (nearly 900 in number), produce a lively reaction on the mind of the visitor. The interior of the sanctum cella is rather plain and devoid of architectural embellishments.

---

[19] Percy Brown describes it as appearing like an 'ivory carving' or 'a hanging drapery'. *Ind. Arch.* P. 134.

[20] The carved ceilings may seem to be analogous to the marble shrines at Mount Ābu. But carved ceilings without dome, as observed by O.C. Gangoly, were probably an earlier stage of evolution. *A.C.*, Pp. 18-19.

The above description of the temple complex and its architectural and sculptural details clearly demonstrates that they could not have been produced overnight, nor, as fancifully claimed in the Parmāl Rāso, with the help of the divine builder, Viśvakarmā.[21] Such an excellence could only have been attained by a long evolutionary process.[22] The march of this stylistic development can be traced back to the archaic forms of the architecture prevalent in the late-Gupta period of the 5th-6th centuries A.D., leading to the emergence of the *Nāgara* form in the 8th. Prof. S. K. Saraswati in his recent monograph has very ably described this process of development from the conical roof of the early *Nāgara* type to the embellished *śikharas* of the Candella age.[23] In course of this development impact of influences from the western and the eastern parts of India brought about considerable modifications in the technique of temple construction as well as in style, and ultimately inspired the local genius to display their own merit and skill in producing something which is most distinctive of its kind. Affinities between different component parts of Central Indian temples with those of other regions may be recognised, but still the ingenuity of the builders of Khajurāho cannot be denied nor can they be dubbed as mere imitators. The Khajurāho style, as observed by Prof. O. C. Gangoly, was in many respects an independent growth.[24]

SCULPTURE

In the Mediaeval period the soft plasticity of modelling of the Classical age gave way to an increasingly stereotyped and conventionalised forms and flexions in Indian sculpture.[25] The Khajurāho temples present a wealth of sculptures, which, while sharing the general characteristics of the mediaeval age, display a finesse in carving images, that

---

[21] *P.R.*, Book II, V. 54.
[22] Benjamin Rowland describes it as 'the culmination of the Indo-Aryan genius in architecture'. (*Art & Architecture of India* P. 173), *H. T.*, II, P. 367.
[23] *S.E.*, Pp. 557-72.
[24] *A.C.*, P. 16.
[25] *S.E.*, P. 656.

brings them very close to the living world.[26] One is struck by the profusion of images in high relief noticeable on the outer and inner walls of the temples, as well as in the innumerable niches and lintels, door-jambs and bracket-capitals, at Khajurāho. Of these some are also to be seen at other centres of the ancient Candella dominion, including Mahobā.

Images in the round, fewer in number, exist in the inner sanctums of the different temples as cult icons, of which the more prominent ones are: (*i*) the image of Sūrya (5′ ft. high), wearing high boots and standing on a chariot drawn by seven horses in the Citragupta temple. (*ii*) the four-armed three-headed Viṣṇu image (4′ 1″ high), standing in an ornate *toraṇa* frame in the sanctum of the Caturbhuja temple, (*iii*) the image of the Dwarf incarnation (4′ 8″ high), in the Vāmana temple, (*iv*) the four-armed Viṣṇu image in the Javāri temple, (*v*) a colossal image of Viṣṇu (9′ ft. high), in the temple at Jaṭkāri, and (*vi*) the standing image of Ṛṣabhadeva, a Jain tīrthaṁkara, (14′ ft. high) in a Jain temple at Khajurāho. Some of the cult icons, also found carved in very high relief, include the four Buddhist statues at Mahobā,[27] and the twin gods in the Śāntinātha temple at Khajurāho.

Relievo sculptures in the Khajurāho temples may be classified as,—(*i*) those depicting the principal gods and goddesses and their *parivāradevatās* (*ii*) minor gods and goddesses, *dikpālas*, *navagrahas* and others, (*iii*) *surasundarīs*, *nāyikās* and scenes from life, including those of *mithuna*, and (*iv*) animals, floral and vegetal motifs as well as geometric patterns.

As regards the principal gods and goddesses, they are represented in high relief in the central projected portions of the outer walls and on the middle of the lintel above the doorway to the sanctum cella and in the niches. These include Śiva and Viṣṇu in their different forms and incarnations, with or without their consorts, Pārvatī and Lakṣmī. Images of Sūrya, Brahmā, Agni, Yama, Gaṅgā and Yamunā, the dikpālas and the navagrahas also occur in profusion in the

---

[26] *Indian Temple Sculpture* Pp. 37-38.
[27] *M.A.S.I.*, No. 8.

Brahmanical temples. The Jain group of temples presents images of Jain tīrthaṁakras and their śāsanadevatās and occasionally Brahmanical deities also. References to the general iconographic features of these images have been made in the chapter on Religion.[28] These generally are of the conventional type, but the three-dimensional effect created by the high relief carving has a unique attraction.

The physiognomy of the images show certain characteristics :—The face is generally oval with rounded chins, prominently carved eyes and eye-brows, nose and lips. "Each eye-brow", as observed by Prof. O. C. Gangoly, "is designed in a long beautiful curve—in raised ridges—terminating near the root of the nose, but they rarely touch each other".[29] The treatment of the eye-brows, as described above, is a characteristic of the Candella style. Images are generally in standing form. What makes them really striking is the stylised flexions of their bodies. They are extravagant in *bhaṅgas* or bends. The limbs are treated in linear movements; even the lower parts of the body, and also the arms and hands, normally carved in straight lines, are here presented in a rounded manner. Their lineal character is surpassed by a three-dimensional effect, which is particularly seen in the images of voluptuous young women, and also in some cases in the representations of goddesses. These characteristics endow the Candella sculptures with a unique distinction in Indian art.

The Buddhist images found at Mahobā are however in sitting postures. In them the Candella technique of imagecraft reaches its level of perfection. These sculptures have been described by K. N. Dikshit as 'some of the best specimens of the later mediaeval art'.[30] Of them the image of Siṁhanāda Avalokiteśvara, according to him, may be regarded as one of the specialities of Indian sculpture.

Plastic decorations of the Khajurāho temples include interesting sculptural embellishments on their outer walls.

[28] Vide ante.
[29] *A.C.*, P. 25.
[30] *M.A.S.I.*, No. 8., p.1.

As already stated, two to three rows of sculptured tiers embellish the bāḍa of the temples, like the ornate *mekhalās* worn by fashionable women. Besides the images of gods and goddesses, there are plenty of three-dimensional representations of youthful damsels,—*nāyikās apsarās* and *surasundarīs* (celestial women), brilliantly illuminating the temple walls. These images have been described by some art critics as figures of living beauty, completely liberated from their stony frames.[31] Each unit of these sculptures has its own story to tell, each one of them expresses a particular mood of mind or an action. Surasundarīs are a gay lot; they seem to enjoy life in all its fullness. Some of them are seen putting on ornaments aided by attendants, others absorbed in having their toilet, viz., doing the hair, or squeezing water out of it after bath, putting vermillion marks on the forehead, or at the parting of hair, holding a powder case, or the stick to apply lac dye to their feet, or collyrium to their eye-lids. Again there are images of women engaged in writing love letters or removing thorns from their feet, or in a reclining pose in a reminiscent mood (*alasa nāyikā*), or holding the branch of a tree (*śālabhañjikā*), or lost in self admiration before a mirror held in her hand, sporting with a ball or practising dance movements. In all these what is most interesting is the lively and realistic depiction of womanly characteristics, chiselled delicately by the master sculptors of the Candella territory.

Sculptured panels at Khajurāho do not present any scenes from the Epics and the Purāṇas, as may be seen in some of the important shrines in other parts of India. But these panels depict some highly suggestive scenes from life, particularly alluringly beautiful figures of youthful men and women playing love to each other. These sculptures portray in high relief intimate forms of amorous dalliance and sexual enjoyment. These erotic scenes thus depicted may remind one of the art of love-making technically treated in Vātsāyana's Kāmasūtra.[32] Grace and virility which charac-

---

31 *Indian Temple Sculpture* Pp. 37-38.
32 Vātsāyana's Kāmasūtra, Ed. Panchanan Tarkaratna.

terise these sculptures endow them with a rare dignity, which appeals to our aesthetic sense.

Various suggestions have been made by way of explaining the presence of erotic sculptures (*mithuna*) in different Hindu temples such as those found at Khajurāho. The popular belief is that they immunize the temple from evil forces of nature, like lightning or thunder.[33] Some scholars think that they illustrate the mystic union of *Puruṣa* and *Prakṛti* in accordance with the successive stages of the development of this doctrine, including those connected with the Tāntrik cults[34]. It has been suggested that some of the Tāntrik cults, particularly the Kaulas and the Kāpālikas, or the Somasiddhāntins (mentioned in the Prabodhacandrodaya), had a following in the Candella country[35]. As sex came to play an important symbolic role in Tāntrik worship, the utility of such sculptures can hardly be over-estimated, in the propagation of some of its fundamental doctrines. It is even suggested, although without adequate data, that some of the *mithuna* pictures are carved in such poses that they can be explained as illustrations of 'sexo-yogic practices.'[36] Prof. O.C. Gangoly invites attention to the prescription in the Śilpaśāstras, which requires, for reasons not stated, the insertion of erotic couples on the facades of temples[37]. Such canonical injunctions may account for the presence of *mithuna* sculptures in Indian temples. The erotic element is subdued in several *mithuna* sculptures at Khajurāho, as for example, the Umā-Maheśvara image, now preserved in Allahabad Museum, which have received due praises for their artistic excellence;[38] but in a number of cases Khajurāho sculptors are found to have been carried away by their enthusiasm in treating their subjects in a realistic fashion. But even then their products bear the stamp of genius and a craftmanship of high order.

Khajurāho art is also rich in representations of scenes

---

[33] *Khajurāho*, B.L. Dhama & S.C. Chandra P. 11.
[34] *A.C.*, P. 29; *H.T.*, II., Pp. 346-47.
[35] *Mārg*, Vol. X No. 3, Pp. 59-62.
[36] *Ibid.*
[37] *Rūpaṁ* No. 22-23, 1925; *A.C.*, P. 29.
[38] *Indian Temple Sculpture* P. 38; *A.C.*, P. 30.

portraying musicians and dancers in groups, hunting excursions, animal fights, royal processions, movements of armies, and occasionally domestic life. Such artistic representations seem to be more or less conventional in character, but it is quite likely that they furnish some information about the nature of the costumes and ornaments, musical instruments, military weapons and also domestic implements, which were used in the Candella territory. The Candella artists thus seem to have selected their subjects from various aspects of life, individual and collective, and in representing them in art they attempted to be as realistic as possible judged by the standard prevalent in the country during their time.

Of special interest is the panel portraying in different sections a group of stone workers engaged in their occupation. In one part of the panel is shown a group of porters carrying a long pole to which is tied blocks of stone with a piece of thick rope, and this is followed by a scene in which a stone-cutter is seen using his hammer with great vigour and firmness stamped on his face. Other notable panels include pictures of men and women in different dancing poses, some holding pots of burning incense in their hands, and others playing on flute, cymbals, mṛdaṅga and vīṇā. There is a curious picture of a man with his beard being pulled by a woman, with another woman holding him by the left arm (Pārśvanātha Temple). This scene may probably represent two jealous women claiming the allegiance of the lover.

Animals, vigorously drawn, include elephants, tigers and horses. Some of the hunting scenes include boars, after they are actually killed being carried on the shoulders of huntsmen. The boar in its incarnatory form also frequently appears in the Candella sculptures. Of particular importance is the powerful figure of a boar standing within a maṇḍapa in front of the Mātaṅgeśvara temple. A common motif is the *Leogryph*, which occurs in various forms in different temples, Hindu and Jain. The leogryph appears in the form of a rampant Śārdūla with a woman kneeling in front of it.[39]

[39] *H.T.*, II., Pp. 336-37, 368.

Floral and vegetal motifs as seen at Khajurāho are in the opinion of experts more or less mechanical and conventional in character[40]. Their main purpose is decorative, but they do not attract any special attention because of the abundance of the human and other elements dominating the Candella art. The Candella artists, however, exhibit a special aptitude for geometric patterns. Their achievements in this field is even supposed to have set a standard, which influenced the sculptors of the neighbouring regions.[41]

[40] *S.E.*, P. 645.
[41] *A.C.*, P. 18.

10. *Sculptured panels of the Kandarya Temple*

2. *Lakṣmanji Temple-Pañcāyatana on an elevated adhiṣṭhāna*

11. *Śāntinātha & Consort—Jain Śāntinātha Temple*

12. *Nīlatārā from Mahobā*

3. *Projected balcony—Kandarya Temp*

4. *Śārdūla (Leogryph)*

5. *Niches on the outer wall with Brahmā, Viṣṇu & Umā-Maheśwara (Kandarya Temple)*

7. *Aṅgaśikharas—Kandarya Temple*

6. *Citragupta Temple : Entrance to ↓ the inner sanctum-Sūrya within*

8. *Ornamented Ceiling & Lintle of the Maṇḍapa —Kandarya Temple*

9. *Balarāma & Revatī*

13. *Bodhisatva Siṁhanāda Avalokiteśvara—Mahobā*

14. *Surasundarī*

15. *Surasundarī*

16. *Mithuna*

18. *Surasundarī*

17. *Mithuna*

19. *Mithuna*

20. *Some Candella gold coins in Indian Museum, Calcutta (V & VI Kīrttivarman; I & IV Madanavarman; II Paramardi & III Trailokyavarman)*

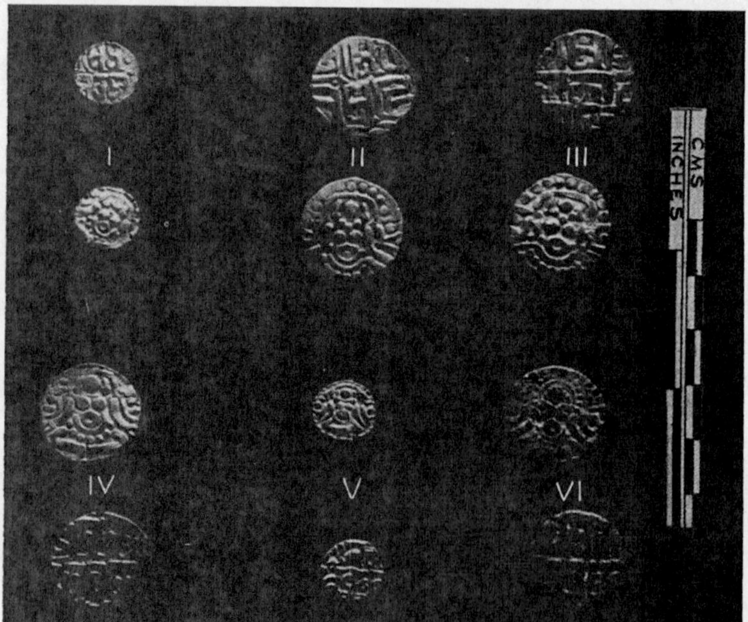

APPENDIX I

INSCRIPTIONS OF THE CANDELLA TIMES

Harṣa.

1. Fragmentary Stone Inscription of Harṣadeva from Khajurāho. Found near the Vāmana temple at Khajurāho—speaks of the princely family of Candrātreya and some of its early rulers, viz., Jejjāka, Vijjāka and Harṣadeva. Either Harṣa or his son, Yaśovarman, placed Kṣitipāladeva (Pratihāra) again on the throne.

The record is undated, but from its similarity with another Khajurāho record of V. S. 1011, it is taken to be also of the same time or a little earlier.

Edited by Kielhorn. E. I. Vol. I. pp. 121-22.

Dhaṅga.

2. Khajurāho Stone Inscription of Yaśovarman of V. S. 1011.

Found amongst the ruins of the Lakṣmaṇjī temple, now built into the wall inside the porch of the temple. Composed by Poet Mādhava, son of grammarian Dadda: written by Karaṇika Jaddha, son of Jayaguṇa of Gauḍa. Records the erection of a temple of Viṣṇu and the installation of an image of Vaikuṇṭha(nātha), received from Devapāla. The record was set up after the death of Yaśovarman during the reign of his son, Dhaṅga. Early ancestors of the family of the sage Candrātreya beginning from Nannuka are also mentioned. At the close it refers to Vināyakapāladeva (Pratihāra) evidently as a mark of allegiance to him.

Edited by Kielhorn E. I. Vol. I. pp. 123-35; commented upon by G. S. Ojhà E. I. Vol. XIV. p. 180; R. C. Majumdar I. H. Q. Vol. XXV. p. 213.

3. Khajurāho Jain temple Inscription of the time of Dhaṅga V. S. 1011.

Inscribed on the door-jamb of the Jīnanātha temple at Khajurāho. Records endowment of a number of gardens to the temple by Pāhilla, who was held in honour by Dhaṅga. It also refers to Mahārājaguru Vāsavacandra.

Edited by Kielhorn E. I. Vol. I. pp. 135-36.

4. Nānyaura Plate 'A' of Dhaṅga. V. S. 1055.

Incised on a copper plate found in the village of Nānyaura in the Hamirpur dist., now in the Asiatic Society, Calcutta.

Records the gift of a village to Bhaṭṭa Yaśodhara, identifiable with the Chief Priest and Administrator of Justice of the same name mentioned in the Khajurāho Record of V. S. 1059. The grant was issued by Pb. M. P. Kālañjarādhipati Dhaṅgadeva, son of Pb. M. P. Yaśovarmadeva, son of Pb. M. P. Harṣadeva, on a lunar eclipse day in V. S. 1055 in the month of Kārttika from Kāśikā (Benares).

Edited by Kielhorn I. A. Vol. XVI. pp. 201-04.

5. Khajurāho Inscription of Kokkala of the Grahapati family. V. S. 1058. Found at the temple of Vaidyanātha at Khajurāho, now built into the wall of the porch of the Viśvanātha temple.

Records erection of a temple of Śiva Vaidyanātha and a set of buildings for pious brahmins by Kokkala of the Grahapati family, who appears to have been a small chief dwelling at Khajurāho. Yaśobala, an ancestor of Kokkala, was settled at Padmāvatī, modern Narwar, Gwālior.

6. Khajurāho Stone Inscription of Dhaṅga. V. S. 1059.

Found in a temple at Khajurāho, now built into the wall at the entrance of the Viśvanātha temple.

Records that Dhaṅga erected a magnificent temple for Śambhu with two liṅgas, one of which was of emerald (marakata) and made grants of land, dwellings, grain, money and cows to pious brahmins. It was set up after the death of Dhaṅga, which is referred to in V. 55, and re-issued by a later ruler, Jayavarman, in Samvat 1173. The origin of the Candrātreya dynasty and its genealogy from Nannuka to Dhaṅga are also mentioned in the record. Written by Kāyastha Jayapāla of Gauḍa country.

Edited by Kielhorn E. I. Vol. I. pp. 137-47.

7. Dudāhi Inscriptions.

Found in the village of Dudhāi, in the southern part of Lalitpur Dist. Records erection of a temple by Candella Devalabdhi, son of Kṛṣṇapa and Âsarvvā, and grandson of Yaśovarman.

Edited by Kielhorn. I. A. Vol. XVIII, p. 237.

Devavarman.

8. Nānyaura Plate 'B' of Devavarman. V. S. 1107.

Records the grant of a village by Pb. M. P. Pm. Kālañjarādhipati Devavarmadeva, son of Pb. M. P. Vijayapāladeva, son of Pb. M. P. Vidyādharadeva from his residence at Suhavāsa, to a brahmin named Abhimanyu, on the occasion of the death anniversary (sāmvatsarika) of his mother, Rājñī Bhuvanadevī. The grant is dated the Monday, the 3rd day of the dark half of Vaiśākha in 1107 V. S.

Edited by Kielhorn I. A. Vol. XVI. pp. 201-02.

9. Chārkhāri Plate of Devavarman. V. S. 1108.

Inscribed on a copper plate bearing the figure of the four-armed goddess Lakṣmī with an elephant on each side pouring water on her head with raised trunk and the sign manual 'Śrīmad-Devavarmadevah svahastah'. Findspot unknown, but preserved in the Chārkhāri State, Bundelkhand. Records the gift of a village situated on the bank of the Yamunā in the Navarāṣṭramaṇḍala-viṣaya to Paṇḍita Kīkkana of the Kṛṣṇātreya gotra by Pb. M. P. Śrī-Kālañjarādhipati Śrīmad Devavarmadeva, son of Vijayapāladeva, son of Vidyādharadeva on the occasion of a lunar eclipse on a full moon day in the month of Māgha in Samvat 1108.

Written by Akṣapaṭalika Yaśobhaṭa.

Edited by Rai Bahadur Hiralal. E. I. Vol. XX. pp. 125-28.

Kīrtivarman.

10. Darbāt Śāntinātha image Inscription of V. S. 1132.

Found in the village of Darbāt near Mahobā in the Hamirpur Dist. Inscribed on a marble frieze containing a sitting lion on each side. The statue once set up on it has now disappeared.

Records the installation of an image of Śānti (Jain Tīrthaṅkara Śāntinātha) by the Śreṣṭhins Pāhila and Jīju belonging to a group of hereditary ministers in the reign of the Candella king Kīrtivarman, son of Vijayapāla. It also refers to Vāsavendu, identifiable with the Jain teacher Vāsavacandra of the Khajurāho Jain temple inscription of V. S. 1011, probably the preceptor of Pāhila and Jīju. Pāhila may be identical with Pāhilla of the Grahapati family, son of Śreṣṭhin Dedu, the father of Sādhu Sālhe, and grandfather of Mahāgaṇa and others, mentioned in Khajurāho Jain image inscription of V. S. 1215.

Edited by D. C. Sircar. I. H. Q. Vol. XXX. pp. 183-85.

11. Kālañjar Inscription of V. S. 1147. (see supplement)

Noticed by N. P. Chakravarti An. Rep. A. S. I., P. 93.

12. Deogaḍh Rock Inscription of V. S. 1154.

Found on a rock near the river gate of the fort in the town of Deogaḍh, overhanging the Betwā.

Records the construction of a flight of steps by Vatsarāja, the Chief Minister (amātya-mantrīndra) of Kīrtivarman, son of Vijayapāla of the Candella family. Vatsarāja claims to have freed the district from the enemy and made the fort 'Kīrtigiri'. It is dated Sunday, 2nd day of the bright half of Caitra.

Edited by Kielhorn I. A. Vol. XVIII. pp. 237-9.

13. Fragmentary Stone Inscription from Mahobā.

Found at Mahobā, now in the Lucknow Museum.

Refers to the origin of the dynasty from the Moon and the early ancestors of the family, Jejā and Vijā, it then eulogises the achievements of Dhaṅga, Gaṇḍa, Vidyādhara, Vijayapāla and Kīrtivarman. Kīrtivarman is stated to have defeated Lakṣmīkarṇa, and revived the glory of his kingdom, just as Puruṣottama having produced the nectar by churning the rolling ocean obtained the goddess Lakṣmī.

14. Ajaygaḍh Rock Inscription.

Beginning with an invocation to Caṇḍikā, it refers to the origin of the Vāstavya Kāyastha family from Brahmā and his son Kaśyapa. Then it mentions Jājuka of this family, who by his services to king Gaṇḍa was awarded the village, Dugauḍa. Finally it records the grant of the village, Pipalāhika, along with the authority over the gates of Kālañjara, to Maheśvara, son of Jājuka, by king Kīrttivarman in recognition of Maheśvara's services, while the king was in distress at Pītādri, which according to the Editor, is the same as Pītaśaila of Ajaygaḍh R. I. of Bhoja, identifiable with Pita or Pet hill of the former Orcchā state.

Noticed by Cunningham, ASR, XXI, p. 54 and by N. P. Chakravarti. ASR, 1935-36, p. 92; edited by S. L. Katare, E.I., XXX, p. 87-90.

Jayavarman.

15. Khajurāho Stone Inscription of 1059 V. S., re-engraved in 1173 V. S. The concluding portion of the inscription records that it was caused to be re-written in clear letters by the illustrious prince Jayavarmmadeva on the 3rd day of the bright half of Vaiśākha in Saṁvat 1173.

Edited by Kielhorn. E. I. Vol. I. pp. 137-47.

Madanavarman.

16. Kālañjar Pillar Inscription V. S. 1186.

The Inscription inscribed on a pillar in the Nīlakaṇṭha temple inside the fort of Kālañjar is fragmentary. Opening with adoration to Nīlakaṇṭha it gives the date, Saṁvat 1186 and the names of Mahāpratihāra Saṁgrāmasiṁha and Mahānācanī Padmāvatī, most probably to record some benefactions.

Edited by Cunningham A. S. R. Vol. XXI. p. 34.

17. Kālañjar broken Pillar Inscription. V. S. 1187.

Fragmentary inscription found on a piece of broken pillar in the Nīlakaṇṭha temple. Besides giving the date (Saṁvat 1187) and the name of the king, Śrīmad Madanavarmadeva, it mentions 'Kālañjarādri Śrī Triśalka'. Probably some benefaction by Śrī Triśalka was recorded.

Edited by Cunningham A. S. R. Vol. XXI. p. 34.

18. Kālañjar Rock Inscription. V. S. 1188.

Incised on the rock to the left of the gateways of the Nīlakaṇṭha temple. Records the installation of the image of Varada in stone by Mahārājaputra Śrī Solunasuta & Vatsa-rājadeva, of the Kumāra family, Śrī Kavidyamka

Achoda and Rāuta Udanah, all worshippers of the lotus feet of Madanavarmadeva, in Saṁvat 1188, Saturday, the 6th Kārttika. The sculptor the son of Rāma, was the same person who made the image of Nīlakaṇṭha.

Edited by Maisey in J. A. S. B. (1848) p. 321; Re-edited by Cunningham in A. S. R. XXI. pp.34-35.

19. Nānyaura Plate 'C' (Augāsi Grant) of Madanavarman. V.S. 1190.

Found in the Augāsi Parganā in the Bāveru Tahsil of the Banda district, now in the Asiatic Society, Calcutta. Bears the Gaja-Lakṣmī emblem embossed at the top of the plate and opens with an eulogy of the princes of the Candrātreya vaṁśa, marked by the appearance of heroes like Jayaśakti and Vijayaśakti. Records the gift of 10 'halas' of land in the village Vamharaḍā in the Sūḍālī viṣaya to a brahmin named Rāhulaśarman, when the king was in residence at Bhaillasvāmin (mod. Bhilsā in Gwālior), by Pb. M. P. Pm. Kālañjarādhipati Śrīman-Madanavarmadeva, worshipping the feet of Pb. M. P. Pṛthvīvarmadeva, worshipping the feet of Kīrtivarmadeva.

The Grant is dated, the full moon day of Māgha in Saṁvat 1190, Monday(this should have been Friday).

Written by Dharmalekhī Thāsisuddha, and engraved by Vijñānika Jalhaṇa.

Edited by R. L. Mitra J. A. S. B. Vol. XLVII. Pt. I. P. 73 ; Re-edited by Kielhorn I. A. Vol, XVI. Pp. 202 & 207.

20. Plates of Madanavarman, V. S. 1192.

Preserved in the Bhārat Kalā Bhavan, Banaras, provenance unknown. Issued by king Madanavarman on Tuesday, Caitra Vadi 5, Viṣuva-Saṁkrānti in V. S. 1192 (24th March 1136 A. D.) from his camp at Pareyī-grāma. Refers to the early heroes of the Candella family, Jaya-śakti and Vijayaśakti and eulogises the reigning monarch, Pb. M. P. Pm. Madanavarman, the lord of Kālañjara, who succeeded Pb. M. P. Pṛthvī-varman, who again succeeded Pb. M. P. Kīrtivarman. Records grant of lands to three donees, viz., Paṇḍita Somaśarman of Kautsa gotra, hailing from the Bhaṭṭāgrahāra of Pāṭaliputra received 2¼ 'padas' of land at Vakṣatapadāṣṭaka in Valahauḍa grāma in the Viṣaya of Mahisineha. The second donee Dīkṣita Nārāyaṇaśarman of Gautama gotra of the Bhaṭṭāgrahāra of Paṇikavaḍa received 4 'padas' of land at Pipalahā-grāma in exchange of some lands in his possession including the plots which had been given to him by Nāḍuka, the priest of Rājñī Lakhamādevī, and Someka (Somaśarmạn). Sahajuśarman, a brother of Somaśarman, was the third donee to receive 1¾ 'padas' of land given to him by Mahārājñī Vālhanadevī and Rājñī Cāndaladevi with King's approval.

Written by Dharmalekhin Sūḍha of the Vāstavya family and engraved by Vijñānin Ūheno, a Rītikāra (brazier).

Edited by Dr. D. C. Sircar, E. I., XXXII pp. 118-23

21. Kālañjar Rock Inscription. V. S. 1192.

Records dedication of an image of Nṛsiṁha by Ṭhakkura Śrī Nṛsiṁha, son of Ṭhakkura Salhaṇa, son of Dīkṣita Śrī Pṛthvīdhara.

Edited by Cunningham A. S. R. Vol. XXI. p. 35.

22. Kālañjar cell Śaiva Inscription. V. S. 1194.

A record of two brahmins of the Bhāradvāja gotra.

Edited by Cunningham A. S. R. Vol. XXI. p. 36.

23. Khajurāho Jain image Inscription of 1205 V. S.

A single line inscription mentioning the names of ŚreṣṭhinPāṇidhara of the Grahapati family and his sons, Śreṣṭhins Trivikrama, Ālhaṇa and Lakṣmīdhara, and the date 'Saṁvat 1205 Vadi 15'. Presumably these worshippers set up the image in question.

24. Ajaygaḍh Stone Inscription. V. S. 1208.

Incised on the jamb of the upper gate in the fort of Ajaigarh.

Records building something (a sirothā ?) by Rāuta Veda, a kṣatriya, during the reign of Madanavarman in Saṁvat 1208.

Noticed by Cunningham A. S. R. Vol. XXI. p. 49.

25. Mahobā Jain image inscription. V. S. 1211.

Records the dedication of the image of Neminātha, made by Rūpakāra Lakhaṇa in the reign of Madanavarmadeva, as incised on the pedestal of the image.

Noticed by Cunningham A. S. R. Vol. XXI. p. 73.

26. Khajurāho Jain image inscription. V. S. 1215.

Records the dedication of an image, probably of Sambhavanātha, in the prosperous reign of Śrīman-Madanavarmadeva, by Sādhu Sālhe, son of Pāhilla, son of Śreṣṭhi Dedu of the Grahapati family. Sālhe's sons, Mahāgaṇa, Mahicandra, Śiricandra, Jinacandra and Udayacandra as well as the sculptor (Rūpakāra) Rāmadeva are mentioned.

Edited by Kielhorn E. I. Vol. I. pp. 152-53.

27. Vāridurga Grant of Madanavarman of V. S. 1219 referred to in the Semrā Plates of his grandson, Paramardideva (V. S. 1223) recording a number of endowments to brahmins, when he was in residence in that

place on the occasion of a solar eclipse on a Thursday, 15th of the dark fortnight of Māgha.

Edited by W. Cartellieri, E. I. Vol. IV. pp. 153 ff.

28. Mahobā Jain image inscription. V. S. 1220.

Dedication of an image with the elephant symbol by Ratnapāla, son of Devaganata on a Sunday, the 8th day of the bright half of Jyeṣṭha in Samvat 1220.

Edited by Cunningham A. S. R. Vol. XXI. p. 74.

29. Māu Stone Inscription of a family of hereditary ministers of the Candella kings. Records the construction of a Viṣṇu temple, excavation of a tank near the village Deddu and some other pious works by Gadādhara, the Chief Minister of Madanavarman. It also gives an account of the rulers of the Candella family from Dhaṅga, who defeated the king of Kānyakubja in a battle, to Madanavarman, and of the ministers belonging to the family of Gautama Akṣapāda viz., Prabhāsa, the Chief Minister of kings Dhaṅga and Gaṇḍa, his son Śivanāga, the minister of Vidyādhara, his son Mahīpala, the minister of Vijayapāla, his son Ananta, a minister under Kīrtivarman and Sallakṣaṇavarman, his son Gadādhara, the Pratihāra of Jayavarman, who later held the post of the Chief Minister of Pṛthvīvarman and Madanavarman. It is undated, but evidently dateable in the reign-period of Madanavarman, i.e., about the middle of the 12th cent. A. D. It is now preserved in the Indian Museum, Calcutta.

Edited by Kielhorn E. I. Vol. I. pp. 195-207.

Paramardideva.

30. Semrā Plates of Paramardideva. V. S. 1223.

Found at Semrā village in the Bijāwār State, Bundelkhand, now in the Lucknow Museum. Inscribed on 3 copper plates bound by a ring. The Gaja-Lakṣmī emblem is embossed on the first plate. Beginning with a reference to the origin of the Candrātreya family from the moon, and the early heroes, Jayaśakti and Vijayaśakti, it eulogises in glowing terms the reigning king Pb. M. P. Pm. Kālañjarādhipati Śrī Paramardideva, meditating on the feet of Pb. M. P. Śrī Madanavarmadeva, who meditated on the feet of Pb. M. P. Śrī Pṛthvīvarmadeva. Records gifts of land, measured in 'pada' (padamekaṁ, padārddhaṁ, padadvayaṁ, &c.,), in the viṣayas of Vikaura, Dudāhi, Vaḍavāri and Gokula, to brahmins of renowned gotras, pravaras and Veda-Śākhas. It was issued from the king's camp at Sonasāra on a Thursday, the 7th day of the bright fortnight of Vaiśākha in V. S. 1223, in confirmation of the grants made by his grandfather, Madanavarman from his Vāridurga camp in V. S. 1219.

Written by Dharmalekhī Pṛthvīdhara of the Vāstavya family and inscribed by Pitalakāra Pālhaṇa.

Edited by Cartellieri E. I. Vol. IV. pp. 153 ff.

31. Mahobā Image Inscription, V. S. 1224.

A single line inscription on the pedestal of a broken Jaina image. It is incomplete, but the date of its dedication, Saṁvat 1224., and the name of the ruler, Kālañjarādhipati Śrīmat Paramardideva, are found from it.

Edited by Cunningham A. S. R. Vol. XXI. p. 74.

32. Ajaygaḍh Stone Inscription. V. S. 1227 (?).

Inscribed on the jamb on the upper gate of the fort. The date was originally read by Cunningham as 1237 V. S., but according to Kielhorn it was 1227 V. S. Records the construction of a Bāuli or well in the fort of Jayapura by Rāuta Śrī Vīra, a kṣatriya, during a famine.

Noticed by Cunningham. A. S. R. Vol. XXI. pp 49-50.

33. Icchāwār Plates of Paramardideva. V. S. 1228.

Found near the village Icchāwār in the Pailani Tahsil of the Bāndā district., U.P. Incised on two copper plates with a figure of Gaja-Lakṣmī embossed on the first plate. It begins with an eulogy of the Candrātreya family, which produced heroes like Jayaśakti and Vijayaśakti, and then refers to the grant of a village named Nandinī in the Nandāvana Viṣaya to Senāpati Madanapālaśarman, a brahmin of the Kṛṣṇātreya gotra at the time of a lunar eclipse on Sunday, the 15th tithi of the bright half of Śrāvaṇa in V. S. 1228., by Pb. M. P. Pm. Kālañjarādhipati Śrīmat Paramardideva, meditating on the feet of Pb.M.P. Śrī Madanavarmadeva, who meditated on the feet of Pb. M. P. Śrī Pṛthvīvarmadeva, while the king was in residence at Vilāsapura.

Written by Kāyastha Pṛthvīdhara and engraved by Śilpin Pālhaṇa.

Edited by Kielhorn I. A. Vol. XXV. pp. 205 ff.

34. Mahobā Plates of Paramardideva. V. S. 1230.

Found in the Mahobā town of the Hamirpur district., U.P.

Incised on two plates bound by a ring with a seal, the Gaja-Lakṣmī emblem is embossed on the first plate. The introductory references to Jayaśakti and Vijayaśakti are similar to those of Semrā and Icchāwār Plates. Records the grant of land measuring 60 sq. 'vādhas' or 5 'halas' (cultivable by five ploughs) in the Dhanaura village in the Eracha viṣaya to a brahmin, Ratnaśarman of the Śaṅkṛitya gotra on the 4th day of the dark fortnight of Māgha in V. S. 1230 when the Sun entered the sign of Makara, by king Paramardi, whose ancestors were Madanavarman and Pṛthvīvarman. The grant was issued from the royal camp at Gahilu. The writer was Kāyastha Pṛthvīdhara and engraver Pālhaṇa, now a 'vijñānin.'

Edited by Rai Bahadur Hiralal. E. I. Vol. XVI. pp. 9ff.

35. Pachār Plate of Paramardideva. V. S. 1233.

A single copper plate bearing this inscription with the emblem of Gaja-Lakṣmī embossed on the top of it was found from the village Pachār, near

Jhānsī, now in the Lucknow Museum. After referring to the early heroes of Candrātreya family, Jayaśakti and Vijayaśakti, it records the gift of some land measuring 10 'halas' in the village of Lauva in the Karigāva Viṣaya, to Paṇḍita Keśava Śarman of the Kāśyapa gotra, on Wednesday, the 8th tithi of the dark fortnight of Kārttika in V. S. 1233, by the illustrious Śrī Paramardideva, whose ancestors were Śrī Madanavarman and Śrī Pṛthvīvarman, from the royal camp at Vilāsapura. Written by Śubhānanda of the Vāstavya family and engraved by Pālahaṇa (Pālhaṇa), mentioned as 'vaidagdhi-viśvakarmmana' (a master of the art and craft).

Edited by Arthur Venis E. I. Vol. X. pp. 44ff.

36. Chārkhāri Plates of Paramardideva. V. S. 1236.

Provenance unknown, preserved in the Chārkhāri durbar, (Bundelkhand). Incised on two copper plates, with the figure of Gaja-Lakṣmī on the first plate. After usual eulogies to the early heroes, Jayaśakti and Vijayaśakti, it records the grant of the village Sagauḍo in the Kīrayiḍa viṣaya to a number of brahmins of the Vatsa gotra, on Monday, the 7th day of the bright fortnight of Caitra in 1236 V. S. by king Paramardideva, whose ancestors were Madanavarman and Pṛthvīvarman, from the royal camp of Vilāsapura. Five 'halas' of land of the same village previously endowed to a Buddhist monastery was however excluded from the present grant. Written by Kāyastha Subhānanda of the Vāstavya family and engraved by Śilpi Pālhaṇa, a 'Vaidagdhi-viśvakarmana'.

Edited by Rai Bahadur Hiralal. E. I. Vol. XX. pp. 128-21.

37. Madanpur Stone Inscriptions, V. S. 1239.

Found inscribed on the pillar of a maṇḍapa of an old temple in the village of Madanpur, '24 miles to the south-east of Dudhāi, 35 miles to the south-south-east of Lalitpur, and 30 miles to the north of Saugor'. The first inscription refers to the devastation of the territory of Paramardi by Pṛthvīrāja of the Cāhamāna family. The second record states that in Saṁ. 1239 Pṛthvīrāja, son of Someśvar, grandson of Arnnorāja, plundered Jejākabhukti (earlier read by Cunningham as Jejākaśukti).

Edited by Cunningham A. S. R. Vol. XXI. pp. 173-74; P. R. A. S., W. I. p. 55.

38. Plate of Paramardin, V. S. 1239.

Preserved in the Bhārat Kalā Bhavan, Banaras,—Provenance unknown. Issued by Paramardi on Tuesday, Phālguṇa—Vadi 4. V. S. 1239 (19th March 1173 A. D.), from his camp at 'Sallakṣaṇa-Vilāsapura.'

Records the grant of the village Vavauḍa-grāma in the Duḍuhi viṣaya to Paṇḍita Padumadharaśarman, a brother of Somaśarman, mentioned in Madanavarman's charter of V. S. 1192. Written by the Dharmalekhin Ṭhakkura Viṣṇuka and engraved by Pālhaṇa, the Pitalahāra(brazier).

Edited by Dr. D. C. Sircar, E. I. XXXII pp. 123-25

39. Kālañjar Rock Inscription. V. S. 1240.

The date of the record, 'Samvat 1240 Vaiśākha sudi 14 Gurau'. and the name of the reigning monarch 'Śrīmad Paramardideva-vijayarājye' could only be read by Kielhorn.

Kielhorn's list No. 178. E. I. Vol. V. (App.); Bhandarkar's No. 400 E. I. Vols. XIX-XXI.

40. Mahobā Stone Inscription. V. S. 1240.

'Found in the fort wall placed upside down as a common building stone' in a damaged condition. Refers to Suhila of the Vāstavya family, probably building a temple (prāsāda). The sculptor was Devarāja, son of Somarāja. Dated in Samvat 1240 Āṣāḍa vadi 9 Some. The reigning king, Paramardi is not mentioned, but it contains the name of 'Nānika' (Nannuka) the founder of the Candella dynasty.

Edited by Cunningham A. S. R. Vol. XXI. p. 72; Smith PASB. 1879. pp. 143-4.

41. Ajaygaḍh Stone Inscription. V. S. 1243.

Found on the jamb of the upper gate of fort. Refers to the building of a Cautrā (raised platform ?) in the Jayapura-durga for all people on Wednesday, the 11th day of the bright half of Jyeṣṭha in Samvat 1243, by Rāut. Śrī Sīhada, son of Rāut. Sāntana of the Kṣatriya caste.

Edited by Cunningham A. S. R. Vol. XXI. p. 50.

42. Plate of Paramardin, V. S. 1247.

Preserved in the Bhārat Kalā Bhavan, Banaras,—Provenance unknown. Issued by Paramardin on Saturday, Phālguṇa Sudi 14, V. S. 1247 (9th February, 1191 A. D.), when he was at the Maṇikarṇikā-ghaṭṭa at Śrī Vārānasī.

Records the grant of 10 'lavas' of land at Iṭalā-grāma in the Pāśuṇi viṣaya to Padmadharaśarman (known to us from a previous charter also, dated V. S. 1239). The concluding portion of the charter, incised on a separate sheet, is however lost.

It may be suggested that the Pāśuni viṣaya was located in the valley of the river Paisuni, which flows through the eastern part of the Bāndā district, before it reaches the Jumna.

Edited by Dr. D. C. Sircar, E. I., XXXII pp. 125-28

43. Baghāri (Baṭeśvar) Stone Inscription. V. S. 1252.

Incised on a stone broken in two pieces, found in Singhanpur-Baghāri, near Mahobā, possibly on the bank of a lake, as suggested by Cunningham and later confirmed by V. Smith and Hoey. Due to some misunderstanding Kielhorn wrote in E. I. Vol. I., P. 207 that it was found at Baṭeśvar (Agra Dist.)

Records the construction of two temples, one for Viṣṇu and the other for Śiva, by Sallakṣaṇa, the Chief Minister of Paramardi. The Second temple was completed by his son and successor in office, Puruṣottama. So this one, like the Māu Inscription, is a record of a ministerial family. An account of the achievements of the successive ministers of this family are given from verses 14 to 29. Lakṣmīdhara, and his son Vatsarāja, great scholars of the Vaśiṣṭha gotra, both were real founders of the line. Lāhaḍa, a son of Vatsarāja, was a chief counsellor of Madanavarman. His son Sallakṣaṇa served in the same capacity under Paramardi, and was succeeded in office by his son, Puruṣottama. Incidentally the record furnishes the story of the origin of the Candrātreyas and refers to the kings Madanavarman, his son Yaśovarman II, and his son Paramardi. The inscription was composed by Poet Devadhara, son of Gadādhara, the Saṁdhāna-vigraha-mahāsaciva of Paramardi, and grandson of Lakṣmīdhara of Gauḍa lineage, and written by Dharmadhara, a brother of Devadhara, and engraved by Mahārāja, son of Somarāja.

Edited by Kielhorn E. I. Vol. I. pp. 207ff; commented upon by Smith and Hoey in JASB. Vol. XXLIV. Pt. I., P. 158. f. n. 1.

44. Kālañjar Stone Inscription of Paramardideva. V. S. 1258.

Found inscribed on a large black stone slab at the entrance of cave temple of Nīlakaṇṭha at Kālañjar. It is a long Sanskrit poem in praise of Śiva and Pārvatī, stated to have been composed by King Paramardi himself out of his innate faith on Purāri. Paramardi is mentioned in the record as 'Daśārṇādhinātha'. It was written and inscribed by an eminent artist, a favourite of the king, named Padma, who was helped by his brother, Deoka. Dated—Monday, 10th day of the bright half of Kārtika, Saṁ. 1258.

Edited by Maisey J.A.S.B. 1848. Vol. XVII. pp. 313-17; Cunningham A. S. R., Vol. XXI. pp. 37-38.

Trailokyavarman.

45 & 46. Gārrā Plates of Trailokyavarman. V. S. 1261.

The records, incised on two copper plates strung together by a ring, which however is not found, were discovered from a tank near the village Gārrā, to the south east of Chātārpur, Bundelkhand, now in the Lucknow Museum. Both the plates bear the emblem of Gaja-Lakṣmī embossed on the top portion. In the usual conventional style they begin with an eulogistic reference to the origin and the early heroes of the family, Jayaśakti and Vijayaśakti, and then refer to the donor, the reigning monarch, Pb. M. P. Pm. Kālañjarādhipati Trailokyavarmadeva meditating on the feet of Paramardideva who meditated on the feet of Madanavarmadeva.

The first Grant records the gift of the village Kaḍohā in the Pāṇiulī Viṣaya on Friday, the 2nd day of the bright half of Vaiśākha, Saṁvat

1261, and the second one of the village Lohasihanī in the Vikraunī viṣaya on Friday, the 2nd day of the dark half of Vaiśākha in the same year as 'Mṛtyukavṛtti', to Rāuta Sāmanta or Sāvanta of the Bharadvāja gotra, son of Rāuta Pāpe, killed at the Battle of Kakaḍadaha, fighting with the Turuṣkas.

Edited by K. N. Dikshit. E. I. Vol. XVI. p. 272 ff.

47. Ajaygaḍh fragmentary Stone Inscription. V. S. 1269.

Found outside the tank at Pātāl-sar in the Ajaygaḍh fort. The name of the reigning king Trailokyavarmadeva, and the date of the issue of the record, Samvat 1269, Phālguna vadi, (tithi is illegible), are points to be noted.

Noticed by Cunningham A. S. R. Vol. XXI. p. 50.

48. Rewā Plates of the time of Trailokyamalla. K. E. 963 (1212 A.D.).

Found at the village Dhureṭi, 7 miles from Rewā town. Incised on two copper plates strung together by a ring, to which a seal is attached bearing the embossed figure of Gaja-Lakṣmī and the sign-manual of the king, 'Śrīmat Trailokyamalla'. It opens with three invocatory verses in praise of Kṛṣṇa and Śiva, the 3rd verse being quoted from Daṇḍin's Kāvyādarśa, and then refers to the reigning monarch Trailokyamalladeva endowed with grandiloquent titles, viz , 'Paramabhaṭṭāraka(ke)tyādi-samasta rājāvalī virājamāna Parama-Māhe-(śva)-ra aśvapati gajapati narapati rājatrayādhipati vividha-vidyā-vicāra-vācaspati Śrī Vāmadeva-pādānudhyāta Kānyakubjādhipati'. (Ll. 5-6). In L. 12 he is mentioned as 'Triśati-rājyādhipati', an unique title not used before. It is a deed of mortgage for the village, Alira in the Dhovahaṭṭa pattana of the Dhanavāhi pattalā, which was pledged by the Śaiva teacher Śāntaśiva, son of Rājaguru Vimalaśiva, to Rāṇaka Dhāreka of the Vatsa gotra on Saṁvat 963 Jyeṣṭha sudi 7 Some dine. The execution of the deed was made by Nādaśiva, brother of Śāntaśiva, witnessed by seven important persons. The record mentions some of the officers of the king, viz., Malayasiṁha the Mahāmāttaka and Māṇḍalika, appointed by the king as his minister; Ṭhakkura Haripāla, the Sāndhivigrahika; Vāhada the Koṭṭapāla ; and the Śreṣṭhin Śrīcanda, the Arthalekhin. Some of these officers were members of the Pañcakūla and the Dharmādhikaraṇa.

Edited by N. P. Chakravarti. E. I. Vol. XXV. p. 1 ff., Mm. V. Mirashi. C. I. I., IV. p. 37 ff.

49. Rewā Copper plate grant of Mahārāṇaka Kumārapāladeva. V. S. 1297.

Incised on two plates not strung together by a ring.

Found in the possession of the Rewā Durbar, now in the British Museum. Opens with three invocatory verses for Brahman, Puruṣottama and

Tryambaka, of which the last is a quotation from Bāṇa's Kādambarī. The reigning monarch, Trailokyavarmmadeva is mentioned endowed with the titles generally associated with the Kalacuri rulers, viz., Pb. M. P. Pm. Vāmadevapādānudhyāta Pb. M. P. Pm. Trikaliṅgādhipati nijabhujopārjjita aśvapati gajapati narapati rājatrayādhipati. Records the gift of the village Rehī in the Vaddharāpattalā to Rāutas Saṅge, Suhaḍa, Mahaita, Rāmasiha, Somivijhu and Sāvantaśarman by Mahārāṇaka Kumārapāladeva of Kakareḍi. A genealogical account of the Mahārāṇaka family is also given, which shows that Kumārapāla was the son of Mahārāṇaka Harirāja. The deed was drawn up by Kāyastha Muktasiṁha, written by Mālādhara and inscribed by the śilpis Jayasiṁha and Pratāpasiṁha on the full moon day of Kārttika in V. S. 1297.

Edited by Kielhorn I. A. Vol. XVII. pp. 231ff.

50. Rewā Copper Plate Grant of Mahārāṇaka Harirājadeva. V. S. 1298.

Incised on two plates provided with ringholes. Found from the Rewā Durbar, now in the British Museum. Begins with invocatory verses as in the earlier record, dated V. S. 1297, and then refers to the king thus,—'Paramabhaṭṭāraketyādi rājāvali-trayopeta-Mahārāja Srī Trelākyamalla' (Trailokyamalla). Records the gift of the village Agaseyī in the Vaddharāpattala to Rāuta Saṅge, Suhaḍa, Mahāditya and Sāmanta by Mahārāṇaka Harirājaḍeva of Kakareḍi in the month of Māgha, Saṁvat 1240. The genealogy of the Mahārāṇakas shows that the donor of this record and the father of Kumārapāla of the earlier record was identical person. Dr. H. C. Ray suggests that the accession of Kumārapāla was due to some court intrigue, which however was suppressed by Harirāja, who recovered his position. (D. H. N. I. Vol. II. p. 728. f. n. 2).

Written by Karaṇika Ṭhakkura Udayasiṁha, and engraved by the son of Kukem, the grandson of 'ayaskara' Dāge (Gāṅge).

Edited by Kielhorn I. A. Vol. XVII. p. 235.

Vīravarman.

51. Chārkhāri Plate of Vīravarman. V. S. 1311.

Provenance unknown, found in the possession of the Chārkhāri Durbar. The copper plate bears the figure of Gaja-Lakṣmī on the top portion of it. Beginning with the conventional eulogies to the early heroes of the family, Jayaśakti and Vijayaśakti, it refers to the reigning prince, the donor Vīravarman with his ancestors, Trailokyavarman, Paramardi and Madanavarman. Records the gift of the village Ṭumṭumā in the Dahī Viṣaya to Rāuta Abhi belonging to the family of Candreśvara of the Kāśyapa gotra, for his services in defeating Dabhyuhaḍavarman in the Battle of Sondhī (identified with the Seondhā fort, now called Kāṇhārgarh on the banks of the Sindh river in Datiā). It was issued from the royal camp of Vilāsapura on Monday, the 8th day of the bright half of Āśvina in Samvat 1311.

Edited by Rai Bahadur Hiralal E. I. Vol. XX. pp. 132-34.

52. Ajaygaḍh Rock Inscription of Vīravarman & his wife Kalyāṇadevī, V. S. 1317.

Inscribed on a rock with a crack dividing it into two parts at Ajaygaḍh. Begins with an invocatory verse in praise of Gaṅgā and then gives the genealogy of the Candella rulers from Kīrtivarman to Vīravarman along with their achievements. Records the construction of a well (nirjara) with perennial supply of water, a hall (maṇḍapa) and a tank within the fort of Nandipura, by the chief queen of Vīravarman, named Kalyāṇadevī. An account of the ancestry of the queen belonging to the Dadhīci-vaṁśa is also given. It was issued during the office of Jetana in the reign of Vīravarman in the year 1317 Samvat, on Thursday, the 13th day of the bright half of Vaiśākha. Composed by Poet Ratnapāla, and engraved by artisan Rāma.

Edited by Kielhorn E. I. Vol. I. pp. 325-30.

53. Jhansi Stone Inscription, V. S. 1318.

Noticed by Kielhorn in E. I. Vol. V. App. p. 33. No. 227.

Refers to the reign of Vīravarman (?) in the year V. S. 1318.

54. Ajaygaḍh Stone Inscription. V. S. 1325.

Inscribed on the wall of a temple at Ajaygaḍh referring to the adoration of Abhayadeva, the son of Aśvavaidya Ṭha. Bhojaka (Bhojuka) of the Vatsa Gotra, in the reign of Vīravarman in Saṁvat 1325. Kielhorn identifies Bhojuka of this record with Bhojuka killed by Vāseka in the reign of Trailokyavarman (E. I. Vol. I. p. 332).

Edited by Cunningham A. S. R. Vol XXI. p. 51.

55. Ajaygaḍh Rock Inscription of the time of Vīravarman. V. S. 1337.

Found on a rock near the figure of a Ganeśa at Ajaygaḍh. Refers to the Candella rulers from Kīrtivarman to Vīravarman, but details are not available as the record has not been edited. Records the setting up of an image of Vināyaka (Ganeśa) by Gaṇapati, a minister of Vīravarman in Samvat 1337.

Noticed by Cunningham A. S. R. Vol. XXI. p. 52.

56. Dahī Plate of Vīravarmadeva. V. S. 1337.

The copper plate bearing the inscription was found from the village Dahī, Bijāwār (Bundelkhand). Begins with the conventional eulogies to the early heroes of the family, Jayaśakti and Vijayaśakti, and then gives the genealogy of the Candella rulers from Madanavarman to Vīravarman.

Records the gift of the village Dahi to one Mallaya of the Kaśyapa gotra for his victories over the lord of Narwar (Nalapurapati) Gopāla, the ruler of Mathurā (Madhuvanakādhīpa) and Harirāja of Gwālior (Gopagiri). Dated the 15th day of the bright half of Vaiśākh in Samvat 1337.

Noticed by Cunningham A. S. R. Vol. XXI. pp. 74-6; Garde I. A. 1918. p. 241 ; commented on by Dr. D. C. Sircar, I. H. Q., XXXII, Pp. 404-05.

56a. Baṅglā Stone Pillar Inscriptions. V. S. 1338.

Fifteen stone pillars have been found in'a rocky waste land covered with thorny shrubs' in a small village named Baṅglā, about 5 miles to the east of Narwar fort (Shivapuri Dist.), and one at the village Sesayi. Some of the records refer to the death of certain warriors who lost their lives fighting on behalf of the Yajvapāla King Gopāla against the Candella monarch Vīravarman. The date of the battle, as given in some of the records, was V. S. 1330, Caitra Sudi 7. Friday (28th March, 1281 A. D.).

Noticed in the Annual Adm. Rep. of Arch. Deptt. of the Gwālior State for V. S. 1991 (1934-35), Pp. 8-12, 25-26 ; H. N. Dvivedi's Gwālior Rājyake Abhilekh, No. 133-39 ; Commented upon by Dr. D. C. Sircar, I. H. Q., XXXII, Pp. 401-05 ; and edited by Dr. D. C. Sircar, E. I. XXXI. p. 326

57. Kālañjar Inscription. V. S. 1340.

It has not been edited. Kielhorn noticed it in his Appendix to E. I. Vol. V., P. 35. No. 241. As it is dated in 'Caitra sudi 3 Budhadine Sam. 1340', it may be taken to belong to the reign of Vīravarman, though the name of the king is not given.

58. Gurhā Satī Stone Inscription. V. S. 1342.

Noticed by Kielhorn in his Appendix to E. I. Vol. V., p. 35. No. 242. It refers to the reigning king Śrīmad Vīravarmadeva, and is dated Caitra sudi 3 Budhe.

59. Kālañjar fragmentary Inscription.

Found inscribed on a piece of yellow stone slab at the entrance of the Nīlakaṇṭha temple at Kālañjar. Records construction of various temples, gardens and ponds, and installation of images of Śiva, Kamalā and Kālī in 'splendid houses' probably during the reign of Vīravarman. It gives a genealogy of the Candella rulers from Vijayapāla to Vīravarman indicating the important achievements of each of them. In Ll. 15-16 we are introduced to Pratāpa, a younger brother of Madanavarman, who was an influential person and looked aft er those 'who were lame and weak, who were sick and who were distressed'. Composed by a person named Vallakīvīra.

Edited by Maisey JASB. Vol. XVII. Pt. I. pp. 317-20; Cunningham A. S. R. Vol. XXI. pp. 38-40.

Bhojavarman.

60. Ajaygaḍh Stone Inscription of Nāna. V. S. 1345.

Found from Ajaygaḍh incised on a slab of stone, now in the Asiatic Society, Calcutta. Records the establishment of a temple at Jayadurga with the image of Keśava by Nāna, a minister of Bhojavarman. Begins with invocatory verses in praise of Murāri and some of the incarnations of Viṣṇu, and then gives an account of the Vāstavya Kāyastha family to which Nāna belonged as originating at Kausamyapura and tracing descent from Kaśyapa. Composed by Poet Amara and engraved by Paṁsuha, a Śrī Vāstavya Kāyastha.

Edited by Prinsep JASB. 1837. Vol. VI. pp. 881-87; Re-edited by H. L. Srivastava E. I. Vol. XXVIII. pp. 98-107.

61. Ajaygaḍh Rock Inscription of the time of Bhojavarman.

Found inscribed 'on a rock near the Tarhāoni or Tirhāwān gate' of the Ajaygaḍh fort. Beginning with a verse in praise of Śiva it makes eulogistic reference to the Vāstavya Kāyasthas of Takkārikā, which was one of the 36 towns famous for the settlement of the Kāyasthas. Members of this caste served successive Candella rulers in various ministerial capacities and recieved grants of villages and distinctive titles like 'Viśiṣa' from them. Records the construction of a temple by Subhaṭa of the same family, the Kośādhikārādhipati, during the reign of Bhojavarman.

Edited by Kielhorn E. I. Vol. I. pp. 330ff.

62. Ajaygaḍh Sati Record of the reign of Bhojavarman. V. S. 1346.

Noticed by R. B. Hiralal. E. I. Vol. XX. p. 135.

Hammīravarman.

63. Chārkhāri Plate of Hammīradeva. V. S. 1346.

The copper plate was found from the Chārkhāri Durbar. It bears the Gaja-Lakṣmī emblem embossed on the top of it. Beginning with the usual eulogies to the early heroes of the family, Jayaśakti and Vijayśakti, it refers to the donor, thus, 'Paramabhaṭṭāraka Sāhī rājāvalītrayopeta-Kālañjarādhipati Mahārāja Śrīmad-Hamīravarmmadeva', meditating on the feet of Pb. M. P. Pm. Sāhī Mahārajā Śrīmad-Vīravarmmadeva, whose ancestors were Trailokyavarman and Paramardi.

Records the grant of a village Ko(or Kī) kaḍagrāma in the Vedesaitha

Viṣaya to two brāhmaṇas on Sunday, the 12th day of the dark fortnight of of Bhādrapada in V. S. 1346.

Written by Paṁ (Paṇḍita) Raum (Rāma)-Pāla.

Edited by Rai Bahadur Hiralal E. I. Vol. XX. pp. 134-36.

64. Bāmhni Sati stone Inscription V. S. 1365.

Found in the village Bāmhni in the Dāmoh District in the reign of Mahārājaputra Vāghadeva, a feudatory of Candella Hammīravarman, described as 'Paramabheṭāraken-ādhirājāvalī-trayopeta Kāliñjarādhipati Śrīmad-Hammīravarmmadeva'. The Sati stone was set up for the wife of 'bhūmipāla' Pālhaṇa of the village Brāhmaṇī in Saṁvat 1365. Written by Paṁ. (Paṇḍita) Jayapāla.

Noticed by R. B. Hiralal. E. I. Vol. XVI. p. 10. f. n. and edited by him. E. I. Vol. XIX. p. 30.

65. Ajaygaḍh fort Sati stone record of the reign of Hammīravarman. V. S. 1365.

Noticed by R. B. Hiralal. E. I. XX. p. 134. f. n. 2.

APPENDIX II

GENEALOGY OF THE CANDELLA DYNASTY

Nannuka (c. 831 A.D.)

Vākpati

Jayaśakti (c. 850 A.D.)

Vijayaśakti

Rāhila

Harṣa = Kañchukā

Yaśovarman = Puppā
(c. 925 A.D.)

Dhaṅga (c. 950—1002-03 A.D.)

Kṛṣṇapa = Āsarvā

Gaṇḍa (c. 1002-03—1018 A.D.)

Devalabdhi

Vidyādhara (c. 1018-1022 A.D.)

Vijayapāla = Bhuvanadevī
(c. 1022-1051 A.D.)

Devavarman (c. 1051 A.D.)

Kīrtivarman (c. 1070-1098 A.D.)

Sallakśaṇavarman
(c. 1100 A.D.)

Pṛthvīvarman
(c. 1125 A.D.)

Jayavarman (c. 1117 A.D.)

Madanavarman = Vālhanadevī
(c. 1129-1163 = Lakhamādevī
A.D.) = Cāndaladevī

Pratāpa

Yaśovarman II (c. 1165 A.D.)

Paramardi (c. 1166-1202 A.D.)

Trailokyavarman (c. 1205—1240-41 or
1247 A.D.)

Vīravarman = Kalyāṇadevī
(c. 1247-86 A.D.)

Bhojavarman (c. 1286-1289 A.D.)

Hammīravarman (c. 1289-90—1308 A.D.)

SUPPLEMENT TO APPENDIX I

11. Kālajñar Inscription of V. S. 1147 (p. 225).

Engraved on a stone slab built into the wall of the sanctum of the temple of Nīlakaṇṭha at Kālañjara.

Records construction of a *maṇḍapa* by Śrīmūrti, the *guru* of Kīrtivarman, for which two 'ploughs' (*halas*) of land was donated at the time of *dhvajārohaṇa* (flag hoisting) to mark the opening ceremony. The donor, according to the editor, may be Sūtradhāra Rāma, who had built it, or Vāsudeva, whose name occurs in the marginal note. Dr. D. C. Sircar however suggests that Kāyastha Devapāla (mentioned 'Devapālena' without the verb) might have donated the land. An interesting point in the record is the mention for the first time of the name of the *guru* of Kīrtivarman and also of his patronage to the Śaivas and the Pāśupatas. The date of the record is Saṁvat 1147, 7th day of the bright half of Māgha.

Edited by S. L. Katare, E.I., XXXI pp. 163-66.

46a. Tehri Plate of Trailokyavarman, V.S. 1264

Found while digging a tank at Laksmipura Mohalla of Saugor (M.P.), now preserved in the Central Museum, Nagpur.

A single plate ($14\frac{1}{4}$" x $10\frac{1}{2}$", wg. 275 tolas) with *Gaja-Lakṣmī* symbol engraved on the top centre. Begins with conventional references to the early Candella heroes, Jayaśakti and Vijayaśakti and then refers to the reigning monarch Pb. M. PM. *Kālañjarādhipati* Trailokyavarmadeva, meditating on the feet of Paramardideva who meditated on the feet of Madanavarmadeva. It omits the name of Yaśovarman II between Madanavarman and Paramardi. Records the gift of the Village Maṇḍaura (Madaira in the Lalitpur Sub-division) in the Vaḍavāri Viṣaya to Nāyaka Kulaśarman of Vatsa gotra, hailing from the village of Raikaura (?).

The grant was issued by Trailokyavarman, while he was residing at Ṭihari (mod. Tehri or Tehri Banapur in the former Orccha State, Bundelkhand), but the announcement of it appears to have been made from the administrative or military camp at Sihadauni or Siyadoni, (*Sihadauni Sainye*), near

Lalitpur. The record is dated V.S. 1264. Bhādrapada Vadi 2, Friday = 29.8.1208 according to expired year calculation. First edited by B. M. Barua & P. B. Chakravarti, JBBRAS XXII (1947) pp. 46 ff; Re-edited by S. L. Katare E.I., XXXI pp. 70-73.

56b & c. Two Inscriptions of the time of Yajvapāla Gopāla of Nalapura (Narwar).

(i) Barauḍi Inscription of V.S. 1336.

(ii) Narwar Inscription of V.S. 1339.

Found at Barauḍi and Narwargarh, both in the Shivapuri district (M.P.) recording excavation of a *Vāpi* (stepped well) in each case.

(i) Devadhara of the Gauḍahara Kṣatriya family, Vatsa gotra (may be Gaur Rajputs), who became the *adhikāri-mukhya* (Chief Minister, according to the editor, but more appropriately a Chief Administrative Officer) of Assalladeva (c. 1254-79), father of Gopāla, caused the excavation of a *Vāpi* in the village of Vaṭapatra (mod. Barauḍi). Incidentally it gives the genealogy of the Yajvapāla dynasty upto Gopāla, the reigning king with Nalapura (Narwargarh) as his capital.

(ii) Gaṅgadeva (Vaidyavaṁśa), a *saciva* (minister) of Gopāla caused the excavation of a *Vāpi* in the Pādonalakṣa Viṣaya (?) as also of repair of temples and gardens in the vicinity. The record mentions the victory achieved by Gopāla over Vīravarman (Candella) and king Lakṣmaṇa of Chandragiri in a battle on the bank of the river Sikatā (or possibly Bālukā mentioned in the Baṅglā Inscription, V.S. 1338). It refers to the rise of Jayapāla (pronounced Jajapella by the common people) the progenitor of the family of Narwar by the grace of Goddess Mahāruṇḍā (probably their tutelary deity) and also to their original home at Ratnagiri (?), may be identical with Ratangarh Khiri in the former Gwalior State.

The composer of both the records was Śivanābhaka of the Mathura Kāyastha family hailing from Gopādri (mod. Gwalior). Edited by Dr. D. C. Sircar, EI, Vol. XXXIII, pp. 31-40.

APPENDIX III

CANDELLA LAND GRANTS AND FEUDALISM

DURING the years of struggle for independence and immediately after its achievement Indian historians frequently emphasised that the Indian history had a unique or distinctive character of its own. When the first exuberance of nationalistic enthusiasm subsided late in the fifties or early in the sixties, attempts have been made by a number of Indian historians to read the history of India in the broader context of the development of human society and civilisation. They believed that since man in India is a part of humanity at large, the same or similar laws of social, economic and political development were operative here as well. While welcoming this new scientific and critical approach to the study of Indian history, it is to be pointed out that these historians fell victim to the Euro-centric ready-made formula of the fourfold development of human society, viz, (i) primitive communism, (ii) slavery, (iii) feudalism and (iv) capitalism.

For our purpose we shall mention one such outstanding work, *Indian Feudalism* (c. 300-1200) by Dr. R. S. Sharma. According to him, "European experience suggests that the political essence of feudalism lay in the organisation of the whole administrative structure on the basis of land; its economic essence lay in the institution of serfdom in which the peasants were attached to the soil held by landed intermediaries placed between the king and the actual tillers who had to pay rent in kind and labour to them. The system was based on a self-sufficient economy in which things were mainly produced for the local use of the peasants and their lords and not for the market" (p. 1). Dr. Sharma acknowledges that various meanings and imports have been given to feudalism, but nevertheless accepts a rather simplicist formulation of the institution. He seems also to ignore the warning given by Ganshoff who points out that analogies of the feudalism as developed in Europe or more particularly in the region lying between the Loire and the Rhine comprising France, Burgundy-Arles and Germany between the 8th & 13th centuries A.D. may be found in other times and at other places also. But a closer examination of the sources has failed to justify their identity. (*Feudalism*, Intro. p. xvi). This is not the place to write a lengthy critique to Dr. Sharma's thesis and we shall confine ourselves to his references to the Candellas only. He has included the reign-period of the Candellas as marking both the climax and the decline of feudalism as a political and economic institution. He has referred to the different kinds of grants of plots of lands and villages made by the Candella kings to the Brāhmaṇas on religious grounds (pp. 167-170, 214, etc.), and also to officers holding high-sounding titles and military beneficiaries, (pp. 167-170, 193, 198 etc.). So far as the grants of villages are concerned, Dr. Sharma is emphatic that these implied not only the right to enjoy the incomes to be derived from them but also a proprietory right over them. The large number of fortresses in the Candella dominion has been taken by him as an unmistakable evidence of feudal organisation, and he believes that towards the close of the Candella rule, the commanders of these fortresses transformed themselves as full-fledged feudal lords (p. 291). Sub-infeudation with or without the permission of the king by the receivers of royal grants is also mentioned by him (p. 229). He further holds that the grant of such villages by a king or a vassal implied the transfer of the villages to the donee. In other words the villagers were tied down to the soil (p. 266). Sharma holds that the condition of the peasants was extremely unenviable, because they had to pay large fees and maintain royal officers of all ranks, whose number seems to be quite large (pp. 237-38).

The grant to temples of cash income from the sale tax and tolls on various commodities has been considered by him as evidence of feudalism of crafts and commerce and likened with the money-fiefs of medieval Europe (pp. 238-241). But he is not sure whether officials under the Kalacuris, Candellas or Cāhamānas were ever assigned such money-fiefs.

It is also during this period that Sharma traces the decline of feudalism. This he ascribes to the expansion of trade and commerce (pp. 247-48) as a result of the large-scale production of cash-earning crops, like sugarcane, cotton and hemp (p. 252). The growth of trade resulted in its turn in the revival and increasing use of money under the Candellas; the mortgage deed referring to 'vitta-bandha' is a pointer (p. 255). Sharma has also noted the gradual change from gold to silver-gilt, silver, silver-bronze and copper coins (p. 260).

The position taken by Dr. Sharma requires careful consideration. But at the outset a question of conceptualisation poses itself. To admit a feudal age in India after the European analogy would demand the recognition of the existence of a stage of primitive communism followed by one of slave economy also. Are we justified in doing so on the basis of sufficient data, archaeological and literary? The main question therefore is whether we are entitled to use the term feudalism at all. In a purely legalist sense of the word, and as it was understood in the land of its origin, feudalism is a contract between the lord and his vassal, the former guaranteeing protection and maintenance, and the latter assuring obedience and service. The contract arose out of an act called 'commendation' by the vassal. It was formalised by paying 'homage' to the overlord and the swearing of an 'oath of fealty' towards him. The lord in his turn assigned a benefice or fief to the vassal through a ceremony of 'investiture' with a staff and a lump of earth in the form of a globe etc. By the acceptance of vassalage a relation of an extremely personal nature is established between the lord and his vassal. The vassal was obliged to render counsel (*concilium*) and aid (*auxilium*) in the form of service chiefly military in character and payment of dues. It will be seen that none of the inscriptions and texts quoted by Sharma in his work contains any explicit or implicit reference to such a contract and personal relation between the parties. Secondly, Sharma himself agrees that unlike the clergy enjoying ecclesiastical benefices in the West, the religious donees owed no military service or for the matter of that any obligation to the donor kings (pp. 84, 271 etc.). Thirdly, Sharma concedes that *concilium*, i.e. to tender counsel to the overlord and assist him in the administration of justice, was not demanded of the vassal in India (p. 192, n. 1). But as has been referred to above, rendering counsel is one of the two kinds of services to be rendered by the vassal to the overlord according to the feudal usage in Europe. Indeed it appears that Sharma has misunderstood the character of the land grants made by Indian kings in general and the Candella rulers in particular. In making grants to the high-ranking officials in lieu of administrative and military services, either rendered or to be rendered by them, there was nothing feudal. These are examples of contract between an employer and an employee, and as such impersonal in character. If such grants are often stated to last till the Sun and the Moon endure, i.e. made permanent and hereditary, this was mere instances of royal condescension, and not wrested away by the donee from an unwilling but impotent overlord. There are also many examples of kings resuming grants made earlier or renewing the charter made by a predecessor but which was abrogated later by an invader or a usurper. All these tend to show that the kings maintained effective control over lands given away as grants to officers, civilian and military. There was thus no question of fragmentation of political authority of the ruler. In Europe, on the other hand, feudalism, when it was fully flourishing, tended to create numerous states within the State (*Imperium in Imperio*) thus reducing the position of the suzerain to the condition of either *Unus enter pares* or at best *primus enter pares*. In India the secular grants brought into existence only a band of officers who, with or without permission or reference to the ruling king, in their turn relegated parts of land and administrative rights granted to them to other persons. This process should not be viewed as subinfeudation, first, because of the absence of any contract of vassalage existing between the donor and the donee, and secondly, because of the absence of any proof of the latter's unquestioning submission to the former to the detriment of the ruling king, or the suzerain. In India there was never a question of a manorial court. What Sharma believes as abandonment of regalian rights, such as policing and jurisdiction, including the right to judge, impose punishments and fines and realising the same, to the holders of land grants (pp. 3-4, 76-79) was instead a process of progressive bureaucratisation of the governmental machinery.

As to the economic contents of feudalism Dr. Sharma notes that, the serfs were tied to the soil. But the expression "along with the villagers" used in connection with the grants of land hardly signifies that they were attached to the soil. What is really intended was that the donee was entitled to a part of the income of all the villagers including craftsmen and traders (Sircar, *Political & Administrative System*, pp. 20-21).

Secondly, besides paying tribute or tax the serfs in Europe had to render obligatory service to the liege-lord. But, as has been mentioned by Dr. Sharma himself, forced labour was not a necessary concomitant of serfdom in India, at least such was the position during the period of the Candellas (p. 243). If the villagers were not tied to the soil and had also not to render forced service to the landlord they cannot be characterised as serfs at all.

Thirdly, it has been observed that feudal economy was a closed one. Production of all sorts was for local consumption, and production of commodities for trade was not flourishing. Consequently money economy was languishing. But the prosperous existence of numerous mercantile groups and communities has been recorded in all ages beginning from the decline of the Guptas down to the 13th century A.D.[1]

These guilds of merchants or Chambers of Commerce traded no doubt in luxuries like magnificent elephants, horses of the finest brands, sapphires, moonstones, pearls, lapis lazuli, rubies, diamonds, emeralds, onyx, topaz etc., and precious articles like cardamom, cloves, bdellium, sandal, camphor, musk, saffron and many other spices and perfumes. But they also engaged themselves in the wholesale and retail trade of goods necessary for everyday consumption (*Ep. Carn.* II. Sk. 118-19). It will also be seen from the Charter of Viṣṇusena and the inscriptions of the Svāmis of Ayyavole that these guilds of merchants or mercantile settlements were often entrusted by the local rulers with the governance of towns and cities. From the Anjaneri grants it appears that the merchants were entrusted with the realisation of the fines imposed for various crimes like abduction of unmarried girls, adultery etc., thus arrogating to themselves certain judicial and executive prerogatives of the State. It will thus be evident that the merchants' corporations as such often presented themselves in the same position as high-sounding officers. Now if they made over a part of their profit for religious purposes, this can hardly be construed as feudalisation of trade and crafts. It may be observed in this context that the State regulated the prices of commodities and checked the weights and measures and collected tolls and duties (*Kauṭilya's Arthaśāstra* Bk II. 16, 19, 21; *Manu* VIII. 402). It has also been observed by Kosambi in connection with Viṣṇusena's Charter that dues and fines were assessed in cash, the unit of currency being *rūpaka* divided into twenties (*JESHO* Vol. 2, p. 285). From the above it is clear that in pre-Candella times in other parts of India trade and commerce, and consequently

1 (i) The charter of Viṣṇusena—(Viṣṇubhaṭṭa) (AD 592), Sircar, *EI XXX* pp. 163-81, D.D. Kosambi, *JESHO* Vol. 2(1959) pp. 285-89, (ii) Anjaneri Plates (A.D. 709-10) *EI XXV*, Pp. 277 ff, (iii) Sudi Inscription of Cālukya Someśvaravarman I Āhavamalla (A.D. 1043 68) *E.I. XV* Pp 77 ff, (iv) *Praśasti* of 500 Svāmis of Ayyavole in an inscription of A.D. 1054 from the Shikarpur Tāluka (Shimoga *Dt.*) *Ep. Carn*, Vol. II, Sk. 118-19, (v) Manigrāmam, *Trivandrum Arch. Series II*, 9, ii; *S.I.I. IV*, No. 147, Fleet *IA*, *X*, p. 189, *EI*, *XVIII* etc.)

a money economy were flourishing (Sircar, *op. cit.* pp. 18-19). There is nothing to show that these coins were issued by the guilds and not by the State. The Rāṣṭrakūṭas were paying their soldiers regularly in cash. This would show that the volume of money in circulation must have been considerable. Hence there is no question of a regeneration of trade and commerce in the 11th-12th centuries. Indeed the absence of forced labour, the extensive production of cash-earning crops and the large scale use of money of different denominations and metals would tend to show that far from being a closed economy centred on the village, there was a notable progress towards mercantile economy, the centre of which were the numerous fortressed townships throbbing under the control and guidance of State officials. It has to be observed therefore that Dr. Sharma seems to be suffering from a sort of contradictions regarding the state of feudalism under the Candellas. He notes that in the period of decline the governors of the fortresses became full-fledged feudal lords (p. 292), which would indicate the zenith of feudalisation of the dominion. But at the same time he records the decay of feudal economy under the Candellas as a result of revival of trade and commerce and currency of money tokens. May we ask how can an institution prosper politically while its economic basis was being corroded ?

Since Dr. Sharma has not touched upon the many social institutions of feudalism like knighthood and chivalry and the consequent pre-eminence in society of the warrior-aristocracy, we may take it for granted that he considered these as non-emergent in India. If the politico-economic pattern of early medieval India was moulded by feudalism, it would be curious not to find here any trace of its social projections.

To close this note, it may be recalled that in spite of his avowed championship of an objective approach to Indian history, Dr. Sharma has practically ignored India south of the Vindhyas in his study of Indian feudalism.

APPENDIX IV

A NOTE ON SOME ASPECTS OF CANDELLA ARCHITECTURE

THE unique celebrity associated with the name of the Candellas is due mainly to their patronage to art and architecture. With their active support and inspiration the art-products of the region came to be designated as the Candella art style with novel features of great aesthetic value.

So far as dating of the temples are concerned there has been some conflict of opinion among art-historians. It is well known that according to epigraphic testimony the temples in and around Khajurāho had been built between the middle of the 10th to the middle of the 11th Century A.D. Krishna Deva in his fairly long article in *Ancient India* (1959) No. 15 has traced the process of evolution of the temple style right from the middle of the 9th century through the different stages of progress to reach its finale in the great Kandariya Mahādeva temple around 1050 A.D. But Professor S. K. Saraswati is of opinion that on stylistic and structural considerations none of the temples at Khajurāho can be dated prior to the second half of the 11th century A.D. (*Struggle for Empire*, pp. 664-66). He believes that the temples suffered irreparable damage during the invasions of Sultan Mahmud, and that the extant temples might have been largely restored and reconstructed by king Kīrtivarman during the period of revival of Candella glory in the second half of the 11th century A.D. I have observed that the view of Professor Saraswati may not be unlikely (*vide ante* p. 211, f.n. 13). But to my mind the following points have to be considered before arriving at any definite conclusion.

(i) The date of construction of one of the earliest developed form of temples, viz., Lakṣmaṇji's is V. S. 1011 (953-54 A.D.) as recorded in the Khajurāho Inscription found *in situ*. The evidence can only be brushed aside if we accept the theory of wholesale damage and destruction by enemy action and thorough renovation during the period of Candella revival, when the inscription in question might have been refixed on the temple wall.

(ii) There is no visible sign of any material damage to this temple or other temples at the hands of the invaders, nor any indication of substantial repair or renovation of the earlier structure at a later date.

(iii) There is also no literary evidence to support the contention that the temple-city of Khajurāho was sacked and the temples were razed to the ground by the invading forces. The Muslim chroniclers would not surely have failed to take credit for such iconoclastic acts of their hero, considered to be highly meritorious according to their religious belief.

(iv) Even if we accept the theory of restoration or construction *de novo*, it has to be clarified first, whether the temple was rebuilt on the same ground plan, in which case the presumption will be that the developed form with its variegations was known and executed at least a century earlier. Secondly, whether any large scale expansion or enlargement was made on the existing plan finding it to be of a less developed type, or thirdly, whether the ground work had been dug up and laid anew in the light of experience and maturity of the architects of the later period.

So long as further evidences are not available to throw light in the matter, determination of the chronology of the Khajurāho temples will remain an open question.

II

The extant temples at Khajurāho built under the patronage of the Candella rulers, include Vaiṣṇava, Śaiva and Jaina. The builder of the brilliant Lakṣmaṇji temple (V.S. 1011), Yaśovarman was evidently a worshipper of Viṣṇu. But from the time of his son, Dhaṅga, to whom goes the credit for the construction of the Viśvanātha temple (V. S. 1059), the Candella rulers professed to be devotees of Śiva. It may be that capture of the fortress of Kālañjara, the abode of Nīlakaṇṭha Śiva might have had a strong influence in the matter of shift in the religious affiliation of the family. In spite of the fact that the Candella rulers were devout Hindus, they were liberal enough not only to tolerate but even to extend patronage to other faiths. This is amply borne out by the large temples dedicated to the Jaina Tīrthaṁkaras, situated in a group to the south-east of the Khajurāho villages. The most nteresting feature to note in this connection is the remarkable similarity in architectural design and structural pattern of these Jaina temples with the Hindu ones. Viewing from outside it would be difficult to distinguish between them. They pertain to a cognate type. This leads us to the obvious conclusion that all the Khajurāho temples, Hindu and Jaina, must have been built by the same community of builders, belonging to a single school of architecture, that is, the Nāgara school of Central India. As craftsmen, they themselves might have had no sectarian bias, and responded equally enthusiastically to the summons of their patrons irrespective of their religious affiliation.

III

It has already been indicated that the Nāgara temple style had its beginnings in Central India, and its successive stages of development are also noticeable in the temple specimens scattered over different parts of the region. The logical outcome of this art movement is witnessed in the evolved temples of Khajurāho, bearing the stamp of ingenuity and creative genius of the master-builders. In plan and elevation as well as in structural embellishments the Candella architects continued their experimentation unceasingly and introduced innovations of new and newer elements with an eye to making the temples more elegant and imposing and at the same time aesthetically more beautiful. In addition to what we have observed in Chapter XIV of the book, a reappraisal of some of the distinctive features of the Candella style may be attempted here.

(i) Even a fully developed representation of the Candella temple, a *pañcāyatana* one on a raised platform, is found to be without any enclosure. It may not be wrong to presume that this departure from the general pattern was deliberately made, in order that the devotees visiting the temple would feel an emotive thrill to find the abode of God approachable from all quarters without any hindrance or barrier.

(ii) The elevation plan points to a conscious effort of the builder to produce the effect of the soaring height of the temple right from the bottom. But they demonstrate their real ingenuity in providing for open balconies with *kakṣāsanas*, by extending the transepts on the northern and southern walls of the temple. This superb treatment of solids and voids considerably lessens the heaviness of the structure to the great relief of the viewer. Here the builders of Khajurāho excelled over their counterparts who built the Liṅgarāja temple of Bhuvanesvar and the Bṛihadīśvara temple of Tanjore.

(iii) The conical tower of the early Nāgara style is developed by the Candella architects to a tall and imposing curvilinear *śikhara*, connected to the wall section by a series of unbroken *rathaka* facets, running upwards almost to touch the crowning *āmalaka* pair. Again the upward movement is emphasised by the provision of miniature turrets (*aṅgaśikharas*) surrounding the principal *śikhara*. Not only that, the setting of the pyramidal superstructures of the *ardha-maṇḍapa*, *maṇḍapa*, and *mahāmaṇḍapa* in graded heights with admirable proportion and symmetry in design, ultimately converging with the spire of the *śikhara*, gives the whole temple an appearance of a mountain range with alternate altitudes and depths. The *śikhara* in silhouette looks like the highest peak almost touching the clouds, the celestial region. This was indeed a creditable achievement of the Candella temple designers.

(iv) Another distinguishing feature of the Candella style is the provision for an inner ambulatory passage round the sanctum cella. It is suggested that incorporation of this element was due probably to the influence of the building traditions of the south (*Struggle for Empire*, p. 568). Even if it is so, the Candellā builders were no imitators, they gave it a reorientation, and it became their own. While the *pradakṣiṇapatha* of the southern temples is dark and ill-ventilated, the balconied openings on either side and even at the back of the Khajurāho temple let in light and air for comfortable ambulation by the devotees.

LIST OF ABBREVIATIONS

A. C.	The Art of the Candellas—O. C. Gangoly
A. I. K.	Age of Imperial Kanauj. (Ed. by R. C. Majumdar & A. D. Pusalker).
Anc. Geog. of India (Cunningham).	Cunningham's Ancient Geography of India. Ed. by S. N. Majumdar.
A. S. R.	Archaeological Survey Reports.
C. H. I.	Cambridge History of India.
C. I. I. M.	Catalogue of Coins in the Indian Museum—V. A. Smith.
C. I. I.	Corpus Inscriptionum Indicarum.
C. R.	Census Report (1931).
D. H. N. I.	Dynastic History of Northern India—Dr. H. C. Ray.
E. H. I.	Early History of India.—V. Smith.
E. I.	Epigraphia Indica.
Elliott.	Historians History of India.
G. L. M.	Gauḍalekhamāla.
H. B.	History of Bengal (Dacca University), Vol I. Ed. by Dr. R. C. Majumdar.
H. C.	The History of the Candellas—Dr. N. S. Bose.
H. I. B.	Some Historical Aspects of the Inscriptions of Bengal—Dr. B. C. Sen.
H. I. E. A.	History of Indian & European Art—Fergusson.
H. I. I. A.	History of Indian & Indonesian Art—Coomarswamy.
H. P., Ganguly.	History of the Paramāra Dynasty—Dr. D. C. Ganguly.
H. T.	Hindu Temples—Stella Kramrisch.
I. A.	Indian Antiquary.
I. B. (III).	Inscriptions of Bengal, Vol III—N. G. Majumdar.
I. G. I.	Imperial Gazetteer of India.
I. H. Q.	Indian Historical Quarterly.
Ind. Arch.	Indian Architecture—Percy Brown.
J. A. S. B.	Journal of the Asiatic Society of Bengal.
J. A. S. B. (Num. Sup.).	Journal of the Asiatic Society of Beng (Numismatic Supplement).

J. A. S. B. (N. S.)	Journal of the Asiatic Society of Bengal (New Series).
J. B. O. R. S.	Journal of the Bihar Orissa Research Society.
J. B. B. R. A. S.	Journal of the Bombay Branch of the Royal Asiatic Society.
J. D. L.	Journal of the Department of Letters (Calcutta University).
J. N. S. I.	Journal of the Numismatic Society of India.
K. A.	Kauṭilya Arthaśāstra.
K. Y.	Kitāb i Yāmini.
K. Z. A.	Kitāb Zainul Ākhbār.
M. A. S. I.	Memoirs of the Archaeological Survey of India
Mbh.	Mahābhārata.
M. K. (Ms.).	The Manuscript of the Mahobā Khaṇḍ (The Asiatic Society, Calcutta).
Mbh., S. P.	Mahābhārata, Śānti Parva.
PASB.	Proceedings of the Asiatic Society of Bengal
Pb. M. P. Pm.	Paramabhaṭṭāraka Mahārājādhirāja Parameśvara Parma-māheśvara.
P. C.	Prabodhacandrodaya.
P. R.	Parmāl Rāso.
P. R. A. S. (W. C.).	Periodical Report of the Archaeological Survey, Western Circle.
Pr. R.	Pṛthvirāj Rāso.
S. E.	The Struggle for Empire (Ed. by R. C. Majumdar & A. D. Pusalker)
S. M. G.	The Life and Times of Sultan Mahmud of Ghazna—Dr. Nazim.
T. A.	Tabakāt-i-Ākbari.
T. F.	Tārikh i Firishtā (Briggs).
T. K. A.	Āl Tārikh i Kāmil bin ul Āthir.
T. N.	Tabaqāt i Nāsiri.
T. Y.	Tārikh-i-Yāmini.
V. S.	Vikraṁ Saṁvat.
Y. Ç.	On Yuan Chwang—Watters.

BIBLIOGRAPHY

Age of Imperial Kanauj. Ed. by R. C. Majumdar & A. D. Pusalker.

Āl Tārikh i Kāmil bin ul Āthir.—Bulak.

Annual Reports of the Archaeological Survey of India.

Annual Administrations Report of Arch. Deptt. of Gwalior State, V.S. 1991.

Archaeological Survey of India Reports, Vol. II, VII, X, XXI.

Art of the Candellas—O. C. Gangoly.

Bhāratiya Vidyā, 1952.

Bibiliography of Indian Coins, Pt. I. (Numismatic Society of India).

Bombay Gazetteer.

Cambridge History of India, Vol. III.

Catalogue of Coins in the Indian Museum. V. Smith.

Census Report, 1931.

Coins of Medieval India—Cunningham.

Contributions to the History of the Hindu Revenue System—Dr. U. N. Ghosal.

Corpus Inscriptionum Indicarum, Vol. IV. (Inscriptions of the Kalachuri Chedi Era)—Ed. by Mm. V. V. Mirashi

Cunningham's Ancient Geography of India. Ed. by S. N. Majumdar.

Development of Hindu Iconography—Dr. J. N. Banerjea.

Dynastic History of Northern India, Vols. I. and II—Dr. H. C. Ray.

Early History of India—V. Smith.

Elements of Hindu Iconography—Gopinath Rao.

Epigraphia Indica.

Gauḍalekhamālā (Bengali)—R. D. Banerji.

Hindu Temples—Stella Kramrisch.

Historians History of India—Elliott.

History of Bengal, Vol. I (Dacca University) Ed. by Dr. R. C. Majumdar.

History of the Candellas—Dr. Nemai Sadhan Bose.

History of Dharmaśāstras—P. V. Kane.

History of Indian & European Art—Fergusson.

History of Indian & Indonesian Art—Coomarswamy.

History of Kanauj—R. S. Tripathi.

History of Medieval India, Vols. I-III—C. V. Vaidya.

History of the Paramāra Dynasty—D. C. Ganguly.

Imperial Gazetteer of India.

Indian Antiquary.

Indian Architecture—Percy Brown.

Indian Historical Quarterly.

Indian Temple Sculpture—K. M. Munshi.
Journal of the Asiatic Society of Bengal.
Journal of the Department of Letters, Vol. X. (Calcutta University).
Journal of the Numismatic Society of India.
Journal of the U. P. Historical Society, Vol. XXIII—Land Grants of of the Candella kings by Dr. R. K. Dikshit.
Kitāb Zāinul Akhbār Ed. by Md. Nazim.
Kitāb i Yāmini.
Kitābul Hind Al Biruni. Trans. by Sachau.
Kauṭilya's Arthaśāstra Ed. by Gaṇapati Śāstrī.
Kauṭilya's Arthaśāstra Ed. by Shamasastry.
Kalhaṇa's Rājataraṁgiṇī—Stein.
Khajurāho (Department of Archaeology, India).—B. L. Dhama and S. C. Chandra.
Kumārapāla-carita—Jayasiṁha Suri (Nirṇayasāgar Press).
Lays of Alha Ed. by Waterfield.
Mārg. (Khajurāho Number), Vol. X. No. 3.
Manu Smṛti.
Mahābhārata—Śānti Parva.
Memoirs of the Archaeological Survey of India. No. 8.
Ms. of the Mahobā Khaṇḍ (preserved in the Asiatic Society, Calcutta).
On Yuan Chwang—Watters.
Parmāl Rāso Ed. by Sri S. S. Das (Kāśī Nāgrī Pracāriṇī Sābhā).
Prabodhacandrodaya—Śrī Kṛṣṇa Miśra (Nirṇayasāgar Press).
Do Ms. with commentary of Rudradeva (Sanskrit College Library, Calcutta).
Pṛthvirāj Rāso Ed. by M. V. Pandia and S. Dass.
Proceedings of the Indian History Congresses, 1951-54.
Rāṣṭrakūṭas and their times—A. S. Altekar.
Rupam. 1925.
Śiśupālavadhakāvya.
Some Historical Aspects of the Inscriptions of Bengal—Dr. B. C. Sen.
State and Government in Ancient India—A. S. Altekar.
Tāj-ul Māthir—Elliott.
Tabaqāt-i-Ākbari-Nizāmuddin. Trans. by B. Dey.
Tabaqāt i Nāsiri—Raverty.
Tārikh i Kāmil bin ul Āthir—Bulak.
Tārikh i Firishtā (Briggs).
Tārikh i Baihāqui. Ed. by Morley.
Tod's Annals and Antiquities of Rājasthān. Ed. by Crooke.
The Life and times of Sultan Mahmud of Ghazna—Dr. Nazim.
The Struggle for Empire (Ed. by R. C. Majumdar & A. D. Pusalker).
U. P. Gazetteer.
Vikramāṅkadeva carita—Bilhaṇa, Ed. by Buhler.

INDEX

L

M

N

O

P

Q

R

S

V

W

Y

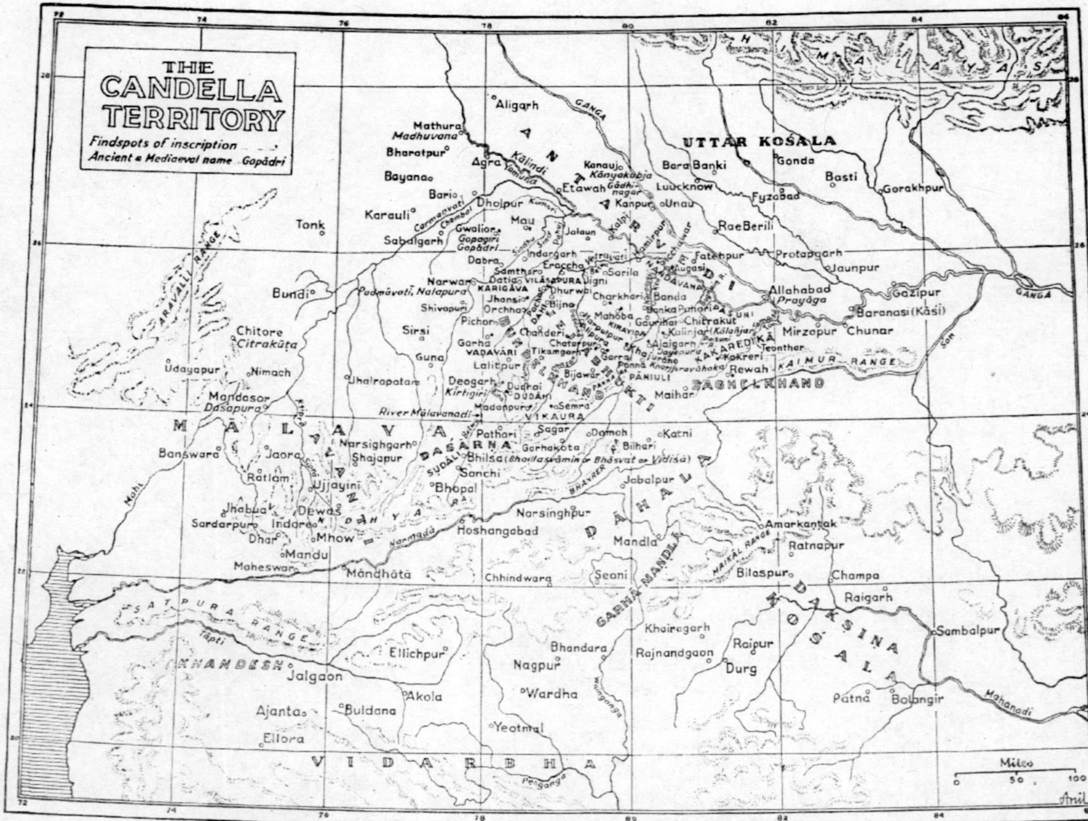
THE CANDELLA TERRITORY
Findspots of inscription
Ancient & Mediaeval name Gopādri
UTTAR KOSALA
HIMALAYAS
GANGA
Aligarh
Mathura
Madhuvana
Bharatpur
Bayana
Bari
Agra
Kālindi
Yamunā
Kanauj
Kānyakobja
Gādhi-nagar
Etawah
Bara Banki
Lucknow
Gonda
Basti
Gorakhpur
Fyzabad
Unau
Kanpur
Dholpur
Karauli
Tonk
Mau
Jalaun
Kalpi
RaeBerili
Gwalior
Gopagiri
Gopādri
Sabalgarh
Dabra
Indargarh
Fatehpur
Protapgarh
Jaunpur
Samthar
Eraccha
Datia
VILĀSAPURA
Narwar
KARIGĀVA
Sarila
Allahabad
Prayāga
Gazipur
Bundi
Padmāvati, Nalapura
Jhansi
Orchha
Shivapuri
Dhurwai
Bijna
Charkhari
Banda
Baranasi(Kāsī)
Mirzapur
Chunar
Pichor
Mahoba
Chitrakut
Kalinjar (Kālañjar)
Sirsi
Chanderi
Garha
VADAVĀRI
Chatarpur
Tikamgarh
Khajurāho
Ajaigarh
KAKAREDIKĀ
Kokreri
Teonthar
KAIMUR RANGE
Son
Chitore
Citrakūta
Udayapur
Nimach
Guna
Lalitpur
Jhalrapatan
Deogarh
Kirtigiri
Dudhai
DUDĀHI
Bijawar
Pannā
PĀNIULI
Rewah
Maihar
BAGHELKHAND
Mandasor
Dasapura
River Mālavanadi
Madanpura
Semra
VIKAURA
M Ā L A V A
Pathari
Sagar
Damoh
Katni
Banswara
Jaora
Narsighgarh
Shajapur
DAŚARNA
Garhakota
Bilhari
SUDĀLI
Bhilsa (Bhaillasvāmin or Bhāsvat or Vidiśā)
Sanchi
Ratlam
Ujjayini
Bhopal
Jabalpur
Mahi
Jhabua
Dewas
Sardarpur
Indore
Narsinghpur
Amarkantak
Dhar
Mhow
Narmadā
Hoshangabad
Mandla
Ratnapur
D Ā H A L A
Mandu
Maheswar
Māndhātā
Chhindwara
Seoni
GARHĀ-MANDLĀ
MAIKĀL RANGE
Bilaspur
Champa
Raigarh
DAKSINA KOSALA
SATPURA RANGE
Tāpti
Sambalpur
Ellichpur
Khairagarh
Bhandara
Rajnandgaon
Raipur
Durg
KHANDESH
Jalgaon
Nagpur
Akola
Wardha
Wainganga
Patna
Bolangir
Mahanadi
Ajanta
Buldana
Yeotmal
Ellora
V I D A R B H A
Penganga
Miles
0 50 100
Anil